E303 English Grammar in Context
Education and Language Studies
Level 3

The Open University

Book 3

Getting Practical
Evaluating everyday texts

Edited by C. Coffin

Units 12–16

Series editor: Caroline Coffin

This publication forms part of an Open University course E303 *English Grammar in Context*. Details of this and other Open University courses can be obtained from the Student Registration and Enquiry Service, The Open University, PO Box 197, Milton Keynes MK7 6BJ, United Kingdom: tel. +44 (0)870 333 4340, email general-enquiries@open.ac.uk

Alternatively, you may visit the Open University website at http://www.open.ac.uk where you can learn more about the wide range of courses and packs offered at all levels by The Open University.

To purchase a selection of Open University course materials visit http://www.ouw.co.uk, or contact Open University Worldwide, Michael Young Building, Walton Hall, Milton Keynes MK7 6AA, United Kingdom for a brochure. tel. +44 (0)1908 858785; fax +44 (0)1908 858787; email ouwenq@open.ac.uk

The Open University
Walton Hall, Milton Keynes
MK7 6AA

First published 2005. Second edition 2006.

Edited and designed by The Open University.

Typeset by The Open University.

Printed and bound in the United Kingdom by Halstan Printing Group, Amersham.

ISBN 978 0 7492 1777 8

2.1

Contents

Introduction to Book 3

Have you ever wondered how some people manage to convince and persuade you to change your mind on an issue, while others have very little influence over your opinions or behaviour?

Perhaps you have noticed that some people – in works of fiction or news stories or in your own lives – come over as more dynamic, while others seem more passive?

More practically, have you ever felt that some of the texts that you have produced – such as academic essays, written reports or formal presentations – could have been organised more effectively?

In Book 3 you will find answers to all these questions – and more! My aim in this book is to enable you to apply what you have learned, and continue to learn, about English grammar in practical and useful ways. In particular, you will find out more about how grammar can help you become a critical reader and listener and an effective speaker and writer.

First, let us briefly revisit one of the most important points that you have learned about grammar so far – namely, the relationship between the cultural and social context of a language interaction and the grammatical and lexical choices a writer or speaker makes. In Books 1 and 2 we saw that:

◆ the field (i.e. the topic or activity) affects the way we use grammar and lexis by, for example, influencing our choice of processes and participants and the degree of technicality in the lexis we use

◆ the tenor (primarily concerned with social roles, relationships and attitudes) influences how formal or informal our use of English is and (among other things) the way in which we use modal resources to position those around us as well as to show how open we are to alternative ideas and opinions

◆ the mode (namely, whether a text is written or spoken) has an impact on how we package and organise information, influencing, for example, the structure of a noun phrase as well as the way in which we arrange information at clause level.

So, by now, you should be well equipped to work out which social contexts the following extracts (Texts 1–4) belong to. More importantly, you should find it easy to pinpoint the key grammatical features that enable you to reach your judgement.

Text 1

CHRIS I'm really struggling with this wretched assignment we've got to do, you know the one about erm the Jackson Pollock painting.

BRIDGET Oh yes, oh me too.

CHRIS Are you? Yeah, it's really, I don't know. I'm staring at this painting and I just can't think of anything to say.

(Data collected and transcribed by the Course Team)

Text 2

The first reason for population movement is employment. In many rural areas of Australia, recession and drought have caused severe hardships in the late 1980's and early 1990's. (sic) As a result many farmers are making losses, not profits.

(Humphrey, 1996)

Text 3

A woman and a child had a narrow escape yesterday when their car left the road. The accident happened at about 9.25am at Marks Tey, near Colchester.

(Biber et al., 1999, p. 264)

Text 4

It's half past ten in the evening, but the light of day still glows through the lime leaves. They are so green that they look like an hallucination of the summer everyone had almost given up expecting. When you touch them, they are fresh and tender. It's like touching a baby's skin.

(Dunmore, 2001, p. 1)

You should have had no difficulty in using your grammatical skills of description and interpretation to work out that the texts come from (respectively) a casual conversation, a piece of student academic writing, a news report and a novel. Key grammatical and linguistic features include the use of noun phrases and nominalisation, choices in processes and participants and theme–rheme patterning.

In Book 3 we continue to recycle much of the grammatical knowledge that you have now built up. At the same time we will extend our exploration of English as it is used in conversation, academic writing, the media and fiction. In Books 1 and 2 you saw that there are many commonalities across texts that belong to these four major contexts of English use. In particular, the corpus evidence of both Longman and the BNC-OU revealed some of the widespread patterns found across these registers. Nevertheless, as we began to discover in Book 2, it is important to recognise that grammatical patterns can be described with different degrees of 'delicacy'. And once we focus on specific texts we may discover that they vary in significant ways from the more general characteristics of conversation, news, fiction or academic writing.

Our exploration in Book 3 will focus, in particular, on how within any one Longman register (such as news or conversation), grammatical and lexical patterns may vary considerably. In other words, once we put specific examples of English use under the microscope we will see that grammatical patterns are far more diverse than might be suggested by large-scale corpus findings. Below, for example, are two texts which are both examples of fiction. However, they differ in terms of their grammatical and lexical choices in quite significant ways. This is because the two novelists (Helen Dunmore and David Lodge respectively) are deliberately creating very different tenor relations between the fictional narrators and their audiences. In addition, whereas Text 5 is unmistakeably written, David Lodge has given Text 6 a spoken feel. Finally, whereas the field in Text 5 is a description of a city (Leningrad), Text 6 is concerned with the narrator's use of a tape recorder to capture internal patterns of thought.

Text 5

Such a late spring, murky and doubtful, clinging to winter's skirts. But this process of spring finally emerging from winter is how it happens in Leningrad. There, under trees which surround the naval academy (the Admiralty), lakes of spongy ice turned grey. There was slush everywhere in the city, and a raw, dirty wind off the Neva, the river that runs through Leningrad. There was a frost, a thaw, another frost.

(Dunmore, 2001, p. 1)

Text 6

One, two, three, testing, testing ... recorder working OK ... Olympus Pearlcorder, bought it at Heathrow in the dutyfree on my way to ... where? Can't remember, doesn't matter ... The object of the exercise being to record as accurately as possible the thoughts that are passing through my head at this moment in time, which is, let's see ... 10.13 a.m. on Sunday the 23rd of Febru – San Diego!

(Lodge, 2002, p. 1)

The relationship between lexicogrammar and aspects of social situations, as captured in the concepts of field, tenor and mode, continues to be an important focus for Book 3. It is the framework which will continue to guide our study of the grammar and lexis of texts in context.

There are five units in Book 3. In Unit 12 we will carry out further exploration of tenor relations and how people use grammar and lexis to persuade and position each other. In Unit 13 we will look at the way in which different world views can be represented through different grammatical constructions and through different lexical choices. Then in Units 14, 15 and 16 we will deepen our exploration of mode to find out how speakers and writers draw on lexicogrammar to produce more or less well-organised and cohesive texts.

In Book 3 you will only do a small amount of hands-on exploration of corpora, although several of the readings will reinforce the role played by corpus-based approaches to grammar. You will, however, do lots of interactive exercises on the CD-ROM to give you practice in recognising and interpreting the meaning-making function of both grammatical and lexical choices.

Throughout all five units you will enhance your skills of grammatical description and interpretation. In addition, you will learn to evaluate texts and to apply your grammatical knowledge to make less effective texts more effective.

By the time you finish the book, I am sure that you will have a better understanding of how English grammar works to represent all our different personas and world-views. For example, you will have gained important insights into how some people are more convincing and persuasive than others, as well as how some texts are effectively organised and others less so. Such understanding will place you in a strong position to use grammar in your own life as a means of understanding and improving the way you communicate with your fellow human beings.

Unit 12

Getting interpersonal: the grammar of social roles and relationships

Prepared for the course team by Peter White

CONTENTS

Materials required

While studying this unit you will need:

> your reference grammar
> the Activities CD-ROM.

Knowledge assumed

You should be familiar with the following before starting on this unit:

> authorial/speaker persona
> communicative standing
> interpersonal meaning
> modality
> personalisation
> question tags
> relative social status
> social contact/distance
> speech act/speech function
> stance
> tenor.

Introduction

As stated in the general introduction to Book 3, the focus in the following set of units shifts from our prior concern – with how grammar and vocabulary vary across different registers – to a concern with the more subtle or fine-grained variations which occur within registers, for example, between different types of conversations, media reports or academic writing. In this unit, our specific topic is the interpersonal function of language, that is, the linguistic means by which speakers and writers:

◆ form and negotiate relationships

◆ act out social roles

◆ represent themselves (for example, as powerful or deferential, assertive or conciliatory, emotionally engaged or uninvolved)

and so on. You were introduced to this interpersonal mode of meaning in previous units under the heading of 'tenor'. Let us return to Figure 2 in Unit 10 and look at the 'map' of tenor (Figure 1 opposite).

In returning to the topic of interpersonal meaning, our objective is both to extend your knowledge of how language operates interpersonally and, in keeping with the book's overall focus, to explore how texts drawn from the same register may differ in interpersonal terms.

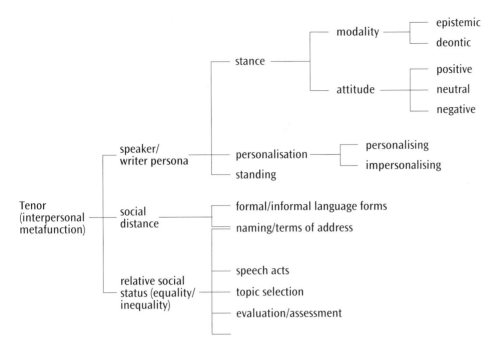

Figure 1 Map of tenor

An understanding of how language operates interpersonally is vital. It enables us to develop systematic analyses which address lots of questions related to the communicative objectives served by grammar and vocabulary. Some examples of what becomes possible once you are equipped with this knowledge include the ability to:

◆ analyse how language is used to form friendships and negotiate alliances, to avoid or provoke conflicts and to indicate deference, respect or animosity

◆ analyse how writers/speakers use language to exercise power or to lay claim to authority, social standing or expertise

◆ analyse the linguistic bases of conventionalised role relations and interactions such as those between doctors and patients, teachers and students, parents and children, etc.

◆ analyse the different linguistic means by which advertisers, politicians, media commentators or academic authors use language to win over their audiences and hence to convince and persuade

◆ analyse the distinctive linguistic properties of texts which seek to popularise expert or technical subjects (for example, the articles in popular science magazines) and thereby to gain a general, non-expert readership for such topics

◆ identify key aspects of the style, tone of voice or textual personas typically adopted in different types of academic prose and thereby to provide an account of what might be expected of academic writers.

① TENOR AND INTERPERSONAL POSITIONING IN SPOKEN INTERACTIONS

We shall begin by comparing and contrasting two face-to-face, interactive spoken exchanges which, in broad terms, can both be classified as 'conversational'. I suspect that, as you read, various differences in the social roles and relationships of those involved in the texts will be fairly readily discernible to you. Our purpose in what follows will be to explore these initial impressions, to develop an account by which it is possible to explain them by reference to a systematic and explicit linguistic account.

1.1 Relative social status (equality/inequality)

ACTIVITY 1 (allow about 20 minutes)

As you read the texts, see whether you can provide possible answers for the following questions:

(1) What type of social setting do you think the original spoken texts occurred in?

(2) Can you connect any of the speakers with any conventionalised social roles (for example, doctor or patient, parent or child, priest or religious congregation, shopper or sales assistant, wife or husband, lawyer or witness, and so on)?

(3) Are the speakers equal or unequal with respect to their social status – for example, with respect to their power, authority or expertise?

(4) Are the speakers socially close or socially distant?

As already suggested, some of the answers may seem rather obvious. If so, consider why this is the case: why is it so easy for you to reconstruct the original social roles and relationships, even when your only evidence is this entirely decontextualised written transcript? What precisely are the linguistic indicators which enable you to deduce the social roles and relationships in this way?

Key to transcription:

(.) indicates a short pause (less than half a second).

‖ ... ‖ indicates that the current speaker and the following speaker overlap here, i.e. both talk simultaneously.

+... indicates that the word has been cut short – the complete word has not been fully articulated or could not be transcribed owing to some overlap or interruption.

S1, S2, etc., refers to Speaker 1, Speaker 2, etc.

Text 1

[The speakers have just watched a film on machines and 'mechanical advantage'. Mechanical advantage refers to ways in which devices such as levers and pulleys can be employed to apply force. The text may be a little difficult at first to follow. This is often the case with transcripts of spoken interactions since there will often be references to items in the immediate physical environment which we will not have any knowledge of, or to other information which the interlocutors have in common but which will probably be unknown to us. In this text, the speakers refer to objects which, in the film they have just watched, were presented as examples of devices which demonstrate this mechanical advantage. Thus when they talk about a *lever*, a *seesaw*, an *inclined plane* and a *baseball bat* they are referring to items which appeared in the film as examples of such devices. (NB: *flying fox* is a term used for a clothesline.)]

S1: Alright, a quick summary of what we have just seen. Quick.

S2: Lever.

S1: Hold on.

S3: Seesaw.

S1: Right. Just wait till we are all here. Have you got enough scrap paper on your desk please? You'll probably only need two or three pieces. Right, you may have to use the stand, Steven and Brad, the sun is shining inside. Alright, thank you. Solved your problem? You'll probably need to see that film tomorrow, as an extra, to get you (.) to get your ideas really sorted out. Right. Let's have a summary of what was the film basically about. They seem to mention two basic machines. Um, Andrew?

S2: Levers. (*pronounces the word with an American accent as in the film*)

S1: It has an Australian pronunciation.

S3: Levers.

S1: Yeah, leave her alone. (*said as a joke – 'leave her' = 'lever' – everyone laughs*) Lever and...(.)

S4: An inclined plane.

S1: An (.) inclined plane. ‖

S5:   ‖ Baseball...

S1: Hold on, hold on, now they extended these two basic machines, (.) into five separate machines. In that movie they extended them out, they extended out some of the machines. They used the lever. ‖

S5:   ‖ Baseball...

S1: Hold on, hold on. Joanne?

S6: Lever.

S1: No, we've done a lever.

S4: Baseball bat.

S1: Baseball bat. (.) Any bat really.

S6: Flying fox. (*said very quietly*)

S1: Pardon, flying fox?

S7: Clothesline.

S1: And what with it?

S7: A wheel.

S1: A wheel. Yeah, no you're right. Clotheslines. That was a... (*interrupted*) what did she use on the clothesline?

SEVERAL: Pulley.

S1: A pulley, which is a type of (.) lever. Except of course, you've got also a what with it? A (.) wind... (*prompting*) ...lass. Anything else that wasn't mentioned that possibly uses the principles of a lever.

S2: Door handle.

S1: A door handle, good one, hey.

Yep. Righto, let's have a look at an inclined plane one (.) well actually that is a type of tool which you have seen in action, come to think of it. Maybe we can get six uses of an inclined plane. Um Aranthi?

S9: Stairs.

S1: Stairs, right. Great answer.

(Adapted from Martin et al., 1997, pp. 88–9; data originally collected by Frances Christie)

Text 2

[The speakers are looking at and discussing a photograph of a British pop group, Hearsay. The group was formed in 2001 as the result of a television talent-quest programme in which young people wanting to become members of a pop group auditioned in front of television cameras, with the auditions being broadcast as part of the *Pop Stars* television programme. Their performances were assessed, on air, by celebrity judges, some of whom became notorious for the negativity of their comments. Halfway through the transcript, the speakers refer to one such judge, Nigel. The speakers begin by discussing the appearance of one of the members of the group, Kym.]

S1: (1) Hold up the picture of her a minute with the (.) I just want to see her hair

S2: (2) She looks stupid, but they look like hair extensions, how can you (.) they're ‖ supposed to look natural aren't they?

S1: (3)   ‖ her extensions look crap but I don't understand why they couldn't do it (.) why they couldn't do it to make it look natural

S2: (4) it looks like ooh ‖ I've got a bob...<*turn continues below – see next S2*>

S1: (5)   ‖ coz it's not that hard ‖

S2: (6)   ‖ then long straggly bits. ‖ What's the point of that?

S3: (7)   ‖ She is quite big actually isn't she (.) ‖ in that picture they all look quite big

S1: (8)   ‖ that's what I was going to say (.) the whole thing is that I don't actually think that they're big (.) but in comparison to say like (.) ‖ <*turn continues below – see next S1*>

S3: (9)   ‖ like ‖

S1: (10)   ‖ Christina Aguillera and Britney Spears and all that lot, even just

S2: (11) Yeah compared to other popstars, exactly ‖ and she's got (.) quite a few things that are like going against her I reckon (.) ‖

S3: (12)   ‖ Are you talking about Kym?

S2: (13) Yea Kym (.) She's like (.) she's not (.) young (.) slim (.) gorgeous type of person is she ‖ which is <*turn continues below – see next S2*>

S1: (14) ‖ she's not ‖

S3: (15) ‖ yeah

S2: (16) really bad to be like criticising her for that but she's not the kind of (.) ideal pop star

S3: (17) yeah but she's the 24-year-old with two kids that's put on a few pound over Christmas (.)

    ‖ that's all the comment is

S2: (18) ‖ but maybe (.) yeah maybe it's good that she's not

S1: (19) How thin do they want them to be as well?

S3: (20) Well he said that they need to have a new diet (.) and a fitness regime, need to go to the gym (.) and all that, doesn't it, doesn't it say ‖

S1: (21)   ‖ in the programme are they talking about that?

S3: (22) yeah yeah

S1: (23) last night

S3: (24) Nigel was yeah

S2: (25) Nige

S3: (26) Nige

S2: (27) Our Nige

S3: (28) And even the lads as well need to go out and

S2: (29) yeah but the thing is actually the pressure's all on the girls not the blokes like (.) the blokes just have to go to the gym, they're already quite buffed up anything, it's just the girls, like, have to get skinny

S3: (30) but the say that they're always, they eat so mu so many takeaways and curries, look (.) here we go.

S2: (31) yeah but then they're like oh they want them to be like (.) normal people that's what normal people do, how much (.) rubbish do we eat all the time, it's like crisps and all that stuff.

COMMENT

Before examining Text 2, let us concentrate on Text 1.

I suspect that you saw Text 1 as clearly involving a relationship of inequality between the primary speaker (S1) and the other interlocutors. Speaker 1 obviously dominates the exchange while the others play a subordinate role. But while this interpersonal state of affairs may be relatively obvious, not all aspects of its linguistic basis may be quite so straightforward. In order to account fully and systematically for how this relationship is enacted linguistically, we need to examine several different aspects of language use.

You may remember that in Unit 8 we indicated that social inequality (communicative participants operating with different levels of power, authority, status or expertise) was reflected in linguistic inequality. By 'linguistic inequality', we refer to disparities in the things which the various speakers can do with language – disparities in the types of words or structures they use, in the types of meanings they create, in the way they address each other, in their control over the direction of the conversation, and so on. There are several different types of such disparity observable in this interaction. We will discuss each of these in turn.

Speech acts

The first disparity operates at a very basic level – in terms of a set of options or choices which apply every time we make an utterance. Here we are concerned with what are known as speech acts or speech functions. You may remember that in Book 1 Unit 3 we discussed how all utterances involve a choice with respect to interpersonal positioning – in formulating any utterance, speakers/writers necessarily position themselves and those they address. There are just a few basic possibilities with respect to this positioning, which depend on options concerning (a) who is positioned as the communicative giver and who the communicative receiver, and (b) whether the communicative exchange involves information or some form of action or behaviour. Thus the speaker/writer can be positioned in the role of either giver or receiver, and likewise the addressee (either giver or receiver). The communication can put at stake information or what we term **goods and services** (some form of action or some provision of a service). Examples of these basic speech acts follow:

	Information	Goods and services
Offer (speaker/writer in role of giver, addressee in role of receiver)	(speech act = **statement**) Fred borrowed my copy of the play *Hamlet*. (offer of information: giver = speaker receiver = addressee)	(speech act = **offer**) Would you like to borrow my copy of *Hamlet*? (offer of service: giver = speaker receiver = addressee)
Request/demand (speaker/writer in role of receiver, addressee in role of giver)	(speech act = **question**) Who borrowed my copy of *Hamlet*? (request for information: giver = addressee receiver = speaker)	(speech act = **command**) Return my copy of *Hamlet* at once. (request for service: giver = addressee receiver = speaker)

In this sense, every utterance is fundamentally interpersonal in that it necessarily involves a particular relationship being established between speaker/writer and the addressee, a relationship which varies according to which interlocutor is placed in the role of 'giver' and which in the role of 'receiver'.

There are obvious differences between the speakers in Text 1 in terms of their use of these different speech acts, and hence in the interpersonal positions they adopt for themselves and for those they address. Thus we observe that Speaker 1 makes free use of statements (offers of information), questions (demands for information) and commands (demands for goods and services), for example:

> They seem to mention two basic machines. (offer of information)
>
> What did she use on the clotheslines? (request for information)
>
> Just wait till we are all here. Hold on. (request for service)

In contrast, the other speakers are confined just to offers of information. Even here there is a clear linguistic disparity in that in their statements these other speakers offer only clause fragments, typically just the one word needed to answer the question posed by Speaker 1. In contrast Speaker 1's statements are typically fully elaborated grammatically. (For a detailed analysis of the speech acts in the text see 'Answers to the activities'.)

Topic choice

Under **topic choice**, we are concerned with who gets to determine the direction of the interaction. Does one interlocutor decide the subject matter or do such decisions seem to be more evenly shared? Here

Speaker 1 is very much in the ascendancy – he/she has absolute control over **topic selection**.

Turn management

Under **turn management**, we are concerned with who gets to speak, when and for how long. Once again Speaker 1's domination seems fairly clear – the sequencing of speaker turns is under his control. Thus he nominates who is to speak, with the other interlocutors largely waiting for Speaker 1's approval or permission before contributing to the verbal exchange. However, there is one point of additional interest here. We notice that Speaker 1's turn-management control is sometimes challenged (though not successfully) by some of the other speakers as they attempt to interrupt or offer information before being invited to do so by Speaker 1. For example:

S4: An inclined plane.

S1: An (.) inclined plane. ‖

S5:   ‖ Baseball...

S1: Hold on, hold on, now they extended these two basic machines, (.) into five separate machines. In that movie they extended them out, they extended out some of the machines. They used the lever. ‖

S5:   ‖ Baseball...

S1: Hold on, hold on. Joanne?

You have probably already deduced that this is a classroom interaction with Speaker 1 in the teacher role and the other speakers the students. It may be a point of interest, then, to note that these particular students can be seen by their linguistic behaviour not as seeing their teacher's turn-management authority as absolute. Such 'resistance' to turn-management control might provide for an interesting point of comparison between different classes, teachers, teaching approaches and even educational systems. This particular classroom interaction took place in an Australian upper-primary science lesson (students 10 to 11 years of age). Were such uninvited offers of information by students something which you recall from your own primary school days? Did your teachers, perhaps, operate with a different interpersonal regime? Do you think that different educational systems and cultures might vary in terms of whether such behaviour by students is allowed or encouraged?

Naming/forms of address

Disparity in the way people are addressed or named is perhaps one of the most salient indicators of the operation of social hierarchies. Most societies operate with honorific titles such as 'Sir', 'Lady', 'Doctor', 'Professor', 'Your Excellency', 'Your Honour' and so on. Such naming devices are very concrete indicators of the addressed person's elevated status or power.

The naming/terms-of-address situation in Text 1 is straightforward: Speaker 1 uses first names to address the other speakers who, in contrast, do not name Speaker 1 at all – clear evidence of a status differential.

Evaluations/assessments

In addition to factual information, Speaker 1 also offers evaluations and assessments. For example, he classifies the offers of information (statements) of the other speakers as right or wrong or praises them (for example, *stairs, right. Great answer*). He also uses modal resources to make assessments about degrees of probability (for example, *You'll probably only need two or three pieces*). In contrast the other speakers are confined to offering only factual information expressed in categorical terms – they make no assessments.

Here then is another type of linguistic disparity, this time relating to the types of meanings which the different speakers seem authorised to make. The more powerful figure here exercises a right to pass various types of judgements and to make assessments, a right which, on this evidence, may not be so readily available to the other speakers.

Deducing social roles and social settings

As has just been indicated, this is a classroom interaction between one interlocutor in the role of teacher and the other interlocutors in the role of (relatively young) students (transcript supplied from research data by Frances Christie). You will probably have deduced this (depending on your familiarity with the cultural context in which the text originally occurred). The reason why the original context can be deduced so easily is because the particular power relationship – the particular pattern of interpersonal positionings just identified – is almost exclusively confined to educational settings of this type. It is not simply a matter of the one interlocutor (the teacher) being so linguistically dominant – there are plenty of other settings in which one interlocutor dominates. It is rather the particular form that the domination takes: the dominant interlocutor poses a series of questions and determines precisely who gets to answer; the other interlocutors are confined to the most minimal of responses; and the dominant interlocutor confirms and sometimes evaluates these minimal responses.

A CTIVITY 2 (allow about 10 minutes)

We can now turn to the second of our two texts, Text 2. In the light of the discussion above, would you say that the social situation is quite as easy to deduce as that in Text 1? Is there any linguistic evidence by which you might make an informed guess about the gender of the speakers or their age? The social setting of the conversation is a Western one (specifically the UK). Are there any aspects of the way in which social roles and relationships are acted out in this text which might be particular to such a cultural context?

You might like to return briefly to Text 2 and consider it specifically in terms of the linguistic aspects we have just observed: speech acts, naming/terms of address, topic selection, turn management, passing of judgements and assessments, as well as any other features which seem relevant.

C OMMENT

I shall now comment on each feature of Text 2 that relates to social status, as described above for Text 1.

Speech acts

The evidence of this extract suggests that all the speakers have equal access to all the speech act types. The exchange is largely made up of offers of information (statements), which the three speakers contribute in roughly equal number. There are just three genuine requests for information, two from Speaker 1 and one from Speaker 3:

(a) S3: Are you talking about Kym?

(b) S1: How thin do they want them to be as well?

(c) S1: ...in the programme are they talking about that?

and two of these (utterances (a) and (b)) amount only to requests for clarification of what the previous speaker had been saying. This is evidence that the speakers are equally able to take the role of 'requester of information', but this particular conversational exchange is not really directed towards the seeking out of unknown information. Rather it is directed towards the sharing of viewpoints – hence the high frequency of statements. There are also several instances of question tags (for example, *they're supposed to look natural aren't they*?) and rhetorical questions which do not function as genuine requests for information (*What's the point of that?*), which will be discussed in more detail below when we turn to considering social distance. We note in passing that once again these seem to be shared out among the three speakers, further evidence of their linguistic equality. There is just one demand for goods and services at the beginning of the exchange by Speaker 1,

Hold up the picture of her a minute. However, this cannot be taken to indicate that commanding is a function which is in some way monopolised by Speaker 1 – one instance of a grammatical feature does not constitute a pattern. We note as well that this command is only incidental to the conversation as a whole and that it imposes only the most minimal imposition (if it imposes any imposition at all) on the person towards whom it is directed.

Topic choice

The topic here seems to have been chosen by mutual agreement and there is some evidence that the three speakers are equals when it comes to introducing new subtopics and hence adjusting the direction of the conversation. Thus we notice:

◆ The topic of the pop star's hair is introduced by Speaker 1 at the opening of the conversation.

◆ Speaker 3 shifts the topic to the subject of the pop star's size/ weight (*She is quite big actually*).

◆ Speaker 2 introduces the issue of whether it is right to be so concerned with women's weight and appearance (*Yea Kym. She's like she's not young slim gorgeous type of person is she which is really bad to be like criticising her for*).

Turn management

This refers to who gets to speak, when, and for how long. There is evidence that all three speakers are equal in terms of determining turn-taking:

◆ They all take turns when turn-handover is offered by the previous speaker – for example, S2 from S1 at (2); S3 from S2 at (17); S1 from S3 at (23).

◆ Perhaps most tellingly, they all interrupt and talk over the top of the other speakers – for example, S1 talks over/takes over from S2 at (3); S3 talks over/takes over from S2 at (7); S2 talks over/ takes over from S3 at (17).

Evaluations/assessments

All three speakers freely offer positive/negative assessments, for example:

> S2: She looks stupid (2)

> S1: her extensions look crap (3)

> S3: She is quite big actually (7).

Deducing social roles and social setting in Text 2

There is strong linguistic evidence to suggest that this is an interchange among social equals. Perhaps you postulated that this was a discussion among friends or family members. This was, in fact, the case – the text was gathered as part of a research project in which the everyday exchanges of members of shared households of university undergraduates were, with their permission, recorded (ages 18 to 21). In general terms the members of such households are, of course, social equals. But what is it about this exchange which suggests 'friends' rather than, for example, students participating in a tutorial session? Perhaps the light-hearted nature of the subject matter – the physical appearance of pop stars – is one indicator. There are, however, more general factors operating here. The fact that we see them as relatively close friends, rather than acquaintances, is a matter of social distance rather than relative social status. We will accordingly take up this matter in a following section.

Perhaps you also postulated that the speakers were female. You would have been correct – the speakers are all young women. You were perhaps relying on a social stereotype, which operates in many cultures, by which it is women rather than men who are seen to be more likely to be interested in discussing other people's appearances, especially questions about their weight. Perhaps you might even have speculated that there is something about the way the conversation is conducted which is more characteristic of females than males. Certainly, there has been a great deal of sociolinguistic research in recent years which has claimed to have found evidence that men and women do use language in systematically different ways (though it should be noted that many of these findings have been the subject of intense debate and questioning in the linguistics literature). Much of this research has focused on casual conversational exchanges like this and has proposed that there are differences between males and females in terms of the frequency with which they interrupt other speakers, give the floor to other speakers, provide other speakers with supportive feedback, seek confirmation from other speakers, compliment other speakers, and so on. Accordingly you might have noted in Text 2 the regularity with which the turn of one speaker interweaves with, or is taken up by, the turn of another speaker and perhaps you postulated that this is more typical of female than male speech. We are not, of course, in a position to test such a proposition here. To do this we would need much more data than this – specifically, we would need an extensive set of similar texts involving both female speakers and, for the purposes of contrast, male speakers. Obviously this would fall well outside the scope of an introductory unit such as this. But the point here is that we may be justified in at least postulating that there is something more female about the ways the speakers are interacting verbally, and accordingly that it may even be possible to deduce a speaker's sex from their linguistic behaviour.

1.2 Social distance

Our analysis provides us with evidence by which we can make clear proposals about the relative social status of the speakers in the two texts and by which, in some cases, we can identify the social roles and identities of those speakers. But, as has been indicated in earlier units, this variable of relative social status (equality/inequality) is only part of the interpersonal picture. We turn now to another equally important parameter by which the tenor of a text may vary – that of social distance. Here, as you will recall from earlier units, we are concerned with the degree of connection or closeness between the speakers, the degree to which speakers by their language suggest they are on familiar, intimate or friendly terms or, alternatively, on not so familiar or friendly terms. You will also recall that some of the key linguistic indicators of social closeness/distance are as follows:

◆ Greater or lesser degrees of closeness, familiarity, friendliness or intimacy are indicated via informal linguistic forms – for example, colloquial slang vocabulary or contracted and elliptical forms.

◆ Familiarity/contact is also indicated by the use of words/phrases which rely on the speaker and addressee having specific or specialised experiences in common.

◆ A different type of familiarity or contact, that of being members of an 'in-group' of experts who share some specialist knowledge, may be indicated by the use of specialist/technical vocabulary.

◆ Social distance or lack of contact is indicated by the use of formal modes of expression.

Social distance in Text 1

Australian primary school teachers and their students are in quite frequent contact – typically five days a week over the school year. Theirs, however, is not typically the closeness or intimacy of family members or close friends. Accordingly, we might classify the tenor of such a relationship as familiar but not intimate. The language choices in Text 1 are in conformity with this scenario. We observe a relatively high frequency of colloquial vocabulary choices on the part of the teacher:

alright, hold on (*in place of the more formal* wait), really (*as a colloquial/ less formal intensifier*), yeah, good one, hey, yep, righto.

We also observe the use of some contractions:

you'll, we've, you're

as well as a few clause constructions involving the types of ellipsis typically associated with more informal settings, for example:

Alright, a quick summary of what we have just seen.
(*in place of the more formal*: Alright, <u>let's do</u> a quick summary...)

Solved your problem?
(*in place of the more formal*: <u>Have I</u> solved your problem?)

The fact that the teacher uses the children's first names to address them is also indicative of some degree of social familiarity. Such usage is customary in Australian schools today, especially at the primary school level.

Remember that above we also noticed that there are a couple of occasions where the students actually interrupt their teacher, or offer answers before being invited to do so. Such interruptions and overlaps are associated with contexts of social closeness rather than distance.

◢ CTIVITY 3 (allow about five minutes)

In the light of this discussion return to Text 2. Can you now systematically identify any specific indicators of social contact/ distance? For example, can you identify instances of colloquial or slang vocabulary, or instances of the contractions and ellipses which we might associate with informal rather than formal contexts?

COMMENT

The language of the text indicates close social contact. The evidence is as follows:

◆ frequent colloquial formulations: *straggly bits*; the use of *like* in the following type of constructions: *quite a few things that are <u>like</u> going against*

◆ vague expressions: *all that lot, all that stuff*

◆ informality: *I reckon* (for the more formal *I think*); *yeah, two kids* (versus the more formal *children*); *the lads, the blokes* (versus the more formal *the boys/the men*); *quite buffed up, skinny* (versus more formal alternatives).

You will also notice the mildly taboo slang word, *crap*. This is significant because such taboo forms are suggestive of quite close social contact.

There is also a high frequency of ellipsis of clause elements and contractions, with the transcription indicating contraction beyond that found in written texts – for example, *the pressure's all* for *the pressure is all*.

There is a very high rate of interruption and overlap which is typically a clear indication of quite close social contact as well as social equality. In fact, in this text, interruption/overlap appears to be the default mode of turn-handover, with most exchanges involving some process of interruption or at least turn-simultaneity.

It is this combination of colloquial and taboo lexis, contraction and ellipsis, and especially the high rate of interruption, which is suggestive of close social contact. Thus, as indicated earlier, the analysis might suggest that the speakers are friends or family members rather than, for example, the members of a newly-formed tutorial group.

❷ ANALYSING TENOR IN NON-INTERACTIVE TEXTS

We turn now from considering tenor in spoken interactions to considering tenor in written texts aimed at a non-specific, unknown or mass audience – for example, media reports, academic articles, textbooks, public information brochures, print advertising and political electioneering materials. It will probably come as no surprise that we need to make some adjustments to our analytical methodology when we make this shift. Obviously there are going to be some fundamental differences in terms of social roles and relationships between texts where there are verbal interactions between multiple communicative participants who are known to each other in some way, and texts where there is just one writer directing his/her words to a mass audience.

For a start, the issue of relative social status (equality/inequality of power, authority, expertise) is no longer quite such a straightforward matter. With spoken interactions we are able to compare and contrast the communicative contributions of the various speakers in order to discover whether there are any interpersonally significant disparities. Obviously this avenue is not available to us with monologic written texts – we have only the words of the text's author to consider. We might postulate that the writers of such texts are all-powerful on the grounds that they do all the communicating, and those to whom their words are directed have no opportunity to contribute to the text's construction and cannot interact with the text producer until after the text has been published or presented.

(This is not to imply that listeners/readers are passive participants: they are actively involved as interpreters of the text.) Yet, against this, there is the obvious point that authors of written texts definitely do not always come across as equally powerful, authoritative or expert. It is quite possible, in fact, for authors to present themselves variably as more or less powerful, authoritative or expert. Accordingly we need an analytical framework for investigating the means by which particular levels of authoritativeness are constructed in written texts.

The issue of social contact/distance poses a similar problem. In the case of spoken interactions it makes sense to consider whether those involved have some past history. Have they had prior social contact? If so, of what type? But such questions are not so readily applicable to the written monologue directed to a mass audience. Our first thought here might be that, since the author does not actually know those to whom their words are directed, there cannot be any prior relationship; accordingly we might expect them to choose language appropriate for communicating with strangers. But we know that this is by no means always the case: there is a great deal of variability in terms of how authors choose to present themselves to their audience. While some may present themselves as distant, having no prior acquaintanceship, others adopt the opposite approach and clearly present themselves as on quite familiar, friendly or even intimate terms. Therefore we need a methodology for explaining how writers of this type of text can construct this sense of connection or intimacy with their unknown, mass audience.

With these points in mind, our approach to analysing the tenor of written, monologic texts will focus on the way in which authors of written texts construct for themselves a particular presence, identity or persona which they present to their readers. In order to conduct analyses of this authorial persona we will examine the following issues:

◆ **Personalisation/impersonalisation** (see Book 2 Unit 10, page 112): To what degree has the subjective presence of the author as the originator of the text been downplayed, obscured or suppressed?

◆ **Standing** (see Book 2 Unit 10, page 114): What communicative role is performed by the writer? What types of meanings does the author present him/herself as having the authority or 'social standing' to create? For example, does the author simply inform or does he/she advise, direct or command? Does the author simply report facts or does he/she evaluate and pass judgements?

◆ **Stance** (see Book 2 Unit 10, page 115): What sort of position does the author take with regard to these various meanings? Does he/she declare them to be categorically the case or does he/she allow for the possibility of alternative viewpoints? To what degree, or in what ways, does the author refer to, or engage with, those who might hold alternative viewpoints?

In order to demonstrate how we conduct a comprehensive analysis of authorial persona we will work with two sets of texts. The first set, which we will turn to in a moment, includes texts which are concerned with the scientific/medical topic of the health effects of foodstuffs which contain caffeine, in particular coffee. The first text (Text 3) has been taken from a mass circulation magazine aimed at a general readership of teenagers and young adults. In analysing this text, our concern will be with what type of presence is constructed by the author in order to communicate expert scientific information to such readers, while at the same time reassuring them of the safety of caffeine consumption. The second text (Text 4) is drawn from a website set up to supply both experts in the field and the general public with scientific information about food-related health issues. We note that the body which publishes the website (The International Food Information Council – IFIC) is largely funded, as the site itself explains, by the 'food, beverage and agriculture industries'. Our concern here will be with the degree of personalisation or impersonalisation which is deemed appropriate for a text which presents the public face of such a body. To what extent is the author's presence downplayed or foregrounded in order to (a) communicate scientific information both to experts and to the general public, and (b) communicate scientific information in such a way that it persuades the general public of the safety of foodstuffs containing caffeine?

Text 3

(1) Whether you're a quivering caffeine junkie or just a casual sipper, there's more to that hair-raising jolt than meets the eye.

(2) What would you say if someone offered you a steaming hot cup of 1,3,7-trimethylxanthine? 'Thanks, but no thanks.'

(3) Well, guess what? You just refused a cup of coffee. 1,3,7-trimethylxanthine is the fancy-schmancy[1] name for caffeine, that go-go ingredient in everything from sodas to snickers[2]. Yet, despite its overwhelming presence, there are many myths brewing about caffeine. So, before you declare yourself a mocha maven[3], test your caffeine chutzpah[4] to see if you're really full of (coffee) beans.

(4) A cup of coffee will keep the love handles[5] away. True or false?

False. Sure, we've all felt that first blast of energy after drinking a fat mug of coffee, but that doesn't mean you're blasting the pounds away. While a moderate dose of caffeine might temporarily jump start your metabolism, it's not an appetite

[1] Different from the ordinary.

[2] A type of chocolate bar.

[3] Expert.

[4] Brazen confidence.

[5] Excess fat around the waist.

suppressant. In fact, in 1991, the FDA banned the use of caffeine in over-the-counter diet pills because, unlike proper nutrition and exercise, it has no proven long-term effect on weight.

(5)   Chemically, caffeine is in the same family as poisonous compounds such as strychnine, nicotine and morphine. True or false?

True. Caffeine is found in the leaves, seeds and fruits of more than 60 plants, including coffee, cacao beans, kola nuts and tea leaves. But, despite caffeine's *au naturel* origins, its chemical make-up belongs to the same family of potentially lethal compounds as emetine. But fear not the hot black brew. A recent study suggests that women who drink two or more cups of coffee a day are less likely to commit suicide than those who don't drink coffee at all.

(6)   The road to an Olympic gold medal is paved with coffee beans. True or false?

Both. By revving up the central nervous system caffeine can temporarily enhance athletic performance. But while your gym teacher might applaud you for your effortless sprint, the International Olympic Committee could hand you your walking papers. Classified as a 'doping agent', caffeine intake is restricted by the committee. Some cardiologists also warn that caffeine before a workout can raise blood pressure.

(*Jump*, August 1998, pp. 46, 48; quoted in Goatly, 2000, pp. 111–12)

Text 4

(1)   Caffeine is one of the most comprehensively studied ingredients in the food supply. Yet, despite our considerable knowledge of this compound and centuries of safe consumption in foods and beverages, some questions and misperceptions about the potential health effects associated with this ingredient still persist.

(2)   This issue of IFIC Review provides background information on caffeine, examines its safety and summarizes key research conducted on caffeine and health.

(3)   **Sources of Caffeine**

(4)   Caffeine is a naturally occurring substance found in the leaves, seeds or fruits of at least 63 plant species worldwide and is part of a group of compounds known as methylxanthines. The most commonly known sources of caffeine are coffee and cocoa beans, kola nuts and tea leaves.

(5)   [...]

(6) **Caffeine and Children**

(7) Contrary to popular belief, children, including those diagnosed as hyperactive, are no more sensitive to the effects of caffeine than adults. Leviton reviewed 82 papers, examining the behavioral effects of caffeine in children, and the results are reassuring. Except for infants, children metabolize caffeine more rapidly than adults; and children in general consume much less caffeine than adults, even in proportion to their smaller size.

(8) [...]

(9) **Physiological Effects**

(10) Caffeine is a pharmacologically active substance, and, depending on the dose, can be a mild central nervous system stimulant.

(11) Any pharmacological effects of caffeine are transient, usually passing within a few hours.

(12) [...]

(13) Individuals tend to find their own acceptable level of daily caffeine consumption. Those people who feel unwanted effects tend to limit their caffeine consumption; those who do not, continue to consume caffeine at their normal levels. In practice, the person who feels adverse effects such as sleeplessness learns not to consume caffeine before bedtime.

(14) Additionally, studies have shown that individuals who consume caffeine may increase memory and improve reasoning powers. Research indicates that those who consumed caffeine scored higher grades on motor skill tests, enhanced reaction times and improved auditory and visual vigilance.

(15) [...]

(16) **Caffeine and Withdrawal**

(17) Depending on the amount ingested, caffeine can be a mild stimulant to the central nervous system.

(18) Although sometimes colloquially referred to as "addictive," moderate caffeine consumption is safe and should not be classified with addictive drugs of abuse. When regular caffeine consumption is abruptly discontinued, some individuals may experience withdrawal symptoms, such as headaches, fatigue or drowsiness. These effects usually are temporary, lasting up to a day or so, and often can be avoided if caffeine cessation is gradual.

(19)   Moreover, most caffeine consumers do not demonstrate dependent, compulsive behavior, characteristic of dependency to drugs of abuse.

(20)   Although pharmacologically active the behavioral effects of caffeine typically are minor. As further elaborated by the American Psychiatric Association, drugs of dependence cause occupational or recreational activities to be neglected in favor of drug-seeking activity. Clearly, this is not the case with caffeine.

(21)   **In Summary ...**

(22)   Because caffeine is so widely consumed, the FDA [Food and Drug Administration] and medical researchers have conducted extensive research and have carefully reviewed caffeine's safety, ever since caffeine was placed on the US FDA's Generally Recognized As Safe (GRAS) list in 1958. In 1978, the agency recommended additional research be conducted to resolve any uncertainties about its safety.

(23)   In 1987, FDA reaffirmed its position that scientific evidence does not indicate caffeine in carbonated beverages creates any adverse effects in humans.

(24)   Furthermore, both the National Academy of Sciences National Research Council and the US Surgeon General's office report there has been no association established between caffeine, as normally consumed in our diet, and an increased risk to health.

(Adapted from *IFIC Review*, 1998, [online])

We shall now consider each of the aspects of speaker persona (personalisation, standing and stance) in turn.

2.1 Personalisation/impersonalisation

There is one aspect of written language which is perhaps taken so much for granted that we may lose sight of some of its key communicative consequences. The written word, being marks on a page, can be impersonal in that it can obscure the fact that these words necessarily communicate the assumptions, beliefs, observations, feelings or viewpoints of a particular person or group of people. With the spoken word, the speaker is always present and is at least some reminder of the subjective, personal presence which underlies all human communication. With the written word, it is possible, by a careful choice of words, to obscure or to downplay this subjective, personal presence. It is this potential of the written word which has enabled the development over the last few centuries of the notion of textual 'objectivity' – the notion by which it is held that it is possible and, in some cases, valuable to produce forms of communication which are neutral and impartial, which are free of authorial opinion or value judgement. This notion of objectivity has been widely influential in many branches of academic enquiry, especially the sciences, and in mass media journalism.

An objective or impersonal text is one from which all indicators of the subjective role of the author in constructing that text have been removed. Entirely impersonal texts are extremely rare, since it is only in exceptional circumstances that absolutely all traces of the author's underlying subjective presence have been removed. In almost all cases there are at least some traces of the author's subjective presence in the text. Accordingly, in most analyses, we will be interested in the degree of personalisation/impersonalisation and in where we might place the texts we are considering along a scale from most to least personalised/impersonalised.

A CTIVITY 4 (allow about 35 minutes)

We will begin by considering personalisation/impersonalisation in our two caffeine texts. We want to determine what approach the two texts take, and whether the authorial presences found in the texts are similar or different in this regard. Look through Texts 3 and 4 above and identify any words, phrases or other elements which can be seen as traces, indicators or evidence of the subjective presence of the author. You should be looking out for the following types of elements:

◆ explicit, direct references to the author

◆ formulations by which the author can be seen as interacting with, or directly addressing, the reader in some way

◆ elements of the text which indicate some relationship between the reader and the writer – for example, that they are on friendly or familiar terms, that they hold similar views, that they disagree, and so on

◆ formulations by which the writer makes some subjective assessment of, or passes some sort of judgement on, the material being presented.

COMMENT

Students who have undertaken this exercise in the past have been quick to see a clear distinction between the two texts, with Text 3 seen as much further along the personalised end of the spectrum than Text 4. Opinion is sometimes divided, however, with respect to how impersonalised students feel Text 4 to be, and especially with respect to which elements of Text 4 can be seen as indicators of its author's subjective presence.

First-person and second-person pronouns

Perhaps the most obvious indicator of personal presence is the use of the first person pronouns (i.e. *I, we, me, us, my, our*) by which the author's presence is directly acknowledged. The use of second person pronouns (*you, your*) gives rise to a similar effect, though more indirectly. By the use of the second person pronoun, reference is made to a world or state of affairs outside the text, to an actual addressee in the case of spoken, face-to-face conversation or to an imagined or intended addressee in the case of monologic written texts of the type we are currently considering. By the use of *you*, an addressee is indicated for which, logically, there must be an addressor. The presence of an addressee implies the personal presence of the writer who does the addressing.

Text 3 is noteworthy for the frequency of the second-person pronoun, *you*. Using this device, the author addresses each reader individually, rather than an anonymous, mass readership. In this she mimics the type of one-to-one personal contact which is typical of face-to-face spoken interaction (we might see this as a form of 'pseudo-interactivity'). As a result, the author's individual, personal presence is strongly felt in this text.

In keeping with this personalisation using personal pronouns, Text 3 also includes an instance of the first person pronoun:

> Sure, <u>we've</u> all felt that first blast of energy after drinking a fat mug of coffee, but that doesn't mean you're blasting the pounds away.

In contrast, Text 4 does not use the second person pronoun to construct this sense of a one-to-one personal connection. Nevertheless, it does contain two instances of a first person pronoun:

> Yet, despite <u>our</u> considerable knowledge of this compound and centuries of safe consumption in foods and beverages, some questions and misperceptions about the potential health effects associated with this ingredient still persist. ... as normally consumed in our diet, and an increased risk to health.

There is just this one instance in the entire text and hence its communicative effects may be only slight. It is also noteworthy that it is the generalised plural form *our*, rather than the more specific *my*. Nevertheless, it still amounts to a direct reference to the author's personal presence as the text's constructor.

In this, there are elements of personalisation in both texts. Clearly, however, they are significantly more salient in Text 3.

Directives

Under this heading, we are concerned with language by which the writer bids to control or direct the actions or behaviours of others. The most obvious means is via the use of commands (as discussed previously under the heading of 'speech acts'.). For example:

> Don't drink too much coffee before going to bed.

Another common means of issuing directives is via the use of modals of obligation and related structures (you explored this category in Book 2 Unit 10 under the heading of 'Deontic modality'), for example:

> You shouldn't drink too much coffee before going to bed.

> It's necessary not to drink too much coffee before going to bed.

> It would be wise not to drink too much coffee before going to bed.

Issuing orders or offering advice are clearly functions which are associated with individual humans. By including these in a written text, the writer once again provides a clear pointer to their subjective presence.

Text 3 has two instances of these types of directive:

> <u>test your caffeine chutzpah</u> to see if you're really full of (coffee) beans

> <u>fear not</u> the hot black brew.

Text 4 has one instance:

> Although sometimes colloquially referred to as "addictive," moderate caffeine consumption is safe <u>and should not be classified with addictive drugs of abuse</u>.

Arguably, the two texts are similar in this respect: both allow for the subjective presence of the author to be revealed, if only occasionally, through this function. I note, however, what seems to me a rather curious paragraph in Text 4:

> Individuals tend to find their own acceptable level of daily caffeine consumption. Those people who feel unwanted effects tend to limit their caffeine consumption; those who do not, continue to consume caffeine at their normal levels. In practice, the person who feels adverse effects such as sleeplessness learns not to consume caffeine before bedtime.

I cannot help wondering how the writer has come to have such certain knowledge about the coffee-drinking practices of coffee drinkers generally. How is it, for example, that the writer is so certain that people who feel unwanted effects are always sensible enough to limit their caffeine consumption or that those who feel adverse effects such as sleeplessness learn not to consume caffeine before bedtime?

The writer offers no supporting evidence at all, a noteworthy omission given that he/she is so scrupulous elsewhere in providing supporting evidence for similar claims and assertions. In fact, I believe it is plausible to see this paragraph as a type of indirect directive. Thus the writer states *the person who feels adverse effects such as sleeplessness learns not to consume caffeine before bedtime* when he/she might, alternatively, have used a directive such as *the person who feels adverse effects such as sleeplessness should not consume caffeine before bedtime*. Using an indirect formulation like this, the writer avoids engaging in a more personalised exchange.

Rhetorical questions and answers

Text 3 is noteworthy for the way in which it frequently asks questions of the reader while, obviously, the reader is in no position to answer. We notice as well that at one point a statement by the author is presented as if it is a response to a comment offered by the reader:

> Sure, we've all felt that first blast of energy after drinking a fat mug of coffee.

We can see this as a form of pseudo-interactivity akin to the use of the second person pronoun discussed above. Once again the writer mimics the sort of interactivity which is most typically associated with face-to-face spoken language and hence evokes the personal contact which is part of such spoken exchanges. The author's presence comes to the fore when they are active as questioner and answerer.

Text 4 is obviously in marked contrast in this respect. It makes no such use of questions and answers.

Informality and social contact

The author of Text 3 has clearly chosen to adopt a friendly, familiar or chatty tone, with extensive use of colloquial words and phrases (for example, *a quivering caffeine junkie*; *that hair-raising jolt*; *Well, guess what?*; *the fancy-schmancy name*; etc.) and contracted forms, which are more typically associated with informal settings (for example, *you're, there's, we've, it's*). Now, as already discussed above, the author does not actually have any familiarity or acquaintanceship with the reader. The author writes *as if* he/she had some degree of social contact or familiarity, mimicking the informal verbal style of casual conversation or communications between friends and family.

This is a strategy which is widely used in the mass media, particularly in lifestyle journalism or when technical topics of this type are being addressed. It is widely favoured in popularisations of science. It serves a number of communicative objectives of which the most obvious is probably that of making the general, inexpert reader feel less alienated by what may seem difficult or abstruse subject matter. The writer presents him/herself as someone who is on friendly, easy-going terms with the reader (rather than being a distant expert) and the subject matter as something which can be thought of in everyday terms, as part of the reader's ordinary, vernacular experience. One by-product of this approach is personalisation. The author is very much obviously present in the text as someone who is putting him/herself forward as a friendly acquaintance, as someone who is on the same level as the reader.

Text 4 clearly contrasts with Text 3 in this regard. There are no instances of casual or colloquial words or phrases and no instances of contractions. Accordingly, no friendly, informal acquaintance between writer and reader is implied. In terms of this aspect of the language, there are no personalising effects, nothing which overtly points to the presence of the author. Note that many past students felt that this text was at least to some degree impersonalised, and certainly that it was more impersonal than Text 3. It would seem likely that a key factor here was this text's formal, socially-distancing style. Perhaps the impersonal, objective text is one which, like Text 4, lacks any indicators of social connection or familiarity.

Conversationalisation

It is worth noting in passing that all the features we have discussed so far (the direct addressing of some respondent, the issuing of directives, the asking of questions and the use of a familiar, informal style of language) are features which, in combination, typically occur in casual conversation. Thus this particular combination can provide the means for writers to give their texts a 'speech-like' quality, and particularly a 'conversational' or 'chatty' tone. In interpersonal terms, the style has two aspects. Firstly, it involves mimicking the interactivity of multi-party spoken exchanges – what we might term 'pseudo-interactivity'. Secondly, it involves the informality which is typical of one particular subtype of spoken language, that of casual conversation – what we might term 'pseudo-familiarity'. In conducting analyses of written texts which operate with such a style, it may be useful to keep these two aspects separate in order to discover whether the style is achieved primarily as a result of pseudo-interactivity (direct address, issuing of directives, asking of rhetorical questions, giving apparent answers), primarily as a result of pseudo-familiarity (use of casual, colloquial language), or by a combination of the two.

Assessment and evaluation

Consider the following:

Each year six per cent of coffee drinkers change over to drinking tea.

This would presumably be classified as an impersonal, objective utterance. Certainly there are no words or phrases which can be singled out as evidence of the subjective presence of the author. The utterance can be interpreted as a straightforward depiction of a factual state of affairs or sequence of events. Compare such a neutral utterance with the following:

1   Predictably six per cent of coffee drinkers change over to tea each year.

2   Bizarrely six per cent of coffee drinkers change over to tea each year.

3   Sadly six per cent of coffee drinkers change over to tea each year.

4   Six per cent of coffee drinkers wisely/foolishly change over to tea each year.

5   Tea is absolutely delicious, much more refreshing than coffee.

6   A substantial number of coffee drinkers change over to tea each year.

7   It's highly likely that the number of tea drinkers is increasing each year.

8   Possibly tea is winning out over coffee.

9   The assertion that a substantial number of coffee drinkers are changing over to tea is inaccurate and false.

10   You really ought to give up coffee in favour of tea.

All these utterances involve the expression of some form of subjective assessment or **evaluation** by the author. These assessments are of various different types: in (1) and (2) the assessment is by reference to notions of what the author sees as expected or unexpected; in (3), (4) and (5) by reference to what is seen as positive or negative; in (6) by reference to some system of measurement; in (7) and (8) by reference to assessments of likelihood or probability; in (9) by assessments of truth; and in (10) by assessments of obligation or requirement. All such assessments necessarily require there to be some human presence at work, some individual (or group) who applies some system of judgement in order to evaluate the phenomenon in these various terms. We can say, therefore, that authorial assessments act, though perhaps to greater or lesser degrees, to point to the underlying subjective presence of the author. A text which features authorial assessments can therefore never be entirely impersonalised, though the degree of perceived personalisation which results from their presence may depend on factors such as the types of assessment which occur, their frequency, and/or their salience.

ACTIVITY 5 (allow about 15 minutes)

Now return to the two texts and see if you can identify any instances where the author makes assessments of these various types. At this stage it is not important to conduct a comprehensive analysis. Just look through quickly to establish whether or not there are at least some instances of authorial evaluations in either or both texts.

COMMENT

The question of how texts communicate authorial evaluation is a complex one. We will return to it in a later section, and it is considered at greater length in the reading for the unit. For the moment we will confine ourselves to the observation that both texts are to a greater or lesser degree personalised by the authors offering various types of assessments and evaluations. For example, in Text 3 we find the following types of authorial evaluations:

◆ An assessment of the intensity of the impact that a cup of coffee can have on the human physiology when the author characterises it as providing a *hair-raising jolt* in *there's more to that hair-raising jolt than meets the eye*.

◆ A somewhat negative, or at least playfully dismissive, characterisation of the technical term *1,3,7-trimethylxanthine* as a way of referring to caffeine is provided when it is described as a *fancy-schmancy* name. (The rhetorical strategy is one of winning over readers to the use of the term by seeming to share with them some mild negativity towards technical, unfamiliar terminology of this type.)

◆ The author passes judgement on various commonly-held beliefs about caffeine by characterising them as *myths* or as directly describing them as *false*.

◆ A positive judgement is passed on coffee itself when the author declares it to be something which is definitely not to be feared – *fear not the hot black brew*.

In Text 4, we find evaluations of the following type (not a complete list):

◆ The author positively assesses the extent of *our knowledge* of caffeine as *considerable*.

◆ Some beliefs about coffee are negatively evaluated when they are characterised as *misperceptions*.

◆ The author passes a positive judgement on the results of a study into the behavioural effects of coffee on children by indicating how these results affect them emotionally – they are characterised as *reassuring*.

◆ The author positively evaluates moderate caffeine consumption as *safe*.

The point is that the authors of both texts step forward, so to speak, to make an assessment or pass some judgement and thereby reveal themselves as the subjective presence behind the text. Both texts, then, are at least to some degree personalised by these authorial evaluations.

Impersonalising the personal

These, then, are the general terms by which the personal, subjective presence of the author of such texts can be signalled. We do, however, need to note that there is one further aspect of the grammar which may somewhat complicate the picture. We have spoken generally about these various types of evaluation but have not made any mention of the various modes of expression by which they may be communicated. One particular way of formulating such assessments is of particular importance. Consider the following pairs:

(1) (a)   I'm disappointed that so many coffee drinkers are turning to tea.

versus

   (b)   It's disappointing that so many coffee drinkers are turning to tea.

(2) (a)   You should give up coffee.

versus

   (b)   It's necessary that you give up coffee.

(3) (a)   I strongly suspect that many of you prefer tea to coffee.

versus

   (b)   It's highly probable that many of you prefer tea to coffee.

Our primary concern here is with the (b) options, in which anticipatory *it* formulations have been used to frame an evaluation which in the (a) options can, unproblematically, be seen as personalised. (For a more extended discussion of these anticipatory *it* formulations, you may remember the paper 'Impersonalising Stance: A Study of Anticipatory "It" in Student and Published Academic Writing' by Hewings and Hewings which you came across in Book 2 Unit 10.) Such *it* structures are frequently felt to have an impersonalising effect. Thus Hewings and Hewings propose that they function:

> to express opinions, and to comment on and evaluate propositions while allowing the writer to remain in the background. Such strategies add to the impression of the presentation of objective, impersonal knowledge.
>
> (Hewings and Hewings, 2004, p. 4)

The interesting point here is that, in interpersonal terms, two apparently incompatible (or at least opposite) effects seem to be simultaneously in play. As Hewings and Hewings themselves observe, such formulations clearly act to express opinions and to evaluate. In this sense they are unavoidably subjective and personalising since, obviously, opinion and evaluation require individual subjective consciousness. Yet at the same time there is a contrary impersonalisation being carried out via the effect of *it* concealing the source of the opinion. What this means is that, while such formulations may not have the potential to efface fully the subjective presence of the author from the text, they may well have the potential to obscure it in some way, to make it less salient and hence less strongly felt. Accordingly, it may be necessary to note the use, especially the consistent use, of such formulations when we are conducting this type of textual analysis.

Personalisation/impersonalisation: conclusions

To conclude this section, we can say that both Texts 3 and Text 4 are to some degree personalised. In both texts there are overt indicators that these are the words of a human individual (or group of individuals) who has a view on the matters being discussed and who seeks to communicate this to the reader. There are, nevertheless, some key differences which turn largely on the use of a conversational, familiar tone of voice in Text 3 and the much more formal, distanced style of Text 4. If Text 3 is seen as the more personalised, less impersonalised text, it seems plausible that this may largely be the result of this conversational style, of the decision by the writer to construct a pseudo-interactive, pseudo-familiar authorial presence.

2.2 Standing

Here we are concerned with the communicative roles performed by the writer and with the type of authority they claim for themselves in adopting these roles. For example, is their role that of storytelling, providing or seeking information, advising, commanding, interrogating, offering a service, debating, persuading, passing judgement, and so on?

A number of the features which were considered above in connection with personalisation/impersonalisation will be relevant here because elements which act to personalise a text will also often relate to the communicative role being performed. For example, we analysed the use of directives in the two texts above. We were interested in such formulations because when writers seek in this way to influence their readers to act in certain ways, they put themselves forward as an individual presence seeking to interact with the reader. Obviously directives will also be a sign that the writer is playing a particular role – that of advising or commanding. In the earlier analysis we found directives in both texts, pointing to the fact that both writers saw their function as going beyond simply providing information about coffee and caffeine to advising and seeking to influence their readers' behaviour.

We also considered the issue of the writer's use of evaluative language to approve, praise, criticise and condemn. We are now going to take this analysis a few steps further.

Evaluative language is of considerable interest in connection with the writer or speaker's role and standing. In informal, casual conversational exchanges between close friends or family members, evaluative language is often used freely, with speakers passing all sorts of judgements on people, places, objects, institutions and happenings, at least in the Western cultural contexts with which I am familiar. However, within the public sphere there are all manner of conventionalised constraints on the use of evaluative language. In fact, in the public domain, certain types of evaluation are legally prohibited under the laws of libel and slander – those evaluations deemed unjustly damaging to someone's reputation. Many discourse types, and the communicative roles associated with these, operate with what can be thought of as an evaluative etiquette. Conventions apply by which certain types of evaluation are authorised while others are excluded. Many school-level students struggle, for example, to understand what is required in terms of evaluation in the standard English literature essay. They offer up how they feel about the book under study, how it affects them emotionally, when, in fact, the conventions of the English essay require that they provide rather different types of evaluations – for example, aesthetic judgements of the writer's style and compositional skills, or ethical judgements about the moral standing of the characters. The news media provide another context in which clear constraints on the use of evaluative language operate and where particular roles are associated with different types of evaluation. For example, the role of the hard news reporter is supposedly to avoid all evaluation and simply to record the 'facts'. It is only the high-status commentator or columnist who is authorised to commend or condemn.

ACTIVITY 6 (allow about two hours)

Now read the chapter 'Subjectivity, Evaluation and Point of View in Media Discourse' in the course reader, which provides a detailed discussion of evaluative language in general and its role in news reporting. The article sets out a framework for the analysis of evaluative language which attends to such issues as whether evaluations are explicitly stated or implicitly activated, whether they are asserted or assumed and whether they are grounded in human emotion or are construed as matters of ethics or taste.

We are going to apply the analytical framework set out in the reading to an investigation of evaluative standing of the authors of the two caffeine texts. We are going to use it to compare and contrast the two texts in terms of what types of judgements the authors present themselves as authorised to make.

Return to Text 3 and consider the following questions:

(1) Are there any positive or negative assessments indicated by the text?
(2) If so, against what sorts of targets are they directed?
(3) Are they implied or explicitly stated?
(4) Is there a pattern with respect to whether the author herself makes the assessment or, alternatively, devolves responsibility for the evaluation to some outside source?

COMMENT

The text contains observations which assess caffeine both negatively and positively. Thus, by means of explicit evaluation, it is assessed as not effective in weight reduction, as entirely safe to drink under normal circumstances, as having the positive effect of reducing suicides and as having the negative effect of raising blood pressure.

The author's standing is such that she readily takes responsibility for much of this material, especially the purely informational content. In fact we observe that in the first half of the text (sections 1 to 3) all the material is directly attributed to the writer. She thereby represents herself as something of an expert on the subject, equipped with the necessary knowledge to make assertions of a general nature about coffee. However, we note that some external sources are introduced in the second half.

These sources seem to be used to introduce material by which the negative and positive assessments of caffeine mentioned above are introduced in the text. Thus the FDA (the United States Food and Drug Administration) is cited as the source for the proposition that caffeine is not effective in weight reduction; a *recent study* is cited as the source of the proposition that coffee may be beneficial in reducing suicides; and *some cardiologists* are introduced as the source of the proposition that caffeine may have the negative effect of raising blood pressure. However, it is not the case that all such evaluations of caffeine are attributed to outside sources. The author, on her own behalf, informs readers that they should not *fear the hot black brew*.

By this the author presents herself as an expert on the subject, but nevertheless an expert who also calls on others to provide additional material or supply supporting evidence for some of her claims, particularly evaluations.

A CTIVITY 7   (allow about 10 minutes)

We now turn to Text 4. How does it compare with Text 3 in terms of evaluative language and the author's standing? Briefly run through the text and consider the questions from Activity 6.

C OMMENT

The text's evaluative orientation is similar to that found in Text 3, although its assessments are more weighted to the positive aspects of caffeine than the negative. Thus, for example, caffeine is positively evaluated as having no adverse effects on even hyperactive children, as increasing memory and improving reasoning power, motor skills and reaction times, as non-addictive and as being generally safe for consumption. Once again there is a pattern in which the author takes direct responsibility for both informational and evaluative content but tends, also, to devolve responsibility for some of the evaluative elements to outside sources. Thus the proposition that caffeine increases memory, reasoning and motor skills is attributed to *studies* and to previous *research*; the proposition that caffeine has no adverse effects on health is attributed to the FDA; and the proposition that there is no link between caffeine and an increased risk to health to the National Academy of Sciences and the Surgeon General's office. Once again, this is the communicative standing of an expert in the field who is equipped to convey knowledge of a generalised nature and to pass judgements, but who nevertheless does also bring in outside sources to lend support for at least some of his/her more evaluative assertions.

Texts 3 and 4 compared: some conclusions

Our analysis has demonstrated that the two texts are broadly similar in terms of the authors' standing, but that they differ substantially with respect to personalisation. It is of some interest to consider how these differences in personalisation might relate to differences in the nature of the publication (a lifestyle magazine aimed at young readers versus a public information website) and in the nature of the audience for which the texts were intended.

As we demonstrated, Text 3 was highly personalised by means of various conversational elements. Although we can only speculate on the author's motives, it would seem plausible to expect that the text's intended audience of young readers is likely to react well to such a friendly, chatty approach. These readers, it is assumed, react well to an approach in which technical terminology is debunked as unnecessarily complicated or obscure and in which the scientific information being communicated is interpreted in everyday, down-to-earth terms. A crucial element of this approach is that the writer actively represents herself not as an elitist 'boffin' but as an 'ordinary' person, operating on the same level as the reader. The authorship of Text 4 is rather different. The website is the mouthpiece of the International Food Information Council, a body funded by large companies from the foodstuffs and agriculture sectors. Its purported purpose is to provide scientific information about food-related health issues. As a representative of such a body, the author adopts a much more distanced, impersonalised tone of voice, largely free of the pseudo-interactivity or pseudo-familiarity which is found in Text 3. We might speculate that the impersonalisation of the text is assumed to lend the text a certain 'objective' authority or credibility. Note, however, that the text's impersonalisation is not complete in that the author does allow him/herself certain subjective assessments when reporting on the safety of caffeine.

Another important difference between the two texts should be noted. While Text 3 is ultimately positive in its view of caffeine, it does nonetheless provide space for consideration of its negative aspects – for example, the fact that it is banned by the International Olympic Committee as a 'drug'. Text 4 also mentions some negative aspects of caffeine but does so in a way which downplays them.

2.3 Stance

We turn now to the final aspect of authorial persona – stance, which you first came across in Unit 10. The term 'stance' is sometimes used in the linguistics literature in a very general way to refer to all language which has an evaluative function. In this course however, we use 'stance' to refer more specifically to the way in which writers position themselves with respect to the material they are presenting and with respect to those who are known to have, or who might possibly have, views on the subject under consideration. We are concerned with such issues as whether the writer presents a proposition as absolutely and undeniably the case; whether they acknowledge the proposition's contentiousness; or whether they indicate that they themselves are uncertain, or acknowledge that others may not agree. We are concerned with how strongly the writer is committed to the material presented, with whether he/she assumes that the reader holds a similar viewpoint, and with whether he/she engages with those who might see things differently.

A CTIVITY 8 (allow about 10 minutes)

In order to explore these issues, we introduce our third set of written texts, this time from the world of journalism. The first of these is a text from a newspaper editorial concerned with a visit to the UK in 1989 by the Chinese president, Jiang Zemin – the same subject matter covered by the three news reports which were explored in the reading for the unit.

How would you characterise the tone of the article? What sort of authorial persona is constructed here? What are the linguistic means by which these effects are achieved?

Text 5

The behaviour of the Government and the police during the visit of Chinese President Jiang Zemin was nothing short of disgraceful.

To see police brutally manhandling demonstrators was not only shocking but representative of more repressive regimes, such as China.

As for Labour's 'ethical foreign policy' the visit exposed that as a sham. The message from Labour is clear: ethics, morals and ideals are not a consideration in foreign policy when exports have to be contemplated. [...]

Having behaved so dishonourably, one would have thought the Government would decide to keep its head down, if not to avoid the flak then at least in shame.

But no. Outrageously un-named Cabinet Ministers have spoken of their displeasure at the behaviour of Prince Charles for not attending the official banquet given by Mr Zemin at the Chinese Embassy last Thursday.

[...]

The Prince felt duty-bound to attend the state banquet given for Mr Zemin at Buckingham Palace on Tuesday but his conscience obviously led him to snub the Chinese President later.

While such a snub was embarrassing to the Government, the Foreign Office and the Monarchy, it was the act of a man who felt that to sup with the devil once was his duty but twice was morally wrong.

However, the Prince's ethical stance and support for such basic ideals as human rights has clearly upset Labour.

'It is not Charles's job to cause this kind of grief for us or for the Cabinet,' a Minister was reported as saying yesterday.

But if the Government places the heir to the throne in a position where he has to meet and rub shoulders with the head of one of the most infamous and brutal regimes in the world can they really expect him to kowtow without an objection?

[...]

What Prince Charles did struck a chord both with civil rights groups and with a much wider section of the public who were rightly infuriated that such hospitality should be given to a dictator.

Mr Tony Blair has realised the sensitivity of the visit but has refused to make a clear public statement on human rights and the visit of Mr Zemin.

In this instance Mr Blair has put trade before ethics, economics before human lives.

(Adapted from *The Birmingham Post*, 1999, p. 14)

COMMENT

This is a typical example of a newspaper editorial. It is forthright, confident and assertive in tone. The writer claims the right to pass extremely negative judgements on the government and the police force in this very public setting, presenting him/herself as an arbiter of right and wrong. This is achieved through the use of categorical assertions to accuse the government baldly of wrongdoing. Thus, for example, the writer declares categorically that:

The behaviour of the Government and the police was disgraceful.

The police's treatment of the demonstrators was shocking and representative of repressive regimes.

Labour's foreign policy has been exposed as a sham.

The people are rightly infuriated by the welcome given to the
Chinese leader.

The Prince's actions embarrassed the Government.

The Prime Minister Mr Blair is putting trade before ethics and
economics before human lives.

This is relatively straightforward. However, when we look at the
evaluation patterns overall in the text, we discover that the picture
is somewhat more complicated with respect to stance. You may
remember from the reading for the unit that it is possible to distinguish
between evaluations which are asserted and those which are assumed.
To assert an evaluation is to present it as being open to discussion or
argument. We can demonstrate this by considering how such assertions
might be taken up in an argument, for example:

S1: The government has behaved dishonourably.

S2: No they haven't, they did what was necessary.

or

S1: Labour's foreign policy is a sham.

S2: No it isn't.

S1: Yes it is.

or

S1: The police manhandled the protesters.

S2: No they didn't, their treatment was entirely reasonable given
the circumstances.

The evaluations from the editorial which I listed above are all instances
of such **asserted evaluation**. They are all propositions which the writer
presents as being at issue, as being the point he/she is seeking to get
across to the reader.

In contrast, the **assumed evaluation** is not so directly available for this
type of interaction. It is presented as a universally accepted given, which
is therefore not at issue and not up for discussion. To demonstrate this
further, consider the following:

Kim Yat Sun has already used these weapons and has made it clear
that he has the intent to continue to try, by virtue of his duplicity
and secrecy, to continue to do so.

Here the proposition that Kim Yat Sun is duplicitous is treated as a
given, a view which is not up for discussion. Accordingly, to reject or
challenge the offering as a whole would not be to reject or challenge

the evaluation of Kim Yat Sun as duplicitous. That proposition would remain. Consider the following:

S1: Kim Yat Sun has already used these weapons and has made it clear that he has the intent to continue to try, by virtue of his duplicity and secrecy, to continue to do so.

S2: No he hasn't, he hasn't made it at all clear that he intends to continue to try to use his weapons. (That Kim Yat Sun is duplicitous is not negated.)

We find a similar situation with the assumed evaluation in the following text:

After nine years of the government's *betrayal* of the promised progressive agenda, Canadians have a gut feeling that their country is slipping away from them.

(Canadian Hansard, 1 October 2002, [online])

In this instance, it is the evaluation of the Canadian government as having 'betrayed' its promised progressive agenda which is assumed and which is thereby treated as an uncontentious given, not up for discussion.

We can now see that this distinction between asserted and assumed evaluation involves a difference in stance on the part of the speaker/ writer. In asserting an evaluation, he/she adopts the position that the evaluative proposition is at issue, and is up for discussion. In contrast, in assuming an evaluation, he/she adopts the position that the evaluation is not at issue, and that it is a universally agreed position which can be taken for granted.

ACTIVITY 9 (allow about five minutes)

Now return to the text and identify any assumed evaluations. You should find six. Can you identify any pattern in which evaluations are asserted and which assumed?

COMMENT

The following excerpts have assumed evaluations:

1. To see police brutally manhandling demonstrators

2. more repressive regimes, such as China

3. Having behaved so dishonourably, the Government...

4. the Prince's ethical stance

5. the head [Jiang Zemin] of one of the most infamous and brutal regimes

6. rightly infuriated that such hospitality should be given to a dictator [Jiang Zemin].

These assumed evaluations include negative assessments of both the British authorities (police and the government) and the Chinese leader, as well as a positive assessment of Britain's Prince Charles. However, I note with interest that while these assumed evaluations of the British authorities are matched elsewhere in the text by asserted evaluations, this is not the case with the assessments of the Chinese leader and his government. All the evaluations of Jiang Zemin are assumed, which is revealing, I believe, of the writer's stance towards the Chinese leader: it is presented as entirely uncontentious, universally held and therefore taken for granted.

To develop the analysis of stance further, we turn now to another journalistic text. In this extract, the editor of the arts review section of British newspaper *The Guardian* responds, in an open letter published on a website, to criticisms that a film review was 'racist'. (The review was by Charlotte Raven, who is mentioned in the letter.)

Text 6

Dear (angry) reader,

I apologise for not replying to all of you personally, but since most of you have made similar points about Charlotte Raven's column, I hope you don't mind if I address them together.

Broadly most of you have written or mailed me to say that you thought Charlotte's column about Crouching Tiger Hidden Dragon was racist because it invoked the old stereotype of the Chinese being inscrutable.

Some of you made more specific points about Charlotte's lack of appreciation for Chinese cinema, and someone went as far as to suggest that by using the phrase 'it seemed to contain multitudes' to describe the performance of the cast, Charlotte was alluding to Western images of 'Chinese masses'.

In e-mail correspondence and conversations with some of you I have defended Charlotte's column quite robustly.

It is absolutely clear to me that what Charlotte was arguing was that Crouching Tiger was a bad film to which liberal audiences imputed a significance shaped by their own prejudices about Chinese cinema and the Chinese in general.

I thought it was a good point and, interestingly, so did the actor David Yip when we discussed this issue on BBC Scotland's The Mix last Sunday.

Given the number of you who were offended by the column, I think it's now pretty clear that the column wasn't as clear as I thought.

I also think that we perhaps underestimated the offensiveness of the word 'inscrutable' when used in a Chinese context – even though I am satisfied that Charlotte was using the word to describe the audience's perception of the performances in Crouching Tiger, rather than describing them herself.

To put it another way, putting quotation marks around the word inscrutable would have made Charlotte's intended meaning clearer (though I suspect many of you would still have felt its use unacceptable.)

I still think several of the points made about Charlotte's column have been misguided, most conspicuously the one about her reference to multitudes.

(Katz, 2001 [online])

 ACTIVITY 10 (allow about 10 minutes)

How would you characterise the tone of this text? Is it as forthright or as assertive or as accusatory as the previous text? Does it use categorical declarations to the same degree? Answer the following questions:

(1) Are there instances where the writer's viewpoint is presented as only possible or probable rather than as absolutely the case?
(2) Are there instances where the author explicitly acknowledges that these are only his opinions and hence that others may hold a different view?
(3) Does he characterise any of his propositions as involving some degree of speculation and hence as not categorical?
(4) Are any of his propositions attributed to an external source, hence allowing for the possibility that, while at least some people hold this to be the case, others may take a different view?

COMMENT

This text clearly includes many more non-categorical declarations than was the case in the previous text. You will probably have noticed the repeated use through the text of framing devices by which the writer explicitly represents his propositions as his subjective viewpoint. In particular, I expect you noticed his use of *I think* and *I thought*:

> *I thought* it was a good point

> *I think* it's now pretty clear that the column wasn't as clear as I thought

> *I also think* that we perhaps underestimated the offensiveness of the word 'inscrutable'

> *I still think* several of the points made about Charlotte's column
> have been misguided

Notice, as well, that the proposition that the writer and his colleagues
underestimated the offensiveness of the word *inscrutable* is explicitly
cast as a possibility, rather than an absolute, by means of the term
perhaps:

> we perhaps underestimated the offensiveness of the word
> 'inscrutable'

He also stops short of declaring himself able to say categorically how
the 'angry readers' would have reacted had the word *inscrutable* been
contained in inverted commas. He states that he suspects they would
have found the word unacceptable, rather than declaring this to be
absolutely the case.

Notice as well the use of *pretty* in *I think it's now pretty clear that the
column wasn't as clear as I thought*. By this the writer somewhat
moderates the force of the utterance.

What do these various devices indicate about the writer's stance? To
get a sense of what is at stake here, it may be useful to consider how
the text would have come across without them, for example:

> What Charlotte was arguing was that Crouching Tiger was a bad
> film to which liberal audiences imputed a significance shaped by
> their own prejudices about Chinese cinema and the Chinese in
> general.
>
> It was a good point.
>
> However, the column wasn't clear in one respect.
>
> We underestimated the offensiveness of the word 'inscrutable' when
> used in a Chinese context – even though Charlotte was using the
> word to describe the audience's perception of the performances in
> Crouching Tiger, rather than describing them herself.
>
> Putting quotation marks around the word inscrutable would have
> made Charlotte's intended meaning clearer (though many of you
> would still have felt its use unacceptable).
>
> However, several of the points made about Charlotte's column have
> been misguided, most conspicuously the one about her reference to
> multitudes.

We might argue that the writer's stance in the original is somewhat less
forthright than this modified version. He certainly comes across as
less dogmatic in the original. Most tellingly, in the original, his stance is
less confrontational and more negotiatory. This is because he does not,
for example, baldly declare that the angry readers are misguided, but

rather represents this as being his point of view – *I still think several points have been misguided*. This is also the case when he argues in his own favour. He does not simply declare the reviewers' claims about liberal audiences to be *a good point*, but once again explicitly grounds this proposition in his own point of view.

This is not to suggest that the writer in any sense presents himself as uncertain or as less than fully committed to his own case: he is still forceful in presenting his arguments and justifications. It is just that, in using these framing devices, he states his position subjectively, and hence recognises it as only one of the possible positions which might be adopted. There is an obvious reason for this more negotiatory stance. Clearly, the point of the letter is to placate, at least to some degree, the outraged readers. *The Guardian* is the sort of paper which would take seriously accusations that it had been guilty of racism. Therefore the editor has an interest in achieving some sort of rapprochement with these readers, or at least in demonstrating that the newspaper is listening to and responding to their complaints. Accordingly, it makes rhetorical sense for the writer to adopt this less than categorical stance and thereby to be represented as engaging with the readers' alternative point of view.

ACTIVITY 11 (allow about 45 minutes)

You are now going to practise analysing the interpersonal style (the tenor) of a text taken from a popular computer magazine. In its authorial 'persona' and in the way it positions the reader, it is a good example of a writing style widely found in texts which popularise some expert domains – for example, popular science magazines and computing publications of this type. Read it and address the following questions:

(1) What sort of relationship is constructed between writer and reader (given the fact that, of course, there is in reality no actual, established relationship, since the writer directs his words towards an unknown, mass audience)? What sorts of communicative objectives might be served by such a constructed relationship?

(2) What sort of persona is adopted by the writer? Does he present himself as expert or inexpert, and if so, in what areas? To what degree is he authoritative, assertive, dogmatic or alternatively, flexible, uncertain or open to alternatives?

You will be analysing this text in more detail in the CD-ROM activities.

Text 7

Computers are bad for you – RSI

Martin Gittins looks at the damage computers can do to your body, and how to avoid it.

'RSI' stands for 'repetitive stress injury'

Computers get blamed for a lot of things. Whether it's a stock market crash, our children getting fatter or the decline in the state of the Top 40, you can bet it's all the fault of the PC. Sure, we all know computers are bad for us, but just how much damage can they do to this delicate wetware of flesh, bones and organs we all call home?

To put it simply: The physical problems that arise with using computers are the problems that arise with doing any activity repeatedly for prolonged periods. You put stress on a part of the body that then doesn't get time to heal properly.

In this article, I'll be looking at the way in which using your PC may be damaging your physical health – leaving aside any discussion of the psychological effect of using computers – and what you can do about it. We'll also be looking at how you can arrange your workspace to help minimise risks and help improve efficiency – after all, if you're comfortable you're also likely to work better.

It really doesn't matter if you are typing up huge documents in a wordprocessor or trying to get to the next level on Quake II; if you use a mouse, joypad or keyboard for long periods it can cause damage to your wrists, lower arms and indeed the rest of your body.

Writer's cramp and tennis elbow are two colloquialisms for RSI – repetitive strain injury – and the symptoms can range from a stiffness or pain in the hand and wrist to severe, debilitating pain throughout the body.

To prevent or reduce the effects of RSI you should first make sure that your input devices such as keyboard and mouse are as comfortable to use as possible. Many of the keyboards supplied with PCs can be pretty atrocious, with poor key action, and nothing will lead to RSI quicker than having to fight with your mouse just to get it to move across the screen.

Many of the problems with typing stem from keeping the wrists bent while the fingers hover over the keys. This is very bad for you and can lead to one of the most common forms of RSI – Carpal Tunnel Syndrome. The hands should be straight and rest lightly over the keyboard.

There are a number of models on the market where the keyboard is split into two sets of keys aligned at a much more natural angle for comfortable typing. I am a huge fan of the Natural Keyboard Elite by Microsoft (http://www.microsoft.com/products/hardware/

natkeybd/). This is an excellent piece of industrial design that facilitates correct hand positioning and encourages touch-typing – it is almost impossible to use if you are a hunt-and-peck two finger typist. Otherwise you might find a wrist rest helps to keep your wrists level and resting on a padded surface.

With mice, there is inevitably a huge range of ergonomic styles, but again I find the Microsoft mouse as good as any. Hold a mouse lightly – never wrestle with it – and it should be OK for light to moderate usage. [...]

The other way of preventing RSI is to take regular breaks: this will give your limbs a chance to recover. This applies to all the ailments described here; regular breaks are the best way to reduce their likelihood. If you have trouble remembering to take breaks there are a number of software solutions which run in the background on your PC and prompt you, at set intervals, to take a break.

Of the programs available, I like BreakTime because it is unobtrusive and doesn't take up many system resources (http://www.isotopemedia.com/breaktime/).

Also take a look at my 'Total Hands, Neck, Eyes and Back Workout' section for some suitable exercises and check out the links sections for some good resources regarding RSI on the Web.

(*PC Basics*, December 1998, p. 30)

COMMENT

The author uses various speech acts (i.e. statements, commands, questions and offers) but not in equal proportions.

When considering commands, it is useful here to group them together with other forms of directives, for example, uses of modals of obligation and related structures such as 'You must take breaks', 'You should take breaks', 'It is advisable to take breaks'. When considering statements, it is useful to note which are categorical and which are non-categorical. Categorical statements are those which take the form of a bare assertion – for example, 'Computers are damaging to your health'. In contrast, non-categorical statements are those under which the possibility of some alternative position or viewpoint is in some way recognised or allowed for. A statement may be non-categorical because:

◆ the proposition is presented as only possible or probable: 'Computers may be damaging to your health', 'Computers are almost certainly damaging to your health'

◆ the proposition is presented as not always being the case: 'Computers sometimes damage your health', 'Computers often damage your health', 'Computers will usually damage your health'

◆ the proposition is presented as only a deduction from the available evidence and hence still not absolutely certain: 'It seems that computers are damaging to your health', 'The evidence suggests that computers are damaging to your health', 'Computers must be damaging to your health'

◆ the proposition is attributed to some external source and hence depends on the reliability of that source: 'A new report has just been published which argues that computers are damaging to health', 'Many experts believe that computers are damaging to your health'

▸ the writer acknowledges in some way their subjective involvement in formulating the proposition, thereby allowing for the possibility that others may not share their view: 'In my view, computers are damaging to your health', 'I think computers are damaging to your health', 'I am convinced that computers are damaging to your health', 'It is my contention that computers are damaging to your health'.

It is still possible for a writer to adopt a non-categorical mode of expression and at the same time to indicate that they are highly committed to the proposition. Thus in a case such as 'I am absolutely certain that computers damage your health', the writer simultaneously indicates that that this is a strongly held belief on their part, and yet still doesn't declare the proposition categorically. Hence they still allow, if only minimally, the possibility that others may not hold this view. This is an apparent paradox: 'I am absolutely certain that computers damage your health' is less certain than 'Computers damage your health'. We only explicitly declare that we are certain when there is some doubt, or at least some debate, associated with the proposition under consideration.

In the last section we have looked at a framework for analysing tenor in non-interactive, single-party, written texts. However, it is important to realise that some aspects of this framework could also be applied to analyses of interactive, multi-party spoken texts, particularly the concepts of stance and standing.

A CTIVITIES CD-ROM (allow about two hours)

Now do the activites for this unit on the Activites CD-ROM, where you will analyse in more detail Text 7, *Computers are bad for you – RSI.*

Conclusion

In this unit we have explored a framework for exploring how both interactive and non-interactive texts operate interpersonally. That is, we have explored how we can relate particular linguistic features of texts to the social roles and relationships which actually hold, or which are presented as holding, between the communicative participants involved in those texts.

First, we explored the interpersonal aspects of interactive texts such as conversations, interviews and classroom exchanges. We demonstrated how the interpersonal aspects of those texts can be related to the relative social status of the communicative participants (equality/inequality) and the social contact/distance between them.

Secondly, we explored the interpersonal aspects of non-interactive, mass communicative texts. A framework was proposed for characterising the authorial persona which writers construct for themselves in such texts. It was proposed that key aspects of authorial persona are:

◆ **Personalisation/impersonalisation**: the extent to which, or the ways in which, the underlying subjective role of the author is indicated or revealed.

◆ **The author's standing**: the author's communicative role; what it is the author undertakes, or assumes the authority, to do through his/her language – for example, informing, arguing, advising, evaluating and so on.

◆ **Stance**: how the author positions him/herself with respect to the material being presented and with respect to those who might hold alternative views.

Finally, let us bring together in a comprehensive manner all the aspects of tenor that we have now covered (see Figure 2 on p. 58).

Learning outcomes

After completing this unit, you should have developed your knowledge and understanding of:

◆ the relationship between social context, specifically tenor, and the grammatical and lexical features of a text

◆ the way in which we can systematically analyse interpersonal meaning in terms of social status, social distance and authorial persona (personalisation/impersonalisation, standing and stance).

In the light of your increased understanding, you should now be able to:

◆ identify grammatical and lexical features relating to tenor
◆ intepret the social and cultural meaning of the tenor constructed
◆ begin to evaluate the communicative effect of different tenor constructions.

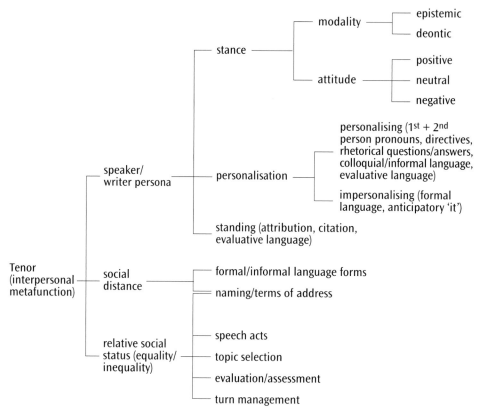

Figure 2 Map of tenor (complete)

Key terms introduced and revisited

asserted evaluation	relative social status
assumed evaluation	social contact/distance
authorial persona [speaker/writer persona]	speech acts [speech functions]
evaluation	stance
goods and services	standing [communicative standing]
interpersonal meaning	tenor
modality	topic choice [topic selection]
personalisation/impersonalisation	turn management
question tags	

Near equivalents are given in [ ].

Answers to the activity

ACTIVITY 1

Key:

offer of information – standard font/type-face

request/demand for information – <u>underlined</u>

request/demand for service/action – <mark>black background</mark>

offer of service/action – <u>coloured underline</u>

Text 1: speech–act analysis

S1: Alright, <mark>a quick summary of what we have just seen.</mark>
[*demand for service – note that although this takes the form of a declarative clause (and may therefore at first appear to be an offer of information), it functions as a demand/request that the students do something, that they provide the summary. This is made clear by the next move, where the teacher indicates that the students should be* quick *about providing a summary.*]
<mark>Quick.</mark> [*demand for service*]

S2: Lever. [*offer of information*]

S1: <mark>Hold on.</mark> [*demand for service*]

S3: Seesaw. [*offer of information*]

S1: Right. <mark>Just wait till we are all here.</mark> [*demand for service*]
<mark>Have you got enough scrap paper on your desk please?</mark> [*demand for service – notice once again that the form here is that of a an 'indirect' command. Although this initially looks like a request for information, the 'please' at the end reveals that it is actually functioning as a command that the students get out some scraps of paper and put them on their desks.*]
You'll probably only need two or three pieces. [*offer of information*]

Right, you may have to use the stand. [*offer of information, though might also act to direct them to use the stand, hence may function as a demand for an action*]

<mark>Steven and Brad, the sun is shining inside.</mark> [*demand for service – indirect command, declarative form used not, in fact, to provide information but to direct the students to take their hats off*]
Alright, thankyou. <u>Solved your problem?</u> [*request for information – though notice that this seems to be more about the teacher controlling the behaviour of the students – getting them to take their hats off – than actually requesting information*]

You'll probably need to see that film tomorrow, as an extra, to get you (*pause*) to get your ideas really sorted out. [*offer of information*]
Right. Let's have a summary of what was the film basically about. [*demand for service – note the use of the 'let's' form of the imperative*]
They seem to mention two basic machines. [*offer of information*]
Um, Andrew? [*Here the teaching is eliciting a response from a particular student so a request for information is combined with demand to that particular student that they respond – so, in a sense, 'request for information' is combined with 'demand for service'.*]

S2: Levers. [*offer of information*] (*pronounces the word with an American accent as in the film*)

S1: It has an Australian pronunciation. [*demand for service – once again an indirect command. The utterance appears to be an offer of information but the student treats it as if the teacher is demanding that they perform a particular service.*]

S3: Levers. [*not really so much an offer of information as an act of compliance with the teacher's previous directive that he use an Australian accent*]

S1: Yeah, leave her alone. (*said as a joke and the class laughs*) [*a word play here – lever sounds like leave her*]
Lever (*writes on the board*) [*more here a physical act – that of writing on the board – than any substantive offer of information; though does act to confirm the previous offer of information by the student*]
and ... (*pause*) [*request for information – another eliciting move, acting both as a request for information and a directive to the class that they respond by providing some information*]

S4: An inclined plane. [*offer of information*]

S1: An (*pause*) inclined plane. [*offer of information – though note that this is not new information, just a confirmation of the information just provided*]
(*The teacher repeats the word as he writes it on the board and a child calls out.*)
Hold on, hold on, [*demand for service*]
now they extended these two basic machines, (*pause*) into five separate machines. [*offer of information*]
In that movie they extended them out, they extended out some of the machines. [*offer of information*]
They used the lever. [*offer of information*]
Hold on, hold on. (*A child is calling out.*) [*demand for service*]

S1: Joanne? [*request for information and a directive – another eliciting move*]

S6: Lever. [*offer of information*]

S1: No, we've done a lever. [*offer of information*]

S4: Baseball bat. [*offer of information*]

S1: Baseball bat. (*pause*) Any bat really. [*offer of information*]

S6: Flying fox. (*said very quietly*) [*offer of information*]

S1: Pardon, <u>flying fox?</u> (*writes on the board*) [*request for information – actually more a request for clarification than for the supply of a specific piece of information*]

S7: Clothesline. [*offer of information*]

S1: <u>And what with it?</u> [*request for information*]

S7: A wheel. [*offer of information*]

S1: A wheel. [*offer of information*]
Yeah, no you're right. Clotheslines. [*offer of information*]
<u>That was a ...</u> (*interrupted*) <u>what did she use on the clothesline?</u>
[*request for information*]

SEVERAL: Pulley. [*offer of information*]

S1: A pulley, which is a type of (*pause*) lever. [*offer of information*]
<u>Except of course, you've got also a what with it?</u> [*request for information*]
A (*pause*) wind (*prompting children*) lass. [*request for information*]
<u>Anything else that wasn't mentioned that possibly uses the principles of a lever.</u> [*request for information*]

S8: Door handle. [*offer of information*]

S1: A door handle, good one, hey. [*offer of information – confirming*]

S1: Yep. (*writes on board*) Righto, let's have a look at an inclined plane one. [*demand for service*]
(*pause*) well actually that is a type of tool which you have seen in action, come to think of it. [*offer of information*]
<u>Maybe we can get six uses of an inclined plane. Um Aranthi?</u>
[*another elicit – combining a request for information about what might be some of the additional uses of inclined plane with a demand to the student that she supply a response*]

S9: Stairs. [*offer of information*]

S1: Stairs, right. Great answer. [*offer of information*]

Unit 13

Construing human experience: grammar, representation and point of view

Prepared for the course team by Peter White

CONTENTS

Materials required

While studying this unit, you will need:

> your reference grammar
> the course reader
> the Activities CD-ROM.

Knowledge assumed

You should be familiar with the following before starting this unit:

> actor
> ergative verb
> experienced
> experiencer
> goal
> intransitive
> long passive
> material process
> mental process
> nominalisation
> relational process
> sayer
> short passive
> transitive
> verbal process.

Introduction

By our language we represent, make sense of, and interpret the world around us. This, of course, is an obvious and key function of language. The commonsensical view is probably that our language simply reflects the world of experience in a relatively passive way. The world impinges on our senses and our language simply provides a means for recording and reporting on these sense impressions. Whether or not this is, in fact, the relationship between language and 'reality' has been a topic of animated debate throughout the history of intellectual thought, providing a topic for discussion within philosophy and a number of religious traditions. In this unit, not surprisingly, we are not seeking to provide any definitive conclusions as to the nature of reality. However, we are going to be demonstrating the crucially-active role which language plays in determining how we interpret, understand and ultimately evaluate events in the material world.

In previous units we explored some of the ways in which language provides for particular representations or interpretations of the world of human experience. We explored analyses which reveal the degree of technical or specialist terms. We also considered the types of clauses which are used in a text (whether transitive or intransitive, active or passive, and so on). Finally, we also examined the types of processes, participants and circumstances which are used to depict and characterise particular events and states of affairs. Let us now return to the diagram which was presented in Book 2, Unit 11 and which shows how language is used to create the field of a text.

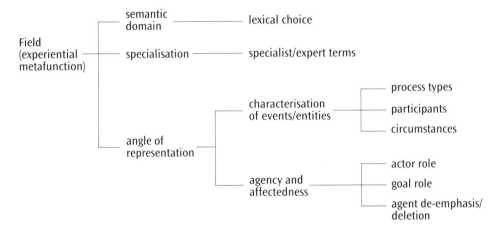

Figure 1 Map of field

In this unit we will build on the material we came across in Book 2 (particularly Unit 8.3 and Unit 11) in order to deepen our understanding of the representational and interpretive function of language. We will provide further evidence that grammatical choices with respect, for example, to clause type or process type are not 'neutral', that differences at this basic level of grammatical structure can result in significantly different characterisations and interpretations. In so doing, we will further develop the argument that there are connections between the use of certain grammatical structures and the expression in a text of a particular value system or point of view.

There is an array of interconnected linguistic features which are relevant to this issue of representation and interpretation. Thus, for example, we may be interested in what type of process occurs most frequently in a text. Do material processes, for example, predominate? In which case the text is likely to be primarily concerned with action, providing a concrete depiction of dynamically unfolding sequences of events. Or do relational processes predominate? In which case the text is likely to be concerned with static states and conditions, with providing descriptions and classifications rather than with depicting action. Similarly, we may be interested in whether there are any patterns under which particular individuals, social groupings or entities are consistently associated with a particular participant role. For example, is there a pattern by which one individual or grouping most typically plays the role of actor in material processes, or experiencer in mental processes, or sayer in verbal processes, and so on? By such patterns a particular entity can come to be characterised as primarily concerned with action, as primarily concerned with communication, as primarily concerned with cognition or emotion, and so on.

Our focus in this unit, however, will be somewhat narrower. We will single out one specific experiential issue for consideration, which we term **agency and affectedness**. Here we are concerned with investigating texts to determine who or what is presented as most 'agentive' – that is, most active, effective or dynamic – and, alternatively, who or what is presented as most 'affected' – that is, most passive, inert or acted upon.

You have already been introduced to the analytical significance of this issue in Book 2 Unit 11, especially in the reading for that unit. The author, Andrew Goatly, proposed that choices about agency and affectedness can have implications for how we view the natural world and for our awareness of current threats to the natural environment. Other writers and researchers have applied similar analyses in investigations of texts from the domains of literary fiction, children's fiction, political rhetoric, news reporting, and academic research in the physical sciences, medicine and the humanities. In all these contexts, key insights into the point of view or way of thinking advanced by the text can be provided by discovering which participants are represented as most active or effective, and which are represented as most passive or acted upon.

My purpose in this unit will be to ensure that you have the tools to conduct close analyses of texts in terms of agency and affectedness, and to use these analyses to compare and contrast texts which, for example, may be concerned with the same or similar subject matter but which provide for different interpretations or ways of thinking about that material. By reference to the reading for this unit (by Michael Stubbs), we will also look at how issues of agency and affectedness can be explored in larger collections of texts by the application of the tools of corpus analysis.

In order to set out this framework, we will explore the differences in agency and affectedness which can be observed in two news items which report on precisely the same incident. We will demonstrate how, by subtle differences in grammatical choices, such apparently similar texts can provide significantly different interpretations and evaluations.

In order to conduct such analyses, it is necessary to be able to:

◆ identify instances of material process clauses

◆ classify these clauses as transitive or intransitive, and as active or passive

◆ identify any instances of ergative verbs

◆ classify the participants in these clauses as actors or goals

◆ identify whether there are any significant patterns by which particular individuals or groupings are more likely to be actors than goals, and vice versa

◆ identify whether there are any uses of structures (for example, short passives, ergative verbs, nominalisations) by which the text obscures or de-emphasises who or what is responsible for a particular action or happening.

① AGENCY AND AFFECTEDNESS – REPRESENTATIONAL AND EVALUATIVE EFFECTS

As I said in the introduction, in this unit we are concerned with the issue of agency and affectedness – i.e. with grammatical patterns by which some participants can be represented as more active, influential or effective, as having more of an impact on the world around them – and, alternatively, by which other participants can be represented as more passive or inert, as being acted upon rather than as acting.

We will begin by returning to the news report of the anti-Blair street protest to which you were introduced in Unit 11. You will probably remember that we discussed at some length the following extract from the opening of a report published in *The Times* newspaper:

Text 1

Bullets wreck Blair visit

FOUR people were wounded in a gunfight between political extremists and police about 100 yards from Tony Blair in Cape Town yesterday after officers spotted men handing out guns to demonstrators baying for the Prime Minister's blood.

(Adapted from Kiley and Sherman, 1999, p. 1)

We are now going to extend that discussion by comparing this extract with one from another British newspaper, *The Guardian*. The opening to its coverage of the same incident took the following form:

Text 2

South African police open fire on anti-Blair protesters

The crack of shotguns was heard in the streets of South Africa's parliamentary capital yesterday as police opened fire on protesters demonstrating against a visit by Tony Blair.

(Adapted from Beresford, 1999)

In the discussion of *The Times* text in Unit 11, we noted the significance of such features as the choice of *Bullets* as the actor in the headline and the use of the short passive *Four people were wounded...* in the opening sentence. We saw how such choices enabled the text to intensify the sense of danger, to imply a greater degree of threat to Prime Minister Blair than the facts might otherwise have indicated. Now we want to take a further analytical step and consider how this text and its equivalent from *The Guardian* influence the reader to evaluate and pass judgement on those involved in the incident, specifically the police and the protesters.

ACTIVITY 1 (allow about 20 minutes)

Look at the two texts again and think about issues of evaluation and interpretation. Then briefly answer the following questions:

(1)   Are the two texts similar or different in terms of the view they take of the police and the protesters? If they are different, in what ways?

(2)   Does either of the texts contain words or phrases which are explicitly evaluative of the police and/or the protesters, i.e. which explicitly characterise the police or the protesters in positive or negative terms? If so, what are these words or phrases?

(3)   Does either of the texts suggest more indirectly or implicitly a negative or positive view of the police and/or protesters? For example, is a negative or positive assessment indirectly suggested or implied, rather than directly stated? If so, how is this implication achieved?

(4)   The two texts present different actors as the primary instigators of the events under consideration. In what ways do the texts differ in this regard and does the choice of actors have any consequences, at least potentially, for the way in which the police and/or the protesters are likely to be viewed?

COMMENT

The Times

I believe most readers would see *The Times* as positioning the reader to take a negative view of the protesters. This negative perspective is perhaps most obviously communicated via the use of the explicitly negative term *extremist* and the explicit and strongly critical *baying for blood*. In this second formulation the protesters are equated with wild animals, obviously an extremely negative association.

The claim that men apparently associated with the protesters *handed out guns* is not of itself explicitly evaluative (it does not feature any actual positive or negative assessments), and yet it obviously has a strong potential to influence the reader's view of the protesters. Here, of course, the protesters are not only represented as active, and hence as in some way responsible for the events which subsequently transpired, but, more crucially, as responsible for an action which is highly likely to be viewed negatively by the typical *Times* reader. The protesters would therefore be seen as having fomented any subsequent violence by providing its means. In this light we can see the further interpretive significance of the use of the short passive *Four people were wounded in a gunfight...* and the formulation *Bullets wreck Blair visit*. Given that the protesters have been characterised as *extremists*, have been likened to wild animals and have been said to be equipped with guns, there is at least a good chance that readers will see them as the most likely source of the shooting which *wounded* the four people and *wrecked* the Prime Minister's visit. Here we see that the grammatical vagueness associated with the short passive and the choice of *Bullets* as actor serves a particular rhetorical purpose. It enables the text to blame the protesters without actually naming them as the shooters. Here, we see how choices at the level of clause structure combine with more explicit choices at the level of word and phrase to contribute to a particular evaluative stance.

The Guardian

The interpretive picture presented by *The Guardian* is, obviously, rather different. It differs markedly both in terms of explicitly evaluative elements (there are none) and in terms of the elements which have the potential to imply a negative view of the police and/or the protesters. The key contrast here with the extract from *The Times* is in terms of agency, of which participants are represented as most actively involved in initiating or causing the events which took place. In the *Times* report, the most active agents were the protesters (who *handed out guns* and *bayed for blood*) and the bullets which, by implication, were associated with those protesters. In marked contrast, in *The Guardian* report the situation has been reversed. Now the primary actors are not the protesters or their bullets but the police who are presented as *firing on the protesters*.

This is not to suggest that *The Guardian* is necessarily indicating a positive view of the protesters and a negative view of the police. It is possible that some or even many *The Guardian* readers will view the action of the police as possibly necessary in order to maintain public order and prevent worse violence. This will depend on such factors as whether the reader already has a positive or negative view of Prime Minister Blair, whether they already have a positive or negative view of the South African police, whether they are generally supportive of, or opposed to, protests of this type, and so on. The difference here is more a matter of potential. In contrast with *The Times*, *The Guardian* text chooses a grammatical structure which clearly refrains from suggesting any wrongdoing on the part of the protesters and, perhaps most importantly, leaves the way open for blame to be subsequently attributed to the police as the most active participant in these events.

The choice of actor has clear representational effects. The differences between the two texts have the potential to result in rather different understandings or interpretations of what took place that day. In the first instance (the *Times* report) it is the protesters who are most active, who initiate and hence who are likely to be seen as most responsible for the violence. In the second instance (the *Guardian* report) it is, in contrast, the police who are presented as most active, as initiating events and who thereby have the potential to be seen as to blame for the day's violence.

Of course, whether or not the two texts maintain these different interpretative standpoints is a question which can only be answered by looking at the texts in their entirety, and this is precisely what we will be doing in the following sections. Before we do this, it is necessary to set out in more detail the analytical framework which we will be employing.

② AGENCY AND AFFECTEDNESS

2.1 Agency and material processes

In exploring agency and affectedness, we typically confine our attention to material process clauses and put aside clauses involving the other process types. The reasons for this are as follows. As you may remember, material processes are 'doing' verbs, which represent physical actions. Such processes always involve some entity which is depicted as initiating, causing, or giving rise to the material action (the actor) and they frequently (though not always) also include an entity which is depicted as being changed, moved, created or influenced in some way by the action (the goal). Through material process clauses, then, entities are represented as dynamically involved with the physical world, as directly effecting change to their material conditions. Similarly, they also provide the means by which entities are represented as being directly acted upon and changed by the world around them. Accordingly, when exploring agency and affectedness, it makes sense to focus attention on clauses of this type since it is here we find the most directly effective, influential and dynamic participants.

It is worth noting, however, that we might also want to take account of other process types and at least some of the participants associated with them. It is possible for the experienced entity in mental process clauses to have a sense of agency, for example:

He (*experienced*) was terrifying (*mental process*) the children (*experiencer*) with his ghost stories.

The sayer in some verbal process clauses can also be seen as active, as effecting change in the world, for example:

He (*sayer*) ordered (*verbal process*) a new design for the front cover.

Nevertheless, such experienced and sayer roles are always less directly agentive – their action upon the world is always to some degree indirect, and accordingly it is reasonable to conduct analyses which exclude such in favour of a more narrow focus on material processes and their participants.

This is the approach we will adopt here. In Unit 11 we conducted such an analysis on the first of our anti-Blair protest reports, from *The Times*. Remember that, for this type of analysis, we provide a version of the text in which we insert any participants which have been left understood in the original text. Thus, if the original text were:

The police formed their vehicles into a barricade and began to unload riot shields

we would provide the following for the purposes of analysis:

The police formed their vehicles into a barricade ‖ and {they = police} began to unload riot shields.

We will look at *The Times* report in detail and so supply the process-type analysis from Unit 11. Clauses with material processes are are underlined.

Text 3

(1) Bullets wreck Blair visit

(2) FOUR people were wounded in a gunfight between political extremists and police about 100 yards from Tony Blair in Cape Town yesterday ‖ (3) after officers spotted [[(4) men handing out guns to demonstrators [[(5) {demonstrators} baying for the Prime Minister's blood.]]]]

(6) Mr Blair's convoy of cars had been held up by the demonstration [[(7) {demonstration} organised by a group [[(8) {the group} calling itself Against Global Oppression,]]]] ‖ (9) and he was smuggled in through a side entrance of the Castle ‖ (10) moments before shooting broke out.

(11) The police said ‖ (12) that they had seen [[(13) two men distributing arms to protesters]] ‖ (14) who {protesters} held up placards [[(15) {placards} condemning the British and American airstrikes against Iraq ‖ (16) and saying 'Death to Blair' and 'One Blair, one bullet'.]]

(17) The officers said ‖ (18) that they {the police} gave the crowd five minutes ‖ (19) {in order for the crowd} to disperse ‖ (20) before {the

police} firing teargas ‖ (21) and {the police} throwing stun grenades at the demonstrators. (22) They {the police} then opened fire ‖ (23) after {the police} being shot at themselves. (24) Officers took deliberate aim with shotguns [[loaded with lightweight birdshot]] ‖ (25) as others [[armed with automatic rifles]] crouched with their weapons at the ready. ‖ (26) But Superintendent Wicus Holtzhausen said ‖ (27) the police did not use sharp-point ammunition. (28) Two members of People Against Gangsterism and Drugs – a vigilante group with its own armed wing – were arrested: ‖ (29) a man who had been wounded in the neck and shoulder ‖ (30) and a woman grazed on the head by a bullet. (31) A child was also seen ‖ {child} being carried away from the scene, ‖ (32) and a reporter [[(33) {a reporter} running for cover]] was caught in the crossfire ‖ (34) and {a reporter was} shot in the legs by a police gun. (35) Ordinary civilians fled the scene ‖ (36) and {ordinary civilians} dived for cover behind an ornamental wall ‖ (37) as the demonstrators, <<(38) some of them women wearing long dresses>>, attempted to hide their firearms. (39) Mr Blair ignored the pandemonium on the street ‖ (40) and {Mr Blair} continued with his programme, (41) {Mr Blair} presenting British soldiers with medals for their work in [[(42) {British soldiers} retraining the South African Army.]] (43) But members of his entourage said ‖ (44) that they heard the gunshots and the sounds of [[(45) police and ambulance sirens wailing through the city.]]

(Adapted from Kiley and Sherman, 1999, p. 1)

2.2 The actor role

Once we have isolated material process clauses in this way, our attention turns more specifically to agency and affectedness. Specifically we are interested in which individuals or groups are represented as most agentive and which as most acted upon. In this case, the groups which are of most interest are the police and the protesters. We are interested, therefore, in whether we can observe any patterns by which one or other of these two participants (the police or the protesters) is significantly more likely to be given the actor role, or, alternatively, to be given the role of goal. We will begin by conducting an analysis to investigate such a possibility.

A CTIVITY 2 (allow about 20 minutes)

This analysis is straightforward enough. It is simply a matter of drawing up a list of those clauses in which the police play the actor role and another list in which the protesters have this function. Before you undertake this, you may want to review the following briefly.

The actor is the participant which initiates, causes or gives rise to the action in material process clauses. It can be thought of as the 'doer'. Remember that actors occur in the following types of clauses – intransitives, transitives and long passives. In intransitive clauses, they are the sole participant, for example:

Intransitive (*actor – no goal*):

Ren Hua (*actor*) bowed (*process*) to my grandfather (*circumstance*).

Everyone (*actor*) jumped (*process*) in fright (*circumstance*).

The vase (*actor*) broke (*process*).

The cake (*actor*) is cooking (*process*).

Violence (*actor*) erupted (*process*) outside the embassy (*circumstance*).

In transitive clauses, the actor occurs with another participant, the goal, which the actor in some way acts upon, targets or affects. For example:

Transitive (*actor and goal*):

King Alfred (*actor*) cooked (*process*) the cakes (*goal*).

The thieves (*actor*) broke (*process*) the vase (*goal*).

The police (*actor*) provoked (*process*) the violence (*goal*).

In long passives, both actor and goal are present, with the goal now occurring as subject and the actor relegated to a more marginal position in a prepositional phrase beginning with *by*, for example:

Long passive:

The cakes (*goal*) were cooked (*process*) by King Alfred (*by-phrase actor*).

The vase (*goal*) was broken (*process*) by the thieves (*by-phrase actor*).

The violence (*goal*) was provoked (*process*) by the police (*by-phrase actor*).

You may like to make use of a table like Table 3 for this identification process. Look back at the text as set out in the previous section and insert clauses in the appropriate column.

Text 3 – actor analysis

Police as actors	Protesters as actors

See 'Answers to the activities' for feedback.

COMMENT

Rather interesting findings emerge from this analysis. We observe tellingly that the protesters are represented as significantly more active, or agentive, than the police in that (a) it is the protesters who are exclusively assigned the actor role for almost the entire first half of the extract, and (b) there are more protester actors than police actors – nine protester actors versus seven police actors. If we exclude clause 18 (*the police gave the protesters five minutes...*) on the grounds that the police did not actually engage in a material action, then the difference is even more marked – nine protester actors to six police actors. We notice, as well, that in its final stages, the extract again favours protester actors – so the text both begins and ends with protesters in this role.

This is only the first stage of our analysis. So far, all we have done is look broadly at which participants are assigned the actor role. There is a further important distinction to be observed with respect to actors – whether or not they co-occur with a goal. This is a matter of whether the clause is an intransitive or, alternatively, a transitive or a long passive, for example:

Actor without goal:

Intransitive: The police (*actor*) opened fire (*process*).

Actor with goal:

Transitive: The police (*actor*) shot (*process*) the protesters (*goal*).

Long passive: The protesters (*goal*) were shot (*process*) by the police (*by-phrase actor*).

For ease of reference I will use the term **transactional actor** (because there is a 'transaction' between the actor and the goal) to refer to those which occur in clauses where there is also a goal (transitives and long passives) and **non-transactional actor** (because there is no transaction indicated) to refer to actors which occur in clauses without a goal (intransitives).

This transactional versus non-transactional distinction can be significant for investigations of agency and affectedness. As already discussed, the key point here is that the transactional actor is represented as having an impact upon some second, typically separate entity, while the non-transactional actor is not. While the transactional actor is shown to be directly affecting the world around it, the non-transactional actor is typically represented as affecting only itself, i.e. its own condition but not the condition of any external entities. In this sense, the non-transactional actor can be seen as less 'effective' than the transactional actor. Both types of actor initiate, cause or give rise to actions, but differ in the degree to which they effect change upon the world around them. To illustrate this difference, consider the following short text which I have concocted using only non-transactional actors:

> Ren Hua awoke. She stretched. She yawned. She washed. She ate. She stretched again. She pounced. She preened. She luxuriated. She slept. Another full day in a cat's life.

Here, I believe, a certain representational effect follows from the exclusive use of non-transactional actors. The cat is depicted as self-contained and self-sufficient, as active but not as acting upon or with the world around it.

In summary, we can say that transactional actors are maximally agentive in that they not only initiate or cause actions but also act directly upon other entities, while non-transactional actors can be seen as somewhat less agentive, in that while they also initiate and cause actions, they do not have this direct impact upon the world around them.

The point of this discussion is that we may want to go beyond simply identifying actors in clauses to noting whether those actors are transactional or non-transactional. That is, we will be interested in observing whether there are patterns by which particular individuals or groups are more likely than other individuals or groups to be represented as transactional actors (and hence as maximally agentive) or, alternatively, as more likely to be represented as non-transactional actors (and hence as less agentive, at least in relative terms).

◢ **A CTIVITY 3** (allow about 10 minutes)

We return to our analysis of the *Times* report. Work through either your own previous analysis of the text or the one provided in 'Answers to the activities' and identify all instances of transactional actors. Once you have completed this, consider whether there are any patterns which might be significant with respect to agency and affectedness.

C O M M E N T

In our analysis, we found seven instances of protesters as transactional actors and only two instances where the police clearly and unproblematically occupied this role. (See 'Answers to the activities' for the detail of this analysis.) This obviously makes for an even more marked contrast between the agency of the police and the protesters than that revealed by our earlier analysis. Tellingly, when it comes to actions which directly have an impact on the world around, it is overwhelmingly the protesters who are represented as having this potential.

Clearly, certain patterns have emerged for our analysis of actors generally and, more narrowly, of transactional versus non-transactional actors. But how are we to interpret or explain such patterns in terms of rhetorical effect, and the potential of this particular text to support a particular view of the events being depicted? Well, a central concern of the report is with the attribution of blame. Violence has occurred and a number of people have been injured, including possibly a child. Does the reader hold the police or the protesters responsible? The preference of the text for protesters as actors would seem to increase the possibility that blame will be assigned to them. As the group represented as the primary initiators and causers of events, the protesters are more likely to be seen as the instigators of any violence and hence as the more likely candidates for culpability. This interpretation is strongly supported by the pattern in which the numerous protester actors are almost all transactional actors while the less numerous police actors are almost never transactional actors. (As indicated above, there are seven transactional-actor protesters to two transactional-actor police.) Thus the protesters not only act but also have a direct impact on the world around them. In contrast, while the police do sometimes act, they are represented as having less direct impact on the world about them. While the police are depicted as *taking deliberate aim*, as *crouching with the weapons*, as *opening fire* and as *firing tear gas at demonstrators*, they are never actually depicted as shooting or wounding or injuring anyone.

2.3 Agent deletion and de-emphasis

Up to now our analysis has operated by identifying patterns by which particular individuals or groups are cast by the text in the role of actor, that is, by which they are represented as initiating or causing actions and events, and hence as the agents of that action. When considering such patterns, it is also important to take into account various grammatical structures by which the agent (the initiator or cause) of some action can go unmentioned. You were introduced to such structures in Unit 11 in the context of a discussion of how texts can act to emphasise or obscure different informational aspects. Specifically, Unit 11 discussed the representational effects potentially associated with short passives and with certain nominalisations. We will now briefly review that material.

Short passives

In short passive structures, the actor (the agent) goes unmentioned, for example:

1   Several shots (*goal*) were fired.

2   Several factories (*goal*) were closed down in the 1970s.

Clearly such a formulation has the potential to obscure or at least de-emphasise the role or involvement of the unmentioned initiating agent. If that action is likely to be viewed negatively by the reader/listener, then such a formulation can act to deflect criticism from those responsible for the action. For example, in example (2) above, the use of the short passive means those responsible for the factory closures – for example, the company management or perhaps the government – are not brought into the picture and hence are less likely to be negatively assessed. Short passives, then, may be used to present a given social entity in a more positive light, or at least to mitigate negative evaluations of that social actor. Thus we might expect a formulation such as *Several factories were closed down* to occur in a text which reflects a pro-business or pro-company ideology and which, for example, views factory closures as necessary and even beneficial if they protect profits and increase financial returns to shareholders. (There is a very extensive literature in which writers develop this type of analysis. See, for example, Trew (1979) or Clark (1992).)

It must be stressed, however, that not all short passives will have such an evaluative functionality. It is always necessary to take into account the textual context in which the formulation occurs. It may be that the initiator is unknown, or has been clearly indicated elsewhere in the text. Consider the following example:

> The company then undertook a programme in which it shut down the majority of mines in the north of the country.
>
> In the 1970s, 10 were closed, and in the 1980s a further 15.

Here, the second sentence makes use of a short passive (*10 were closed*). Yet the responsibility of the company for this action has been clearly indicated in the previous sentence. It would therefore be rather difficult to suggest that this text as a whole acts to deflect attention from the company's role.

This is not to say that the use of the short passive in such contexts is entirely without rhetorical effect. To illustrate this point, compare (1) with (2) below:

1   The company managers then undertook a programme in which they shut down the majority of mines in the north of the country.

    In the 1970s, 10 were closed, and in the 1980s a further 15.

2   The company managers then undertook a programme in which they shut down the majority of mines in the north of the country.

    In the 1970s, the managers closed 10, and in the 1980s they closed a further 15.

Arguably, version two has a stronger impact, or more sharply focuses the reader's attention on the involvement/responsibility of the managers by explicitly presenting them as the initiators of this programme of closures in both sentences.

Nominalisation

Nominalisation is another mechanism by which the role of those responsible for an action may be obscured or suppressed. As you may remember, nominalisation is a way of presenting actions not as verbs but as nouns and noun phrases. Compare, for example (1) and (2) below.

1   The company management closed several factories in the 1970s.

2   The 1970s saw several factory closures.

In (1), the action at stake is presented via a verbal group (as a process) with those responsible for the action, *the company management*, clearly in the role of actor. In (2), a nominalisation (*closures*) is used to present the action and, simultaneously, to omit mention of those responsible for the action.

Example (2) has a similar positioning power to that of the short passive. Once again the reader's attention can be drawn away from those who initiated the action, thereby, at least potentially, deflecting criticism from that entity.

It is arguable that nominalisations of this type are more effective rhetorically than short passives, which can be seen as leaving an information gap which may be noted by the reader. Thus in the case of

Several factories were closed in the 1970s.

it is possible that the short passive structure itself may provoke the reader to ask who closed them, since the sentence so obviously lacks a by-phrase actor which would provide this information. In contrast, no 'gap' is quite so obviously present in a formulation such as *The 1970s saw several factory closures.* Accordingly the reader is less likely to be alerted to the rhetorical manipulation which has occurred.

Of course, it must also be stressed that nominalisations are like short passives in that they by no means always act to suppress or obscure agency in this way. Instances of nominalisaton vary in the degree to which the responsible agent is retrievable from the context or from elsewhere in the text. And of course, agent suppression is not a necessary feature of nominalisation since there are various options within nominalisation by which the actor can be explicitly stated, for example:

The closure of several factories <u>by the government</u> provoked much debate.

Ergatives

We need to discuss one further option by which the role of those who initiated or caused the action (the agent) can be obscured or suppressed. The reading for this unit (by Michael Stubbs) describes what can be seen as a further subtype of actor. Here we are concerned with clauses in which the entity that we might logically think would be the goal (the affected party) is, in fact, presented as the actor. This occurs in the context of what, as Stubbs explains, are termed ergative verbs. You may remember from Unit 11 that ergatives are a special type of verb which allows for the following alternation:

(1)   Transitive: <u>The government</u> (*actor/initiator*) <u>closed</u> (*process = ergative verb*) <u>several mines</u>. (*goal*)

(2)   Long passive: <u>Several mines</u> (*goal/affected*) <u>were closed</u> (*process = ergative verb*) <u>by the government</u>. (*by-phrase actor/initiator*)

(3)   Short passive: <u>Several mines</u> (*goal/affected*) <u>were closed</u>. (*process = ergative verb*)

(4)   Ergative intransitive: <u>Several mines</u> (*actor/undergoer*) <u>closed</u>. (*process = ergative verb*)

Such verbs are noteworthy because they allow for the affected entity (in this case, *several mines*) to be variously represented as (1) the goal in a transitive clause, (2) the goal in a long passive clause, (3) the goal in a short passive clause, and, most importantly for our current concerns, as (4) the actor in an intransitive clause. In this they are different from most transitive material process verbs where the fourth option set out above is not available – that is, where it is not possible for the goal of the transitive clause also to act as the actor of an intransitive clause.

Thus we have:

Transitive: <u>The Goths</u> (*actor*) <u>destroyed</u> (*process*) <u>the city</u> (*goal*).

and

Long passive: <u>The city</u> (*goal*) <u>was destroyed</u> (*process – passive voice*) <u>by the Goths</u> (*by-phrase actor*).

and

Short passive: <u>The city</u> (*goal*) <u>was destroyed</u> (*process – passive voice*).

but not

Ergative: *<u>The city</u> (*actor*) <u>destroyed</u> (*process*).

As Stubbs observes in the reading, this ergative option is notable in that it enables the text to represent the affected entity as in some way giving rise to the action by which it is affected. At the very least, such ergative formulations enable the process to be presented as in some way automatic, as not having any particular causal agent.

Given the right ergative actor and an appropriate verbal process, such formulations may give rise to a rhetorical effect similar to that associated with short passives. Such structures enable any actual initiator/cause (a potential actor) to be entirely effaced from the representational picture. Thus, in *15 mines have closed*, the process of a mine closing is presented as in some way uninitiated or uncaused, as an action which somehow simply emerges from within the mine itself, without external agency: a mine closing is presented as the result of an almost spontaneous process. Obviously, in the right circumstances such formulations can be highly rhetorical in enabling the texts to obscure the responsibility of some social actor for a given action or event. As Stubbs argues in the reading, such formulations are even more effective rhetorical devices than short passives because, with the ergative structure, there is absolutely no trace at all left of the unmentioned initiator of the action. They are similar to nominalisation in this respect.

ACTIVITY 4 (allow about 1–2 hours)

Now read the chapter 'Human and Inhuman Geography' by Michael Stubbs in the course reader. Alternatively, you could read it when you have completed the unit. In order to focus your reading, consider what his study tells us about the use of ergative verbs in:

(1)   a secondary-school Geography textboook

(2)   a secondary-school environment textbook

(3)   the LOB corpus.

How does Michael Stubbs interpret his findings?

ACTIVITY 5 (allow about 20 minutes)

We return now to the *Times* text to consider it from the perspective of agent deletion and de-emphasis. Reread the text, and try to identify any formulations which can be seen as in some way obscuring, backgrounding or de-emphasising the agency of either the police or the protesters. Consider any instances of short passives, nominalisations and ergative verbs, or any other structures which might be seen as having this effect. Write notes commenting on whether you can observe any instances of agency suppression which could be seen as supporting the apparently pro-police and anti-protester perspective which has been indicated elsewhere in the text.

COMMENT

We notice firstly that there is just one instance of a short passive where the agency of the protesters is de-emphasised:

after {the police} (*goal*) <u>being shot at</u>

and three instances where, at least arguably, it is the agency of the police which is being de-emphasised:

1   FOUR people (*goal*) were wounded (*process*) in a gunfight between political extremists and police.

2   Two members of People Against Gangsterism and Drugs... (*goal*) were arrested.

3   A man [protester] (*goal*) had been wounded in the neck and shoulder.

In (1) there is some ambiguity. The writer has been careful to leave open who was responsible for the wounding. Accordingly, we cannot say definitively that the text here suppresses the agency of either the police or the protesters. However, one possible interpretation could be that it is more likely that the police did the wounding, since we would expect any protesters to shoot the police rather than their own people. This is an instance in which the agency of the police is de-emphasised by a newspaper following a particular editorial stance.

There are two additional sentences which, even though they involve long passives rather than short passives, can nevertheless be seen as downplaying the agency of the police. They are:

4   A woman [protester] (*goal*) grazed on the head (*circumstance*) <u>by a bullet</u> (*by-phrase actor* – bullet *rather than* police)

5   and {a reporter} (*goal*) shot in the legs (*circumstance*) <u>by a police gun</u> (*by-phrase actor* – police gun *rather than* police).

These are interesting in that, rather than entirely omitting the police in the actor role, the author has replaced them with a more neutral, less evaluatively charged actor – *a bullet* and *a police gun*.

Our analysis of passivisation in Text 3 has revealed that there is significantly more de-emphasis of the police as initiator/agent than of the protesters. Accordingly, in this case it is possible to argue that by underplaying the agentive role of the police, the text makes it less likely that they will be seen as responsible for the violence which occurred. Thus this agent-suppression is part of a general tendency by which the text favours the police over the protesters. But, as already noted, we need to be careful that we do not assume that instances of agent-suppression or de-emphasis necessarily indicate anything about the evaluative position being adopted by the text. Some agent-omissions may be innocent in rhetorical terms. It could be argued, for example, that the omission of the police as agent in *Two members of People Against Gangsterism and Drugs were arrested* is innocent: it is obvious from the context which participant did the arresting and the act itself – that of arresting – puts less at stake evaluatively than other actions described in the text. But the omission of the agent in *A man had been wounded in the neck and shoulder* is significantly less innocent: the omission clearly has implications for how the reader views particular participants. Similar arguments hold for the agent-replacement involved in *A woman had been grazed on the head by a bullet* and *A reporter was shot in the legs by a police gun*. This last replacement seems particularly noteworthy. Why did the reporter not simply write, *A reporter was shot in the legs by police*? It would seem to be the more obvious or straightforward way of describing what happened. After all, it would be extremely unexpected to encounter similar formulations along the line of *Police guns yesterday opened fire on protesters* or *Several police were yesterday wounded by protesters' guns during a demonstration*. Here, by using the formulation *police gun*, there seems to be a deliberate attempt to imply that the incident must have been accidental, that the wounding was in some way out of the control of the police, since it was the gun which caused the injury, not the policeman who fired it.

Although nominalisation does not play a major role in this text, there are just a couple of instances which are worthy of further attention:

> 6   FOUR people were wounded in a <u>gunfight</u> between political extremists and police about 100 yards from Tony Blair in Cape Town yesterday ‖

> 7   ...and he was smuggled in through a side entrance of the Castle moments before <u>shooting</u> broke out.

In (6), the writer states that people were wounded *in a gunfight* rather than stating that this occurred as a result of, for example, *the police opened fire as they fought against political extremists* or *political extremists using guns as they fought the police* or *the police and protesters fired guns at each other as they fought*. Here the nominalisation *gunfight* (in place of, for example, *they fought with guns*) is intriguing in that, at least at first glance, it appears to be de-emphasising the agency of both the police and the protesters. In this sense, it might be seen as evaluatively impartial or neutral. Upon closer analysis, it is possible to argue that certain evaluative purposes are served by this formulation. To begin with, the phrase *gunfight between political extremists and police* suggests that the police and the protesters were equally matched in terms of their ability to fight, since it is usually the case that gunfights take place between two more or less equally-equipped opponents. By implication, the police are represented as having confronted a formidable opponent, one capable of engaging them in this way in the relatively protracted action of a gunfight. Accordingly there is an implication that the police action of opening fire is to be seen as reasonable and well-motivated. Secondly, the formulation enables the writer to avoid stating who it was who initiated the firing which led to the gunfight. But, as we have already noted, other elements in these opening few sentences act to position the reader to see the protesters as the most likely instigators. Hence the ambiguity of the phrase *in a gunfight* serves the writer's purpose of casting blame on the protesters without having to explicitly accuse them of wrongdoing.

The second instance of nominalisation – *shooting broke out* – operates in a very similar way. Here, even though no agent is indicated (the writer does not state who fired the initial shots), the surrounding text operates to influence the reader to see the protesters as the most likely instigators.

2.4 Goals and affectedness

ACTIVITY 6 (allow about five minutes)

As a final step, let us now investigate patterns of goal choice (who gets to be represented as acted upon or affected) in order to determine whether there are any rhetorically significant tendencies.

Return now to the *Times* text, and draw up a list of (1) police acting as goals, and (2) protesters acting as goals. In conducting this analysis, you might like not only to classify the goals but also to make a note of who or what acts as the actor in these clauses. Write down any conclusions about how the reader may be influenced in evaluating either the police or the protesters.

COMMENT

We find the following pattern:

Police as goal	Protesters as goal
	FOUR people (*goal*) were wounded (*process passive*) in a gunfight between political extremists and police (*circumstance*)
after {the police} (*goal*) being shot at themselves	
	Two members of People Against Gangsterism and Drugs... (*goal*) were arrested
	A man [protester] (*goal*) had been wounded in the neck and shoulder (*circumstance*)
	a woman [protester] (*goal*) grazed on the head (*circumstance*) by a bullet (*actor*)

Not surprisingly, the analysis reveals that the protesters are more acted upon than the police. Nevertheless, it is perhaps significant that protesters are represented as affected in only four out of the 44 clauses which make up the text. Thus it is only in a minority of instances that they are represented as being on the receiving end of some action and hence construed as potential victims who might attract the reader's sympathy. But other factors are even more indicative of the text's evaluative point of view. In none of these four instances are the police represented as actor. Thus the protesters are never represented as being directly on the receiving end of some harmful action by the police. We note rather interestingly, as well, that in three of the four instances the affected protesters are not named as such. They are, instead, somewhat ambiguously described as *four people, a man* and *a woman*. Imagine the shift in rhetorical effect if the opening sentence had stated *Two protesters and a reporter were wounded in a gunfight between police and demonstrators*. By this strategy the text lessens the likelihood that the protesters will be seen as victims.

2.5 Text 3: conclusions

Our analysis of agency and affectedness has provided us with evidence for an argument that the grammar of the text supports or even advances a particular viewpoint towards the events, a point of view from which it is the protesters rather than the police who are likely to be seen as responsible for the violent sequence of events, and therefore as more to blame. Of course, grammatical structures of this type are not the only means by which texts can reflect evaluative viewpoints. In this instance we noticed that there are more explicit indicators of negativity towards the protesters, namely the writer's classification of them as *extremists* and his use of the metaphorical *baying for the Prime Minister's blood* to characterise their protest action. In this, we see that the underlying grammar combines with, and supports, certain explicitly evaluative lexical choices to advance a negative view of the protesters.

❸ THE SECOND TEXT – DEVELOPING A TEXTUAL COMPARISON

With the analysis of Text 3 completed, we are now in a position to apply a similar analysis to the second anti-Blair protest text (the *Guardian* report). The text ran as follows:

Text 4

(1) South African police open fire on anti-Blair protesters

(2) The crack of shotguns was heard in the streets of South Africa's parliamentary capital yesterday as police opened fire on protesters demonstrating against a visit by Tony Blair.

(3) At least three people were injured with rounds of birdshot, including a local journalist, as police resorted to strong-arm tactics to break up the protest outside Cape Town's castle. (4) The British

prime minister, accompanied by his wife Cherie, was attending an awards ceremony involving British military advisors in the 17th century fort.

(5) Police also used rubber bullets, stun-grenades and tear-gas to disperse about 150 demonstrators, many of them women. (6) They were brandishing threatening placards – 'one bullet, one Blair', 'death to Tony Blair' – protesting against Britain's role in the recent airstrikes against Iraq.

(7) Officers at the scene said police had come under fire, but there was no confirmation of this. (8) Security was tight for the visit, coming as it does after last week's pipe bomb explosion at the Victoria and Albert Waterfront shopping centre, Cape Town's premier tourist attraction.

(9) Police used apartheid-era security laws to control access to the city's airport for the prime minister's arrival in Cape Town on the third and last day of his first official visit to South Africa. Roads into Cape Town were blocked by armoured vehicles. (10) A smaller demonstration at the airport was allowed to pass off peacefully. (11) Blair's schedule was not disrupted and he moved on to the Cape Town parliament to deliver an address in the same chamber where Harold Macmillan made his famous 'Winds of Change' address predicting an end to white rule on the continent.

(12) On his arrival at parliament the minister for water affairs and forestry, Kader Asmal, offered a government apology, saying: (13) 'We express our regrets at the events that took place outside the castle this afternoon.' (14) The prime minister flew on to Kuwait from South Africa last night.

(Adapted from Beresford, 1999)

Once again we will begin by seeking to discover if the text displays any significant patterns with respect to actor and goal choices. We will then compare any patterns we observe with the patterns we discovered in the *Times* report. We will then attempt to reach conclusions as to what rhetorical purposes such patterns might serve.

ACTIVITY 7 (allow about 40 minutes)

We need to repeat the analysis we applied to Text 3. Since for comparison purposes our primary concern is with how the police and the protesters are represented, we can confine our investigations to those clauses where they are mentioned. Once again we will also confine our analysis to material process clauses since these are of most immediate relevance for our current concern with agency and affectedness. In order to begin this investigation, we provide below an analysis in which we identify (a) clauses where mention is made of police and/or the protesters, and (b) clauses which involve a material process.

(Underlining has been used to identify material process clauses with either police or protester participants or which in some other way involve either the police or protesters.)

(1) South African police open fire on anti-Blair protesters

(2) The crack of shotguns was heard in the streets of South Africa's parliamentary capital yesterday ‖

(3) as police opened fire on protesters [[(4) {protesters} demonstrating against a visit by Tony Blair]].

(5) At least three people were injured with rounds of birdshot, including a local journalist ‖

(6) as police resorted to strong-arm tactics ‖

(7) {police} to break up the protest outside Cape Town's castle.

(8) The British prime minister, [[accompanied by his wife Cherie]] , was attending an awards ceremony [[involving British military advisors]] in the 17th century fort.

(9) Police also used rubber bullets, stun-grenades and tear-gas

(10) {police} to disperse about 150 demonstrators, many of them women.

(11) They were brandishing threatening placards – 'one bullet, one Blair', 'death to Tony Blair' – [[(12) {placards} protesting against Britain's role in the recent airstrikes against Iraq.]]

(13) Officers at the scene said ‖

(14) police had come under fire, ‖

(15) but there was no confirmation of this.

(16) Security was tight for the visit, ‖

(17) coming as it does after last week's pipe bomb explosion at the Victoria and Albert Waterfront shopping centre, Cape Town's premier tourist attraction.

(18) Police used apartheid-era security laws ‖

(19) {police} to control access to the city's airport for the prime minister's arrival in Cape Town on the third and last day of his first official visit to South Africa.

(20) Roads into Cape Town were blocked by armoured vehicles.

(21) A smaller demonstration at the airport was allowed to pass off peacefully.

(22) Blair's schedule was not disrupted ‖

(23) and he moved on to the Cape Town parliament ‖

(24) to deliver an address in the same chamber [[where Harold Macmillan made his famous 'Winds of Change' address ‖ predicting an end to white rule on the continent.]]

(25). On his arrival at parliament the minister for water affairs and forestry, Kader Asmal, offered a government apology, ‖

(26) saying: ‖

(27) 'We express our regrets at the events [[that took place outside the castle this afternoon.]]'

(28) The prime minister flew on to Kuwait from South Africa last night.

You should now work through the text to identify instances of police actors versus protester actors, and instances of police goals versus protester goals. You might like to use some form of mark-up (for example, coloured pens) in order to pick out the different actors and goals graphically – one colour for police actors, another for protester actors, and so on.

Now use the analysis to fill in a table like the following. You should indicate any instances of transactional actors.

Police as actors	Protesters as actors

Once you have completed this initial analysis, write down any possible conclusions that the analysis suggests about how the police and the protesters are represented and evaluated.

COMMENT

Your analysis should have revealed that in this case it is very clearly the police who are represented as the more active and influential – there are nine instances of police actors against just two instances of protester actors (see the table in 'Answers to the activities'). Notice also that the police actors here are mostly transactional (acting directly upon some second entity) with six out of nine police actors falling into this category.

Thus we can conclude that, in terms of agency and affectedness, Text 4 is in marked contrast with Text 3. In fact, it is almost the exact reverse of Text 4 in these terms. In Text 3 it is protester actors which predominate (nine protester actors to five or six police actors) while in Text 4 it is police actors which dominate (nine police actors to two protester actors). Similarly, we note the significant difference with respect to transactional actors. In Text 4, when police occur as actors, it is much more often in this more dynamic role (six out of the nine instances); while in Text 3 instances of police actors are relatively evenly distributed between non-transactional and transactional actors (two or three instances of transactional actors versus three instances of non-transactional actors).

3.1 Agent deletion/de-emphasis

ACTIVITY 8 (allow about five minutes)

Now reread your analysis and identify any instances of formulations which could be seen as de-emphasising the agency of either the police or the protesters. How does this text compare in this respect with Text 3?

COMMENT

Interestingly, we notice that this text makes significantly less use of short passives than Text 3 – and none of these involves either the police or the protesters as participants. There is only one structure which can be seen as rhetorically significant in that it downplays the agency of police or protesters. This is the formulation *police had come under fire* which occurs in the following context:

> Officers at the scene said <u>police had come under fire</u>, but there was no confirmation of this.

We notice here that, rather than using a passive form such as *police were shot at*, by which the police would clearly be represented as the acted upon/affected, the writer has chosen this *come under fire* formulation. Although not strictly speaking an ergative verbal formulation, it nonetheless has a similar representational function. By this grammatical device the police are presented as actors, as the participant which initiates some action – they do the *coming* – and yet in terms of the underlying meaning, they would clearly not be the initiating participant but rather the acted-upon or affected party. (Strictly speaking, the verb *coming* is probably best seen here as having a relational meaning with the clause presenting the police as being in a certain abstract location – that of being *under fire*.) Thus, as in the case of ergative constructions, the action is presented as in some way arising from, or being engendered by, the affected participant. The ultimate communicative effect may be subtle, but nonetheless it can be seen here as acting to deflect attention from the likely source of any such firing, away from the protesters as possible guilty parties.

Accordingly, we observe that the one clear instance of agent de-emphasis in the text acts to support a view which is more positively disposed towards the protesters and more negatively disposed towards the police.

3.2 Goals

As the final step in our analysis, we need to consider patterns with respect to goals. We observe the following:

◆ no instances of police goals

◆ three instances of protester goals: (1) *At least three people* (goal) *were injured with rounds of birdshot*; (2) *{police} to break up the protest* (goal); (3) *{police} to disperse about 150 demonstrators (goal)*.

In this respect there are no clear differences between the two texts – remember that there was one instance of a police goal in Text 3 and four instances of protester goals. Nevertheless we do note that in Text 4, two of these protester goals are acted upon by police actors. This contrasts with Text 3 where none of the police actors were presented as directly acting on the protesters. Thus Text 4 indicates a more direct role for the police in acting on the protesters. Some closer consideration of that one instance of a police goal in Text 3 may also provide further insights. Remember that in Text 3 the formulation at issue was *{police} being shot at*. Although there is just this one instance of a police goal, it is nonetheless potentially quite significant in terms of the way the incident is represented. According to this, there is the potential for the police to be seen as victims, as the aggrieved party, and hence for their subsequent actions against the protest to be seen as justified. We note that a somewhat similar meaning is provided in Text 4, but that, tellingly, it is by the formulation which we have just been discussing:

Officers at the scene said police had come under fire, but there was no confirmation of this.

Perhaps the most obvious difference is that while the police being shot at was presented as a fact in Text 3, here it is presented as just a claim on the part of the police, a claim which the reporter explicitly characterises as in some way open to doubt. Added to this are the grammatical properties which we just outlined – the use of an ergative-like structure in which the affected party is in some way represented as giving rise to the action, and hence as in some way responsible.

3.3 Text 4 analysis: conclusions

The analysis we have conducted has provided us with systematic, detailed and objective linguistic evidence for an argument that the grammar of Text 4 (the *Guardian* report) supports an interpretation by which the police are viewed more negatively than was the case in Text 3, and by which the protesters are more positively evaluated. This evidence, as we have seen, derives from the way in which the text construes agency and affectedness. Since it is the police in Text 4 who are presented as the more active and influential participant, a potential exists for them to be seen as responsible and hence as 'to blame' for the violence which occurred. Once again there are other more explicit indicators of this viewpoint in the text. We notice, for example, that Text 4 refrains from using the negative label *extremist* when describing the protesters and that an explicitly negative formulation is used to indicate criticism of the police actions. They are described as using *strong-arm tactics*, thereby indicating an assessment by the writer that the police used excessive force and making connections with contexts in which the police act without restraint on behalf of totalitarian regimes. The way in which the words of the police are cast into doubt in Text 4, as discussed above, is a further indicator that Text 4 is less supportive of the police than Text 3. So once again we see how the underlying grammar acts in concord with more obvious aspects of the text to establish a particular way of viewing the events at issue, a particular evaluative framework for interpreting what happened that day.

It must be stressed, however, that this is not to suggest that the participant which is represented as most active and agentive is necessarily represented as to blame. As it turned out, this causal connection did apply in both these texts – the participant which was clearly presented as most agentive happened to be the participant which was positioned to be seen as most blameworthy. However, this effect was an entirely contingent one. It depended entirely on the particular meanings which operated in the two texts. In other texts, the connection may be between agency and praise rather than blame, as would be the case if the event under consideration were seen in positive rather than negative terms – for example, in a description of the police involved in some form of rescue. It is also possible to conceive of texts in which the more active participant is seen as the aggrieved rather than the offending party, on the basis that they have been compelled to act against their will by, for example, some prior wrongful act by a second party. In other contexts the issue of praise or blame may not really apply at all. Here agency and affectedness may be involved in more general characterisations of participants, characterisations by which particular participants are represented as more or as less active, as more or as less influential, effective or dynamic but by which they are not, or at least not directly, evaluated in moral terms.

◆ 4 CONDUCTING PROCESS-TYPE AND AFFECTEDNESS ANALYSES

Introduction

This section gives further practice in the grammatical analysis skills necessary for analysing experiential meanings in texts – for exploring relationships between choices at this level of grammar and a text's point of view, interpretive perspective or 'way of thinking/seeing'. That is to say, I want you to develop a methodology for answering questions about how these experiential aspects of grammar can have consequences for representation, interpretation and evaluation. The methodology we shall be rehearsing is thus applicable to analyses of individual texts and, equally, to the comparative and contrastive analyses of either small or large groupings of texts. One obvious application of the methodology is to investigate similarities and differences between texts which seem to cover the same topic but which differ in the ways in which they represent, interpret or evaluate this.

The CD-ROM activity which you will undertake in this final section will take the form of a comparative analysis of two newspaper reports of an incident in which a United States military aircraft entered Chinese airspace and collided with a Chinese military aircraft, sending it crashing into the sea. One of the reports is taken from the website of the US CNN media organisation while the other is taken from the website of the Hong Kong-based *Hong Kong Standard*. Though covering the same incident, the two reports were written by journalists working for rather different media organisations (one American, the other Chinese) and were directed at rather different audiences. Our analysis will be directed towards exploring any similarities and/or differences at this level of grammar. Do the two texts provide essentially the same account despite their different sources and audiences? Or are there significant differences in the sort of picture of the event provided by the experiential grammar of the two texts, i.e. differences in the way in which the two reports represent, interpret or evaluate the issue at stake? First, read the two texts to get a general impression of any differences there may be.

Text 5

U.S. accuses China over air collision

A collision between U.S. and Chinese military aircraft has led to Pentagon accusations that China is intercepting U.S. military aircraft in an 'unsafe manner'.

A U.S. spy plane made an emergency landing Sunday in China after it was clipped by a Chinese jet, the Pentagon said.

China is blaming the U.S. for the collision, which according to the Pentagon happened over international waters.

The Chinese fighter crashed into the South China Sea and its pilot remains missing, according to Beijing.

The U.S. Pacific Command told CNN that in the past two months Chinese officials had been told by their U.S. counterparts that U.S. planes were being intercepted in an 'unsafe manner'.

China's response, the Pentagon said, was 'unsatisfactory'.

The U.S. plane – a Navy EP-3 Aries II – landed on the Chinese island of Hainan. None of the 24 crew members were reported injured.

The U.S. is calling for the immediate return of the plane and crew and warned China not to board the secret high-tech aircraft because it is sovereign U.S. property.

'We've got assurances that our crew is safe and sound and that we'll get to see them soon,' said Joseph Prueher, the U.S. ambassador to China.

'We've got some people on the way down there tomorrow. And we'll continue to work hard both here and in Washington,' Prueher added. 'And it appears also the Chinese have lost an aircraft and we're sorry that occurred'.

Aviation expert, Jim Eckes, managing director of Indoswiss Aviation, dismissed China's claim that the incident was the fault of U.S. pilots.

'Aviation protocol demands that the quicker plane take steps to avoid the larger, slower aircraft, which in this case was the EP-3 belonging to the U.S.,' said Eckes.

The downed U.S. surveillance aircraft represents one of the most technologically advanced aircraft owned by the military, according to Eckes.

'This is a very, very sensitive piece of equipment and one the U.S. will not want sitting in Chinese territory,' he told CNN.

U.S. lawmakers warned the incident could strain diplomatic relations if not resolved quickly. 'We are at a very important and delicate point in our relationship with the People's Republic of China and how this is handled will go a long way as to the future of that relationship,' U.S. Senator Chuck Hagel said in an interview with CNN.

Chinese Foreign Ministry spokesman Zhu Bangzo said two Chinese military planes were following the U.S. plane to monitor it.

The Chinese planes 'were flying normally' about 60 miles (100 kilometers) southeast of the Chinese island of Hainan when 'the U.S. plane suddenly turned toward the Chinese plane,' he said, in a statement. 'The head and the left wing of the U.S. plane bumped into one of the Chinese planes, causing it to crash.'

(CNN, 2001)

Text 6

US spy plane hits China jet

A US Navy EP-3 spy plane made an emergency landing in Southern China after a collision with a Chinese fighter plane (PLA).

A mainland fighter jet crashed after colliding with a United States Navy spy plane over the South China Sea yesterday, while the American aircraft made an emergency landing in Hainan, officials said yesterday.

Foreign Ministry spokesman Zhu Bangzao said the pilot of the People's Liberation Army (PLA) plane was missing.

'The authorities are searching for the pilot whose situation we are deeply concerned about,' the Xinhua News Agency quoted Mr Zhu as saying. Xinhua said the US EP-3 surveillance plane took off from the US military airbase in Kadena, Japan, and that two PLA jet fighters rose to follow it when it was southeast of Hainan.

Mr Zhu said that at 9.07am, 104 kilometres southeast of Hainan, the US aircraft turned towards the PLA jets and hit one of the mainland planes with its nose.

The US aircraft then entered Chinese airspace without permission and landed at Hainan's Lingshui airport at 9.33am, he said.

He said the mainland jet fighters' response to the US military surveillance flight was routine and in accordance with international practice, blaming the crash on the US aircraft's sudden change of direction. 'The responsibility of the incident is entirely on the US side,' Xinhua quoted Mr Zhu as saying.

He said the 24 crew members of the EP-3 were being well looked after, but that Beijing reserved the right to make representations on its intrusion into Chinese airspace.

Colonel John Bratton, a spokesman for the US Pacific Command in Hawaii, said the crew members were not injured.

Colonel Bratton said the EP-3 was on a routine surveillance flight in international airspace when the two mainland jet fighters intercepted it.

The collision appeared to be 'an accident' and the Chinese did not force the plane down, he said.

'The planes actually bumped into each other,' said another Pacific Command spokesman, Lieutenant-Colonel Dewey Ford. The incident came at a touchy time in Sino–US relations, with the administration of US President George W Bush taking a wary tone toward Beijing and the recent detention of two US-linked scholars on the mainland.

Colonel Bratton said he did not know the crew's status, but Beijing appeared to be responsive to US requests that they be well treated.

'We see no problems with retrieving the crew,' he said.

The US embassy in Beijing 'communicated our concern about the incident' to the Chinese government, Colonel Bratton said. US authorities have also contacted China's embassy in Washington.

Experts said it was the first time a US military plane had made an emergency landing after colliding with a mainland aircraft. But they said such run-ins were common because US planes fly along China's coast eavesdropping on military communications.

(*Hong Kong Standard*, 2001)

4.1 A methodology for comparing representations of events

Your next task is a rather specific one – examining the two news texts above with respect to patterns of experiential meanings which may have consequences for representation, interpretation and point of view.

The following steps represent a general methodology for carrying out such a task, and we will be following most of these steps in the CD-ROM activity.

1   Divide the text into clauses.

2   Calculate the proportions of the different clause types (e.g. top-level clauses and embedded clauses).

3   Classify each process according to its functional type (material, relational, verbal and mental).

4   Calculate the proportions of the different process types.

5   Determine whether there are tendencies under which there are associations between particular individuals, groupings or objects and particular participant roles. For example, look for patterns by which one participant is more likely to operate as actor, goal, sayer, sensor, phenomenon or token. (In the CD-ROM activity, you will focus only on the roles of actor and goal.)

6   In the case of analyses focusing on agency/affectedness, determine whether there are any representationally significant instances of

agentless passives, ergatives, nominalisations and similar formulations.

7   Determine whether there are any significant tendencies with respect to the nature of the participants. For example, look for tendencies in terms of whether they are human or non-human, natural or man-made, and concrete or abstract. (NB: in the CD-Rom activity, you will not be carrying out this particular step.)

Interpretation

Depending on the findings provided by the raw text analysis, you will need to reach conclusions about the reasons for, and the communicative effects of, some or all of the following:

♦   proportions of process types

♦   patterns of association between particular participants and particular participant roles

♦   use of passives, ergatives, nominalisation and similar formulations

♦   tendencies in the nature of participants: human versus non-human, concrete versus abstract, etc.

ACTIVITIES CD-ROM   (allow about two hours)

Now do the activities for this unit on the Activities CD-ROM. The activities analyse in detail the two newspaper reports of the April 2001 airspace incident over China (i.e. Texts 5 and 6 in this unit).

Conclusion

We conclude this unit by summarising the methodology that has been developed for exploring how the experiential grammar of texts provides for particular interpretive frameworks or 'ways of seeing'. By now you should feel confident in following such a methodology, as set out below.

1   Basic clause divisions

Break the text into clauses. It is usually best to begin by determining whether sentences (or other textual units) have more than one clause. If they do, it is probably best to divide the sentence (or other unit) into top-level clauses – that is, clauses which are combined via either coordination or subordination (see Book 1 Unit 6). After you have done that, you should determine whether there are any embedded clauses (for example, clauses acting as qualifiers – see Book 1 Units 4 and 6).

2   Process types

(Single out those clauses with material processes if your specific interest is agency and affectedness.)

3   Agency and affectedness

(a)   Grammatical analysis:

Identify patterns by which particular individuals or groups are associated with either the actor or the goal role.

Identify the use of any formulations by which the agentive role of particular participants is de-emphasised (for example by means of short passives, nominalisations and ergative structures).

(b)   Interpretation/argumentation:

Interpret any such findings in terms of what you see as their potential communicative effects. For example, indicate whether you see choices about non-transactional actors, transactional actors and goals as representing particular individuals or groups as more active, effective or influential, or as more passive, inert or acted upon. Are any of the instances of agent de-emphasis evaluatively significant in that they are likely to influence the reader's view of a particular participant?

Learning outcomes

After completing this unit, you should have developed your knowledge and understanding of:

◆   the relationship between social context, specifically field, and the grammatical and lexical features of a text (as summarised in Figure 2)

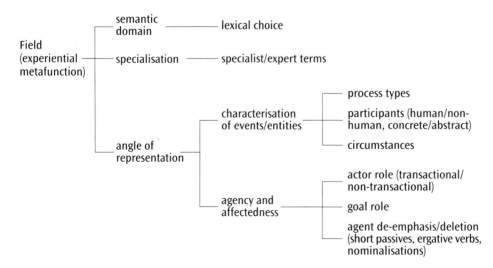

Figure 2   Map of field (complete)

◆ the way in which we can systematically analyse one important aspect of experiential meaning, namely the construction of agency and affectedness.

In the light of your increased understanding, you should now be able to:

◆ identify grammatical features relating to agency and affectedness

◆ interpret the social and ideological meaning of different constructions of agency and affectedness

◆ evaluate the communicative effects of different constructions of agency and affectedness.

Key terms introduced and revisited

actor	mental process
agency and affectedness	non-transactional actor
ergative verb	relational process
experienced	sayer
experiencer	short passive
goal	transactional actor
intransitive	transitive
long passive	verbal process
material process	

Answers to the activities

ACTIVITY 2

Text 3: actor analysis

(Actors are marked in bold.)

Police as actors	Protesters as actors
(18) {**the police**} <u>gave</u> the crowd five minutes to disperse [*Note, however, that this is not actually a material action – the police didn't actually act on anything via this process.*] (20) {**the police**} <u>firing</u> teargas (21) {**the police**} <u>throwing</u> stun grenades (22) {**the police**} then <u>opened fire</u> (24) **Officers** <u>took</u> deliberate <u>aim</u> with shotguns loaded with lightweight birdshot (25) **others** <u>crouched</u> with their weapons at the ready (27) **the police** <u>did not use</u> sharp-point ammunition [*Notice here that the police are, in fact, declared not to be actors – accordingly we might want to exclude such a clause from any analysis of the police's agency.*]	(4) **men** <u>handing out</u> guns to demonstrators (5) {**demonstrators**} <u>baying</u> for the Prime Minister's blood [*This is obviously a metaphorical use of language. As a consequence this is somewhat complicated as far as analysis goes. If we look at the literal meaning, we would analyse this as a material process – baying is an action of doing. However, if we deal with the metaphorical sense, then we may want to see it as in some way verbal – by the baying the demonstrators communicate their hatred for the Prime Minister. This is an instance where the presence of metaphor means that, in fact, the wording carries two meanings – one material, the other verbal.*] (6) Mr Blair's convoy of cars <u>had been held up</u> [**by the demonstrators**] (*by-phrase actor*) (7) {demonstration} <u>organised</u> [**by a group calling itself Against Global Oppression**] (*by-phrase actor*) (13) **two men** <u>distributing</u> arms to protesters (14) {**protesters**} <u>held up</u> placards (19) {**the crowd**} <u>to disperse</u> (38) Some of them **women** <u>wearing</u> long dresses (37) **demonstrators** <u>attempted to hide</u> their firearms

ACTIVITY 3

Police actors	Protester actors
(18) {the police} (*transactional actor*) gave the crowd five minutes to disperse [*Note, however, that this isn't actually a material action – the police didn't actually act on anything via this process.*]	(4) men (*transactional actor*) handing out guns to demonstrators
	(5) {demonstrators} (*non-transactional actor*) baying for the Prime Minister's blood
(20) {the police} (*transactional actor*) firing teargas	(6) Mr Blair's convoy of cars had been held up [by the demonstrators] (*by-phrase transactional actor*)
(21) {the police} (*transactional actor*) throwing stun grenades	(7) {demonstration} organised [by a grouping calling itself Against Global Oppression] (*by-phrase transactional actor*)
(22) {the police} (*non-transactional actor*) then opened fire	
(24) Officers (*non-transactional actor*) took deliberate aim with shotguns loaded with lightweight birdshot	(13) two men (*transactional actor*) distributing arms to protesters
	(14) {protesters} (*transactional actor*) were holding up placards
(25) others (*non-transactional actor*) crouched with their weapons at the ready	(19) {the crowd} (*non-transactional actor*) to disperse.
(27) the police (*transactional actor*) did not use sharp-point ammunition [*Notice here that the police are, in fact, declared not to be actors – accordingly we might want to exclude such a clause from any analysis of the police's agency.*]	(38) Some of them women (*transactional actor*) wearing long dresses
	(37) demonstrators (*transactional actor*) attempted to hide their firearms

ACTIVITY 7

Guardian text: actor and goal analysis

The following formatting has been used to map police and protester participants:

Police = police actor

Police = police goal

Protester = protester actor

Protester = protester goal

(1) South African police (*non-transactional*) open fire (*process*) on anti-Blair protesters (*circumstance/location*)

(2) The crack of shotguns was heard in the streets of South Africa's parliamentary capital yesterday ‖

(3) as police (*non-transactional*) opened fire on protesters [[(4) {protesters} (*non-transactional*) demonstrating against a visit by Tony Blair]].

(5) At least three people (*goal*) were injured (*process*) with rounds of birdshot (*circumstance/means*), including a local journalist, ‖

(6) as police (*transactional*) resorted to (*process*) strong-arm tactics (*goal*) ‖

(7) {police} (*transactional*) to break up (*process*) the protest (*goal*) outside Cape Town's castle.

(8) The British prime minister, [[accompanied by his wife Cherie]], was attending an awards ceremony [[involving British military advisors]] in the 17th Century fort.

(9) Police (*transactional*) also used (*process*) rubber bullets, stun-grenades and tear-gas (*goal*)

(10) {police} (*transactional*) to disperse (*process*) about 150 demonstrators, many of them women.

(11) They (*transactional*) were brandishing (*process*) threatening placards (goal) – 'one bullet, one Blair', 'death to Tony Blair' – [[(12) {placards} protesting against Britain's role in the recent air strikes against Iraq.]]

(13) Officers at the scene said ‖

(14) police (*non-transactional*) had come under fire, ‖

(15) but there was no confirmation of this.

(16) Security was tight for the visit, ‖

(17) coming as it does after last week's pipe bomb explosion at the Victoria and Albert Waterfront shopping centre, Cape Town's premier tourist attraction.

(18) Police (*transactional*) used (*process*) apartheid-era security laws (*goal*) ‖

(19) {police} (*transactional*) to control (*process*) access to the city's airport (*goal*) for the prime minister's arrival in Cape Town on the third and last day of his first official visit to South Africa.

(20) Roads into Cape Town were blocked by armoured vehicles.

(21) A smaller demonstration at the airport was allowed to pass off peacefully.

(22) Blair's schedule was not disrupted ‖

(23) and he moved on to the Cape Town parliament ‖

(24) to deliver an address in the same chamber [[where Harold Macmillan made his famous 'Winds of Change' address ‖ predicting an end to white rule on the continent.]]

(25). On his arrival at parliament the minister for water affairs and forestry, Kader Asmal, offered a government apology, ‖

(26) saying: ‖

(27) 'We express our regrets at the events [[that took place outside the castle this afternoon.]]'

(28) The prime minister flew on to Kuwait from South Africa last night.

Clauses with transactional actors are indicated in bold in the following table.

Police as actors	Protesters as actors
(1) South African police open fire on anti-Blair protesters	(4) {protesters} demonstrating against a visit by Tony Blair
(3) as police opened fire on protesters	**(11) They were brandishing** (*process*) **threatening placards**
(6) **as police resorted to strong-arm tactics**	
(7) **{police} to break up the protest outside Cape Town's castle**.	
(9) **Police also used rubber bullets, stun-grenades and tear-gas**	
(10) **{police} to disperse about 150 demonstrators, many of them women**	
(14) police had come under fire,	
(18) **Police used apartheid-era security laws**	
(19) **{police} to control access to the city's airport**	

Unit 14
Organising messages

Prepared for the course team by Caroline Coffin

CONTENTS

Materials required

While studying this unit you will need:
> your reference grammar
> the course reader
> the Activities CD-ROM.

Knowledge assumed

You should be familiar with the following before starting on this unit:
> demonstrative
> ellipsis
> experiential/topical theme
> interpersonal theme
> lexical density
> mode
> nominalisation
> noun phrase
> stance
> stance adverbial
> textual theme
> theme.

Introduction

> Jane
>
> You really have a problem with this essay. It's almost impossible to see what your main points are. This makes it difficult to work out what your overall argument is. You really cannot continue to hand in such poorly organised work. May I suggest very strongly that you go to the study centre and make more enquiries about essay-writing clinics...

I wonder if any of you recognise the comment made by a lecturer on a student's (Jane's) essay? How many of you at some stage in your education have received similar feedback from a teacher or lecturer? Maybe in your working life you have also felt that some of the texts that you have produced – such as written reports or formal presentations – could have been organised more effectively? In this unit you will find out more about how the resources of theme can help you to organise your ideas at the level of paragraphs and whole texts. Following on from Book 1 and Book 2 Unit 9, you will continue your exploration of grammatical and lexical resources which relate to the textual metafunction (and therefore mode). In particular, you will look at various factors (such as the **channel** of communication) that affect the way grammar is used.

In Book 1, you may remember that our main focus was on exploring the differences between the grammars of spoken and written English. In that book, you learned that these two distinct modes of communication have a major impact on the kind of language speakers and writers use. Thus people engaging in spontaneous, conversational interchange are likely to link clauses together in intricate ways and make considerable use of the resources of ellipsis, the verb phrase, demonstratives and pronouns. A lone writer, in contrast, is less likely to use pronouns and demonstratives and often draws on densely-packed noun phrases to construct clauses which are compact and semantically rich, but structurally simple.

In Book 2, you continued your exploration of how the spoken and written modes have an effect on how speakers and writers organise their information and ideas. In that book (in Units 9 and 11) you focused on the resource of theme as a means of structuring and organising messages at the level of the clause. You looked at a number of different texts located within the four Longman registers to see how speakers and writers angle their messages differently. We saw there that the 'departure points' of clauses are largely influenced by whether participants are engaged in spontaneous conversation or involved in producing carefully planned and edited written texts. The theme analyses that you undertook, for example, revealed that, in conversation, different kinds of information are placed in initial-clause position when compared to written registers. In face-to-face conversations, for example, it is typically the speakers who are in first position in a clause (e.g. *I saw...*, *you know...*). In written English, in contrast, we saw that what comes first in the clause tends to be much more varied. In particular, you discovered from the various analyses that you did that the communicative purpose and field of a text influence what the writer chooses to put in first position. Thus we saw that in academic prose, rather than a writer being the departure point, it is more often the case that abstract ideas and entities are the elements foregrounded in theme position.

In Units 14, 15 and 16 we will build on our introduction to mode as a contextual variable and go a little deeper in our exploration of textual grammar, as illustrated in Figure 1 below. For example, we will explore how the use of grammatical resources such as theme and demonstratives are influenced not just by whether a text is spoken or written, but by the specific channel of communication, for instance, radio, television or book. We will also show how grammatical choices vary according to whether language accompanies physical action (e.g. a sports commentary on a rugby match unfolding in real time) or is used to reflect on events distant in time and space (e.g. a news editorial reviewing the recent performance of the English national team).

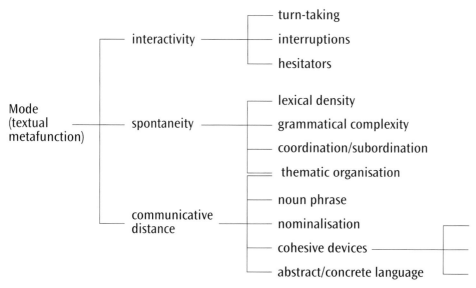

Figure 1 Map of mode

In this unit we will extend and enrich our understanding of mode. We will see that it is not always useful to think of language as either spoken or written. Rather, it can be helpful to see a text as exhibiting, to different degrees, the characteristics that are typically associated with spoken or written language and to see how the degree of 'spokenness' or 'writtenness' has an impact on how information is structured and organised.

The focus on mode in the next three units will, I hope, be of particular use to your work as university students. For many of you, writing a well-organised and coherent essay or extracting key information from a multitude of resources are demanding tasks. However, by becoming more consciously aware of how English texts are typically organised and how they can be structured to achieve greater communicative effectiveness, you will improve your ability both to read critically and to write effectively. Such conscious awareness will also benefit you in your professional and social lives (current or future) where reports increasingly have to be written and read, cases for changes to the workplace/community made, and lengthy written negotiations with local and global partners conducted.

① CHANNELS OF COMMUNICATION

A CTIVITY 1 (allow about 45 minutes)

All speakers and writers of any language use a variety of channels to communicate with others. The most common are listed in Table 1 below.

Read Texts 1–6 and try to judge the channel of communication for each. Place your answer in a table similar to Table 1, noting down any grammatical features that helped you reach your decision. You will notice that all the texts are centred around the artist Jackson Pollock and in particular his painting called *Lavender Mist*. You may find it interesting first to have a look at this painting which can be found on the Activities CD-ROM in the file 'Lavender Mist' (located in Unit 14).

Table 1

Channel of communication	Text no.	Grammatical features
Face-to-face		
Telephone		
Email		
TV		
Radio		
Journal		

Text 1

Jackson Pollock – love him or hate him? In the mid 70s he was in vogue and some people thought he was erm the best thing since sliced bread, others thought he was just throwing paint on canvas in a haphazard, random style. Personally, I've spent some time looking at Jackson Pollock...and looking at his chaotic style gives me some pleasure, gives me some enjoyment. It becomes quite chaotic without without a pattern to begin with and somehow there's detail and pattern revealed the longer you stare at Jackson Pollock. Lavender Mist for instance reveals a kind of aerial photographic style to it, looking like a terrain with pathways and mountains and lakes.

(Open University, 1993)

Text 2

CATHY Well, you know the biggest mystery to me is why on earth this is called Lavender Mist. What...I mean, looking at that. I don't really, really understand what all these...all these things are about.

GEOFF I think...

CATHY I mean that sort of greeny splodge...

GEOFF I think originally looking at the painting the...

CATHY Yeah

GEOFF Oh...it looks like they...that bluey colour...

CATHY You mean that erm that little thing just...this thing here...

GEOFF Well there's a kind of turquoise wash, I think...

CATHY Oh right.

GEOFF I think...

CATHY Gosh I can't see that at all myself.

GEOFF I think Jackson Pollock started with the colour, then did the black lines then the white on top.

CATHY Right.

GEOFF Obscuring the Lavender Mist perhaps.

CATHY Aha, so it's just sort of coming through.

GEOFF Yeah.

CATHY In places.

GEOFF Yeah, whether you call that turquoise lavender I don't, I don't know if I agree.

CATHY I don't think I would have, no.

[...]

But it's not misty, you know, it's quite a heavy splodgy paint, it's not got that ephemeral quality of mist or haziness although actually looking at it now, getting a bit of distance from it you can see how it's...

GEOFF Yeah, I think it's almost misty in the background with the...

CATHY Mmm.

GEOFF ...scrapy, scratchy marks on the top which you know almost sort of, covers up the mist.

(Open University, 2005)

Text 3

One of the things that Pollock's getting out of this kind of surface and this way of working, is an extraordinary, almost like, point by point variation in intensity in that surface. He has made a pictorial surface, err, he has laid down this, what you described as this membrane, this skin of paint, er...what feels like every square millimetre, every square Angström unit of it is different from every other. Er, it's as if this mode of attack has led to an umm extraordinary differentiation of something like the feel of that surface from point to point and the pulverizing of colour that takes place in it, the kind of inmixing of these different paints into one another so that there is almost like, literally, no level of closeness in the viewing of this picture that finally seems excessive to the way it works. Er, I see this surface in those terms. I have no idea to what extent precisely that responds to a set of intentions Pollock had at that time except that one might say that one basic drive of modernist painting from the beginning, or of a central tradition within it, say starting with Courbet or Manet, erm, and on into Impressionism erm involves something like wanting to intensify painted surfaces, to give them something like a maximum of a certain kind of presence effect or, as I would prefer to say, presentness effect and Pollock, I think, represents an extraordinary new stage or breakthrough or new paradigm for a certain sort of intensification of the values of, of surface.

(Open University, 1993)

Text 4

CHRIS I'm really struggling with this wretched assignment we've got to do, you know the one about erm the Jackson Pollock painting.

BRIDGET Oh yes, oh me too.

CHRIS Are you? Yeah, it's really, I don't know. I'm staring at this painting and I just can't think of anything to say.

BRIDGET No, it's just like a complete blur. Every one bit of it is just like every other bit. It looks like one of those fractal things.

CHRIS Yeah, I mean, I was just wondering if we had a chat about it then maybe it would be useful. But, I don't, I don't know if you've got time now or got the painting to hand.

BRIDGET Funnily enough, funny you should mention that but I've got it on the desk. I've been poring over it trying to get this assignment written. Erm, yeah, yeah, well I'd be very grateful for any inspiration you can give me.

CHRIS Well, just, well, do you like it?

BRIDGET I don't actually. I've got to be honest, I don't like it.

CHRIS Do you think it is, I mean, the thing I noticed erm if you've got it in front of you there's erm a kind of small blue splodge...

BRIDGET Yes.

CHRIS In the middle to the right that seems...

BRIDGET To the right? Wait a minute. I've got... Maybe we've got it different ways up but that says a lot doesn't it, what's top, what's bottom?

CHRIS Yeah.

(Open University, 2005)

Text 5

The major paintings possess two qualities which relate to both form and content. First, they create order out of chaos. Without obvious patterning they achieve a total symphonic composition and this speaks of the struggle against alienation, fragmentation and disintegration. Second these compositions 'signify' at many levels – they convey by suggestion a multiplicity of 'meanings', meanings that are social, historical and political in character.

Let us take *Lavender Mist* as an example. [...] It is suggestive of an aerial photograph of a city, but it is a city that has somehow been blasted. Here we must remember that this painting was done from above. It is also suggestive of astronomical photographs of nebulae and galaxies (in *Comet, Galaxy* and other works this is explicit, and Pollock is known to have been an avid stargazer) while at the same time close up details of this and other paintings resemble microscopic photos of molecular structures.

Add to these visual associations that these works were painted in the aftermath of Hiroshima and at the onset of the Cold War, and note Pollock's own statement that 'modern art to me is nothing more than the expression of contemporary aims of the age that we're living in ... the modern painter cannot express this age, the airplane, the atom bomb in the old forms of the Renaissance or of any other past culture. Each age finds its own technique.' Also recall again that this technique was to drip, flick and throw the paint onto the canvas from above. Put all this together and I think the connection between the work and the historical advent of the threat of nuclear annihilation is clear.

(Molyneux, 1999)

Text 6

Hi there

Still struggling with JP...still can't work out why he called it Lav mist. Maybe it's the reproduction I've got but I definitely can't see any lavender - or mist! the thing I'm wondering about at the moment is a green splodge. seems to stand out from the rest of the painting. It's two thirds of the way up from the bottom of the painting and a little to the right. What do you think? Significant? Or not?

anyway just wondering if you want to meet up and talk about it - maybe it might make more sense then?

Are you free this p.m.? Or to-morrow?

Let me know

Cheers

C

(Open University, 2005)

C OMMENT

You should now compare your answer with the one in 'Answers to the activities' and note some of the main grammatical differences across the different texts. For example, which are more grammatically complex and which are more lexically dense?

By carrying out Activity 1 you will have realised that different channels of communication have different effects on language use by creating different barriers between the speaker or writer and their audience, for example, the presence or absence of aural and visual contact. Thus, television permits one-way visual contact but removes any aural response from the audience. Most telephones, on the other hand, remove visual contact but an aural response is maintained. In computer-mediated communication (cmc), such as email and electronic conferencing, there is a delay in a participant's response unless the interaction occurs in real time (referred to as synchronous, as opposed to asynchronous, communication). Figure 2 below shows the effects of different channels on language use and demonstrates how these effects can be perceived as a kind of scale with, at one end, speaker and listener as close as possible and, at the other end, the audience far removed from the writer.

Face-to-face	Telephone	Cmc	TV	Radio	Letter	Journal/book
immediate response	immediate response	written response (often fairly immediate)	no response	no response	delayed written response	no response (apart from review)
+ aural	+ aural		+ aural	+ aural		
+ visual	– visual	– visual	+ visual	– visual	– visual	– aural
		– aural			– aural	– visual (unless illustrated)

Spoken ◄───────────────────────────────────► Written

Figure 2 The effect of different channels on communication (adapted from Martin, 2001, p. 158)

❷ ACTION TO REFLECTION

The channel of communication is one dimension of mode. Another significant dimension is the role played by language in a particular situation. For example, is it an integral part of the action or is it being used to recreate events that happened in the past and/or in a very different geographical location?

◆ **ACTIVITY 2** (allow about 45 minutes)

Look at the Texts 7–12 and decide what they have in common. Then look in 'Answers to the activities'.

Text 7

Hi there C

Just getting in touch about meeting up this wk. still on for the film Sat. night?

J

BTW[1] just watched great rugby match – England totally slammed Ireland. Wilko played brilliantly – at half time I thought we were finished but then he dropped 2 amazing goals. Great game!

[1] = By the way

Text 8

England's only ragged period was in the third quarter. They gave away a few silly penalties and were also forced into some running repairs on the injury front. No help there from an unnecessarily frosty referee, Jonathan Kaplan.

And then it all clicked. Mike Tindall came on to a short, deft pass from Will Greenwood on the hour and hit the after-burners to take him to the try-line. Five minutes later it was Greenwood's turn to get in on the act...

(Cleary, 2003)

Text 9

Much of the development of analysis procedures within British rugby league has been influenced by the work of a leading coach. Larder (1988) advocated the use of accurate video analysis in the coaching process. He suggested that detailed analyses could aid the coach in measuring positive factors (tries, breaks, support play, accurate kicks, solid defence) and negative factors (players with unacceptably low work rates or who made errors, had faulty techniques, made incorrect decisions or worked poorly with other players). The two factors that he believed should be measured during every match were possession count and tackle count.

O'Hare (1995) examined the 'success' of Australian rugby league performance in international competition. He identified the 'collision', defined as the time a person is tackled, falls to the ground, stands and brings the ball back into play, as crucial to Australia's success. Australian players are trained to exploit the collision. O'Hare (1995) reported Clarke's use of computerised notational analysis to objectively quantify the collision.

(Potter, 1998)

Text 10

MARGARET (grandmother of Jessica and Madeleine) Gosh they can go up in the air now

JESSICA (11 year old grandaughter) Oh, he just dropped it, that was rubbish... It's that nice looking guy again

MARGARET don't let them

JESSICA get the ball...oh look

MARGARET go on, go on, go on

ALL hooraaaaaay

MADELEINE (9 year old grandaughter) England's got a try!

MARGARET He's been marvellous.

CHRIS (father of Jessica and Madeleine):   Yes

MARGARET I thought he was finished

JESSICA Gosh he looked pretty happy about that

CHRIS Fantastic! I'd like to see that again.

(Author's personal data, 2003)

Text 11

A: Matt Dawson was punching the air. They've got to try
something out and...Greenwood reads it. Walking almost there.
I don't think Jonny Wilkinson was very happy, the fact that he
made him run into the corner for that but er...

B: I don't think Jonny Wilkinson worries about that, does he?

A: No, maybe not.

B: There you have it. England strolling to the Grand Slam. Will
Greenwood strolling to the line. Who thought that this would be
such a stroll?

(BBC Sport, 2003)

Text 12

It's worth dwelling on the batterings and the blows he takes to illustrate
just how much Wilkinson sacrifices physically in defence of the
English turf. His is essentially a creative role. He is the link between a
monstrous pack and a back division that has become steelier and more
dynamic over the past five unforgettable months. There is a fear that
dare not speak its name. It is that England have become dangerously
reliant on him in that playmaker's role. Charlie Hodgson, of Sale, has
picked up a serious injury, and Grayson is generally thought of as a
competent veteran who lacks Wilkinson's match-winning capability.

(Hayward, 2003)

Now place the texts at the appropriate point on the scale in Figure 3
below. This scale differentiates between language which describes an
activity taking place in the here and now and that being described long
after the event. Using this scale we can categorise language interactions
between, at one end, language as action and, at the other end, language
as reconstruction. This aspect of mode is often referred to as
communicative distance.

Dialogue during match	TV replay during match	Email same day of match	Newspaper report next day	Newspaper editorial next day	Book

Action ← ──────────────────────────────── → **Reconstruction**

Figure 3 Scale: from action to reconstruction

COMMENT

In order to carry out Activity 2 you will have drawn on your knowledge of how grammatical constructions vary according to how close in time they are to the events they are commenting on or reconstructing. Thus, in Text 10, you will have realised how it would only be possible to understand references such as *Gosh they can go up in the air now* if the participants shared the same physical context (thus identifying Text 10 as a dialogue where the speakers are watching the same programme, in this case a rugby match). This principle of shared context would also explain the ability of the spectators to retrieve the identity of the player referred to through the pronoun *he* (*Oh, he just dropped it...*) and the player addressed in the imperative (*Go on, go on, go on*).

Text 11 you will probably have identified as a TV replay in which a sports commentator comments on a significant moment in the game. The use of proper nouns (e.g. *Matt Dawson, Jonny Wilkinson*) and the past tense will have helped you reach this decision.

The text you are likely to have identified as an email to a friend is Text 7. This text shares some of the spoken grammar featured in Text 10, e.g. the use of ellipsis (*BTW just watched great rugby match...*). However, the use of the past tense and the evaluation of the game as a whole indicate the increase in distance between the writer and the events described.

Distance in time and place from the rugby match increases further in Text 8 (a newspaper report on the match) and in Text 12 (a newspaper sports editorial). In these news texts (published the day after the game) there is no use of personal pronouns, demonstratives or ellipsis and the number of content words has increased. Texts 8 and 12, in other words, cannot rely on a shared physical context – unlike Texts 10 and 11. Instead, they must work hard to recreate events for the reader. In addition, they are also able to comment on and evaluate the significance of the game. Text 12, in particular, shows an increase in the use of nominalisation and dense noun phrases as the sports editor reflects on, and evaluates, one of the key English players, Wilkinson. Text 12, in other words, is not merely retelling the events of the game but speculating in a relatively abstract way on the strengths and weaknesses of the English team, e.g. *a competent veteran who lacks Wilkinson's match-winning capability*.

Increased lexical density (a term you came across in Units 1 and 8) is also a feature of Text 9 which you will probably have identified as an extract from a book. In this text, language is independent of a specific rugby match and the writer makes generalisations about the game by using highly abstract and nominalised language.

Figure 4 shows how the movement from face-to-face dialogue to written book can be seen as a movement from, at one end of the scale, *language in action*, to, at the other end, *language as reflection*.

Language in action	Commentary	Reconstruction	Language as reflection

Spoken ←————————————————————————————————→ **Written**

Figure 4 Action–reflection scale

The scales represented in Figures 3 and 4 are helpful in providing a way of thinking about the varying grammatical patterns that characterise different types of spoken and written text. Most importantly, they help us to move away from the idea that there is a simple dichotomy between spoken and written text. That is, whereas some English texts are very clearly spoken and others are obviously written, some blur the distinctions and simultaneously draw on grammatical features associated with both types. In new technologies such as email, for example, written text can exhibit a very spoken style. The movement from more spoken-like to more written-like language (as reflected in the two scales) is often referred to as the **mode continuum**. Indeed you may remember that Ron Carter used this notion (which he refers to as the speech–writing continuum) in the chapter 'Grammar and Spoken English' in your reader.

③ ORGANISING MESSAGES AT CLAUSE LEVEL

In this section we return to the notion of theme which you came across in Book 2 Unit 9. This time we will explore the extent to which thematic patterning is influenced by the channel of communication and how close or distant a text is from the events it is describing. First, let us review how we identify the theme of a clause by analysing some extracts from the texts that you came across in Activity 1.

Remember that all themes include an experiential element. By 'experiential element' we mean a participant, process or circumstance. Examples of a participant and circumstance functioning as theme are illustrated in the following extract from Text 1.

<u>In the mid 70s</u> he was in vogue <u>and some people</u> thought
  circumstance as theme   participant as theme
<u>he</u> was erm the best thing since sliced bread, <u>others</u> thought
participant as theme   participant as theme
<u>he</u> was just throwing paint on canvas in a haphazard, random style.
participant as theme

All themes include an experiential element. Some may also comprise an interpersonal element prior to the experiential theme. Interpersonal themes function to:

◆ express the speaker's or writer's personal judgement on the message such as an adverb expressing stance (stance adverbial), e.g. *clearly, actually,* or polarity, i.e. *yes/no*)

◆ signal the use of a polar question (expressed as a polar finite, e.g. *did* in *did you...?* or as a modal finite, e.g. *may* in *may I...?*)

◆ reveal the degree of closeness between interlocutors (expressed in different forms of address, e.g. *darling, sir*).

In the following extract from Text 4 we can see two examples of interpersonal themes. Notice how the experiential element that follows them is also included as part of the theme. In other words, the rule for identifying theme is to include (from the start of the clause) everything up to and including the first experiential element.

> CHRIS <u>Yeah, I</u> mean, <u>I</u> was just wondering <u>if we</u> had a chat about it <u>then maybe it</u> (*interpersonal + experiential theme*) would be useful. <u>But,</u> <u>I</u> don't, <u>I</u> don't know <u>if you</u>'ve got time now.

> BRIDGET <u>Funnily enough, funny you</u> (*interpersonal + experiential theme*) should mention that <u>but I</u>'ve got it on the desk. <u>I</u>'ve been poring over it trying to get this assignment written. Erm, yeah, yeah, <u>well I</u>'d be very grateful for any inspiration you can give me.

The theme of a clause may also include a textual element prior to the experiential theme. A textual theme functions to relate the message of a clause to other parts of a text. Textual themes are expressed through conjunctions, linking words (referred to as **linking adverbials**) or relatives. In the extract above the linking adverbial *then* in *then maybe it would be useful* is an example of a textual theme. In the following extract from Text 2 we can also see a textual theme (*But*) preceding the experiential theme.

> CATHY <u>But it's</u> (*textual + experiential theme*) not misty, <u>you</u> know, <u>it</u>'s quite a heavy splodgy paint, <u>it</u>'s not got that ephemeral quality of mist or haziness...

Finally, you also need to remember that minor clauses do not have themes (e.g. *Oh right* in Text 2) and that in cases of ellipsis, many analysts leave the ellipsed element unanalysed. For example, in *seems to stand out from the rest of the painting* in Text 6, the subject *it* is ellipsed and is not counted in the theme analysis. Likewise non-finite clauses are not analysed for theme.

A CTIVITY 3 (allow about 60 minutes)

This activity is designed to give you further practice in identifying themes. As a word of warning, you may find it challenging in places. For example, in the case of some of the spoken texts, you may find it difficult to decide where the clause boundaries are. For this reason it may be worth revisiting Book 1 Unit 6, where you learned about different clause types and learned how to recognise clause boundaries. In any case, I do not expect one hundred per cent accuracy but rather I want you to develop your awareness of how writers and speakers can create different frameworks for their messages.

Read Texts 1 to 6 from Activity 1 and underline each of the clause themes (you may find it easier to do this after you have put in the clause boundaries). As you did in Unit 10, it is useful to use colour to show whether there are textual and interpersonal as well as experiential themes. In the case of Text 3 you may want to watch the video version of the discussion (accessed from the Unit 14 page on the Activities CD-ROM). When you have finished the activity, see 'Answers to the activities' for feedback. Then, having examined the themes for each clause, think about the overall pattern for each text and make some notes in a table like Table 2 below (the first box has been filled in as an example). Are there differences across the texts? Can you think of any reasons for why this is the case?

As we noted in Unit 9, researchers follow slightly different practices on this point. In Unit 17 of Book 4, we shall include ellipsed experiential themes in our analysis. You will also find that the activities in the CD-ROM include ellipsed themes.

Although non-finite clauses usually only consist of rheme, e.g. *To avoid delay* ‖ *have your money ready*, they may sometimes contain textual and experiential themes, e.g. <u>*With*</u> (textual) <u>*all the doors being locked*</u> ‖ we had no way in.

Table 2

Channel of communication	Text no.	Thematic patterning
Face-to-face	2	Largely *I* and *you* pronouns with some thematising of linking adverbials (*well, then, so, although*), only one interpersonal stance adverbial (*actually*), some wh-interrogatives (*what, whether*).
Telephone	4	
Email	6	
TV	3	
Radio	1	
Journal	5	

COMMENT

The most significant point that you will probably have noted as you completed Table 2 was the fact that, where language accompanies action and participants operate in shared time and/or space (i.e. in face-to-face conversation), the typical thematic patterning is *I* and *you*. In Texts 2, 4 and 6, thematic patterning is similar in that even though the channel of communication changes, the interaction is spontaneous, unplanned and dialogic. Textual themes, therefore, are used to move the conversation along (*well, so*) and wh-question words and finites are drawn on to create dialogue. Not surprisingly there are no marked or long, densely-packed themes.

In contrast, the semi-planned nature of the TV and radio 'talk' and the fact that it is 'one way', with no audience feedback, leads to greater variety of theme choices. Rather than a to-ing and fro-ing between *I* and *you*, theme choices foreground aspects of Pollock's painting (*the pulverising of colour that takes place in it...and looking at his chaotic style...*). The increased thematisation of nominalisations (e.g. *this mode of attack*) and generalised participants (e.g. *the major paintings*) also indicate a greater degree of distance from, and reflection on, the topic. Rather than the speakers simply exchanging their own personal reactions and opinions in the 'here and now', they stand back from Pollock and make more general statements concerning both the artist and art more generally – *and some people thought...others..., one basic drive of modernist painting from the beginning...*

The shift away from the speakers being in theme position to the artwork itself being the departure point for the clauses is also a feature of Text 5. Here, theme choices not only focus on different aspects of Pollock's work but are used to organise the argument (*First...Second...*) and direct the reader's response (*add, recall, put*).

In sum, your exploration in Activity 3 has shown you how theme organises and packages messages in ways that vary according to both the channel of communication and the degree to which language is being used to generalise and reflect on a phenomenon (i.e. the communicative distance).

I should perhaps stress at this point that, as you have probably gathered from various comments, it is possible to take slightly different approaches to theme analysis. Some analysts, for example, only analyse theme at the level of independent clauses. Some account for ellipted themes. Others do not. You will also see other differences. The point is that different purposes entail different approaches (such as a broad sweep versus a detailed analysis). The important issue is to be consistent once you embark on your analysis.

I should also point out that there are different ways of laying out a theme analysis. You will see from some of the CD-ROM activities that (aside from the use of colour), a useful way of displaying the analysis is to use separate lines for each unit and line up the different types of themes. For example:

Textual	Interpersonal	Experiential	
	Do	you	remember?
	What		is the problem?
		He	laughed
and		< he >	sang
	No doubt	she	is on her way
		The one [[you need]]	is on the table

In the following section we will show how, in written texts, the principle of theme can work at paragraph and whole-text level as well as at clause level. We will explore how such an organising device helps to package information in a way that assists a reader to follow the writer's main ideas. The register we will focus on is academic prose and we will draw mainly on texts produced at the level of secondary school (11 years and upwards) and which would fall towards the written end of the spoken–written mode continuum. In the CD-ROM activities, you will have a chance to compare patterns of theme across academic prose produced at different levels of the education system, some more dense and abstract (at the written end of the mode continuum) and some less so (more towards the spoken end). In addition, the CD-ROM activities will enable you to explore how theme can vary within the Longman news and fiction registers.

ORGANISING MESSAGES AT WHOLE-TEXT AND PARAGRAPH LEVEL

ACTIVITY 4   (allow about 30 minutes)

The purpose of Activity 4 is to explore the effect of a writer choosing different departure points at the level of whole text and paragraph (which we have highlighted) as well as at clause level (which we have underlined). First skim read the text below, which is an extract from a student essay (the first three paragraphs). The essay was written by a secondary school History student in response to the question *To what extent was the 1920s a decade of hope?* After you have skimmed the text and gained a general idea of what it is about, read it a second time and think about:

◆ the relevance of the initial paragraph to the whole text (colour-highlighted)

◆ the role played by the initial clauses in the second and third paragraphs (colour underlined)

◆ the function of the elements underlined in black (the themes) in the clauses in the second and third paragraphs.

Text 13

To what extent was the 1920s a decade of hope?

The 1920s has been called a decade of hope – by the end of the decade the anti-war feeling was very high in most countries and many treaties had been signed to ensure that there would not be another war. However, it can also be argued that the twenties had a pessimistic dimension in that they prepared the world for depression. Evidence which supports both views will, therefore, need to be examined in order to state the degree to which the 1920s can be viewed as a period of hope. This evidence will include an examination of anti-war feeling, the signing of various treaties and pacts and the economic climate.

One of the main forms of evidence that indicates that the 1920s was a period of hope was the strength of anti-war feeling. Soon after World War 1, people around the world realised just how much a disaster the war had really been. They had witnessed the millions of men who had died innocently and they were affected by the millions of dollars that had been spent on the war. As a result, anti-war feeling increased in most countries around the world. Partly as an outcome of anti-war feelings, many treaties were signed so that the same mistake would not be made again. In 1925 the Locarno Pact was signed at Locarno. It was a pact between Germany, France, Belgium, Great Britain and Italy. In it, Germany agreed to accept her western frontier with France and Belgium as final and settled. In 1926 Germany joined the League of Nations. This was very significant because firstly it showed that the other nations accepted Germany as a country and secondly it showed that Germany was prepared to forget about the past and cooperate with the other nations. <u>Generally, Germany's behaviour</u> was a signal for the world to have hope for a peaceful future.

<u>Further evidence for a peaceful future were the Dawes and Young Plans.</u> <u>These plans</u> helped Germany greatly—especially with her economy. <u>Between 1924 and 1929,</u> Germany made the payments required by the Dawes Plan <u>and <ellipsed subject theme></u> expanded her economy. <u>In 1929,</u> an international committee headed by an American banker, Owen Young, reduced Germany's reparations from 6.6 billion pounds to 2 billion pounds to be paid off by 1988. <u>Not surprisingly, the plan</u> was welcomed by Germany.

(New South Wales DSE, 1996a, p. 165)

COMMENT

You will probably have seen that the underlined parts of the text played a significant role in organising and communicating the main messages of the essay.

At the level of whole text the writer uses the opening paragraph to set out the issue to be debated in the body of the essay, i.e. whether or not the 1920s can be described as a period of hope. The student also sets out – in sequential order – each piece of evidence which will be considered: an examination of anti-war feeling; the signing of various treaties and pacts; and the economic climate.

This opening paragraph is crucial in prioritising and emphasising key arguments and ideas which help the reader to make sense of the ensuing text, namely the different pieces of evidence which are elaborated in the body of the text in order to prove the writer's overall thesis or position.

At the level of paragraph the student uses the initial sentence in both paragraph 2 and 3 to introduce the types of evidence that will be the focus of the paragraph – the strength of anti-war feeling (in paragraph 2) and the Dawes and Young Plans (in paragraph 3). In addition, lexical choices signal the significance of the unfolding evidence (*One of the <u>main</u> forms of evidence...*) as well as its staging (*<u>Further</u> evidence...*).

At the level of clause the writer has made choices which serve as:

◆ a point of departure for the process of interpreting or evaluating the message presented in the clause, e.g. the attitude adverbial in *<u>Not surprisingly, the plan</u> was welcomed by Germany* tells the reader that the German reaction was to be expected

◆ a means of linking a clause to the one preceding it, e.g. in the following adjacent clauses the rheme of the first clause (the part of the clause in which the theme is developed) is picked up in the theme of the second:

Further evidence for a peaceful future <u>were the Dawes and Young Plans</u> (*rheme*). <u>These plans</u> (*theme*) helped Germany greatly.

◆ an indication of which part of the message the speaker considers important to the field of the text, e.g. circumstances of time are placed in first position in many clauses (e.g. *Between 1924 and 1929...In 1929...*) as well as circumstances of cause (e.g. *as a result...Partly as an outcome...*). Both dates and causation are key concepts in History so it is not surprising that they frequently serve as points of departure, as a kind of framework for organising the key ideas in the essay.

The grammatical terms for referring to elements placed first in a text, paragraph and clause are referred to respectively as:

macro-theme – at text level

hyper-theme – at paragraph or section level

theme – at clause level.

⑤ IMPROVING YOUR WRITING

5.1 Improving the overall structure of a text

A CTIVITY 5 (allow about 30 minutes)

The purpose of Activity 5 is to develop your ability to recognise and formulate effective macro-themes. First you will need to read the text below to establish:

◆ what the text is about
◆ what the likely relationship is between the reader and the writer
◆ where the text falls on the spoken–written continuum.

After you have established the overall context of the text, think more carefully about the main ideas being communicated by the writer and decide how these would be best highlighted, or 'previewed', in the opening paragraph (the macro-theme). To make this task easier we have provided some sample macro-themes following the text. Which one do you think would be most effective? Why?

Text 14

Reasons for population movements in Australia

[First paragraph, i.e. macro-theme, is missing here.]

The first reason for population movement is employment. In many rural areas of Australia, recession and drought have caused severe hardships in the late 1980's and early 1990's. (sic) As a result many farmers are making losses, not profits. This has led to an increase in unemployment as many services in rural areas have been closed down. Consequently, many people are leaving the rural areas and moving to larger towns or cities in search of work.

Affordable housing is another important cause of population movement. In recent years, more and more higher-income people are moving into the inner-city areas of many Australian cities and renovating the older houses. As the houses are renovated, their value increases. This leads to an increase in the house values and land rates of other houses in the area. Consequently, some of the older low-income residents can no longer afford to live there. They are, therefore, forced to sell their houses and move elsewhere.

A third reason for people moving is urban renewal. During the 1970's (sic), there was a trend towards building larger houses in the suburbs rather than living closer to the city itself. This led to an expansion of the suburbs, which often required large areas of land. This urban sprawl resulted in many problems, including lack of public transport, pollution and lack of basic services. In the late 1980's (sic), the government has tried to attract people to move back closer to the city centres. They have, therefore, encouraged medium and high density housing. As a result, more town houses and units have been built in many areas.

(Humphrey, 1996)

Possible macro-themes

1   Many farmers are currently making losses, not profits and so many of them are leaving the rural areas and moving to larger towns or cities in search of work. Other people are moving to city centres because of problems with suburban living.

2   In Australia, large numbers of people move from one place to another to live. While the majority of moves occur within the same town or city, many people move from the rural areas to the cities and others move out of cities to suburban areas or towns. The main reasons for this are employment, cheaper housing and urban renewal.

3   There are lots of reasons for why people move house. I think one of the biggest reasons is that people can't really afford to live in the city centres these days. It's probably also because out in the country people aren't doing so well so they need to come here to look for work.

COMMENT

On your first reading of the text, you will probably have established that the main topic of the text is factors which cause Australians to move from one part of the country to another (as indicated in the title). You will also have probably worked out that the writer is a school student with a teacher as audience, creating a rather formal, distant relationship. Finally, I expect you placed the text at the written end of the mode continuum since there are no typical features of spoken text.

In terms of selecting a macro-theme, you may have selected (2) as the one that would be most effective in the essay. Certainly this is the paragraph that originally accompanied the essay. The reasons I would put forward for choosing it as an effective opening paragraph include the following:

◆ The three main reasons for population movements in Australia are introduced in the order in which they are discussed in the main body of the essay. Compact noun phrases and nominalisations are used to distil and formulate these three factors (employment, cheaper housing and urban renewal). The opening thus provides a useful general overview without encumbering the reader with too many details too soon. In addition, whereas macro-theme (2) predicts for the reader the three reasons to be discussed, the other sample macro-themes only include one or two reasons.

◆ The reasons cited for population movement are stated in categorical terms in macro-theme (2), whereby the reader is likely to perceive them as factual statements rather than propositions open to debate. The modality used in macro-theme (3), in contrast, makes the writer's case less convincing, e.g. *I think* one of the biggest reasons is...It's *probably* also...

◆ The marked theme in macro-theme (2), *In Australia* (a circumstance of place), picks up on a key term in the title of the text and geographically locates the discussion in the body of the essay.

◆ In macro-theme (2), the writer remains absent from the text, unlike in macro-theme (3). The absence of the personal voice of the writer is more in keeping with the body of the text (and, as we have seen in previous units, with much academic writing).

◆ There are no features of spoken grammar in macro-theme (2). Since the body of the text has a relatively formal written style, macro-theme (3), which has a more 'spoken' style (e.g. the use of colloquialisms and contractions), would be somewhat incongruous.

ACTIVITY 6   (allow about 45 minutes)

The purpose of Activity 6 is for you to draw on your understanding of how you can use the grammatical resources discussed in the comments section of Activity 5 to construct an effective macro-theme.

First read the text below to get a general overview. Reflect on the overall topic, the social relationship between writer and reader, and where the text falls on the spoken–written continuum.

Then think about the key ideas in the text and work out how these could be best captured in a general introductory paragraph. Write a short paragraph drawing on the resources of the noun phrase and nominalisation where appropriate. You should also consider what type of stance to convey, i.e. should the writer construct an interpersonally distant or close relationship with the audience? Which pieces of experiential meaning need to be highlighted?

Text 15

The environmental impact of logging the rainforests

[First paragraph, i.e. macro-theme, is missing here.]

The vegetation of the rainforest is severely affected by logging, especially when the clearfelling method is used. This method involves removing a wide variety of trees and understorey vegetation, including rare species. Often the trees which are planted to replace those taken are the most productive species from a timber point of view, and the diversity of the original forest is lost.

Animals and birds living in the rainforest are killed or left homeless by logging. The removal of trees destroys valuable habitats, shelter and food supplies. Birds and animals that rely on the vegetation of the rainforest are therefore forced to leave the areas that have been cut. As more of the forest is cut, there is not enough adjoining uncut forest left to which the animals can migrate. In addition the movement of vehicles, the falling of trees and the dragging of logs across the ground kill many tree and ground dwelling animals.

Soils are also affected when the trees are removed. Before clearfelling, the soil is protected by vegetation and leaf litter. When the trees are removed the soil is exposed to rain, wind and sunlight. In addition, the movement of trucks and tree felling compacts the soil, thus reducing its capacity to hold water. The water and nutrients are transported out of the area, thus reducing the nutrients available to remaining vegetation and eroding the soil.

Removing large areas of rainforest can also have serious effects on climate. Plant life has the capacity to absorb carbon dioxide and return oxygen to the atmosphere. Logging rainforests destroys a large number of plants and consequently the amount of carbon dioxide in the atmosphere increases. The excess carbon dioxide forms a blanket around the earth and traps heat. This is called the greenhouse effect. The greenhouse effect leads to an increase in global temperatures which in turn may lead to a rise in the level of the sea as the polar icecaps begin to melt.

(New South Wales DoSE, 1996b, p. 87)

COMMENT

You may be interested to look at some sample macro-themes composed by other students, as well as to see the original paragraph: these are all available in 'Answers to the activities'.

5.2 Improving the overall structure of a paragraph

In the activities above you explored how detailed information can be gathered together to form a general overview of the main meanings expressed in a text. In particular, in Activity 5 you saw how the resource of nominalisation serves to compress and package whole sets of detailed meanings into more generalised noun phrases (e.g. *urban renewal*, *employment*). This makes the macro-theme a relatively abstract and dense section in a written text. In English texts (particularly academic prose) the same principle of compression also works at the level of the paragraph, where the initial sentence is often relatively abstract compared to those that follow. As you may remember, this opening sentence is referred to as a hyper-theme in functional grammar, but a similar concept is captured in the term 'topic sentence', a term which you may already be familiar with. The following annotated paragraphs taken from the essay on logging illustrate the typical grammatical resources drawn on in hyper-themes, i.e. the noun phrases *the clearfelling method* and *serious effects on climate* in the hyper-themes for Paragraph 2 and 5 (respectively) are 'unpacked' in the remainder of each paragraph.

The environmental impact of logging the rainforests
Paragraphs 2 and 5

The vegetation of the rainforest is severely affected by logging, especially when the clearfelling method is used. This method involves removing a wide variety of trees and understorey vegetation, including rare species. Often the trees which are planted to replace those taken are the most productive species from a timber point of view, and the diversity of the original forest is lost.

Removing large areas of rainforest can also have serious effects on climate. Plant life has the capacity to absorb carbon dioxide and return oxygen to the atmosphere. Logging rainforests destroys a large number of plants and consequently the amount of carbon dioxide in the atmosphere increases. The excess carbon dioxide forms a blanket around the earth and traps heat. This is called the greenhouse effect. The greenhouse effect leads to an increase in global temperatures which in turn may lead to a rise in the level of the sea as the polar icecaps begin to melt.

ACTIVITY 7 (allow about 30 minutes)

In the following student essay concerning the pros and cons of electronic games you will notice that there is an absence of hyper-themes (indicated by...). As you read through the essay think about the effect this has on your ability to follow the writer's argument. Then select a hyper-theme for each paragraph from the set of possible hyper-themes listed below. (You may then like to compare your selections with the original text in 'Answers to the activities'.)

Text 16

What are some of the concerns people have about electronic games? What arguments are put forward in defence of these games?

...They cover the social, mental, physical and emotional well-being of the people playing the games. In addition, many are ambivalent in their opinions and are voicing both opposing and supporting arguments, making it a complex issue.

...Evidence of anti-social behaviour is observed in the school yard as children try out Kung-Fu-style movements on others. The concern is voiced by psychologists who say that players become desensitised to violent behaviour and hence consider that conflicts are resolved through superior violence.

...Dr Julia Robinson, for example, claims that these games can actually help people combat their problems through dealing with conflicts at a distance. She contends that cancer patients and emotionally disturbed patients, for example, can deal with their emotional problems through these games.

...Those who defend electronic games appear to have the upper hand in this area. The arguments in defence of these games come loosely under the educational banner and are that the players improve their hand–eye co-ordination skills, and develop their concentration skills and problem-solving abilities.

...They state that players can become addicted to the games, mood changes are possible, and that the games can even bring on epileptic fits. In addition, the sedentary nature of electronic games can increase the health risks in children.

(Polias, 1993)

Possible hyper-themes

1   The opponents of the games point to the apparent negative effects on the user's behaviour.

2   The concerns people have about electronic games and the arguments advanced in favour of these games are many and varied.

3   Others say that rather than creating social problems, the games have some problem-solving within the competition.

4   The main concern raised about electronic games such as the ultra-violent *Mortal Kombat* is the development of anti-social behaviour in the players.

5   Another major issue with respect to the games is the physical and mental development of the user.

C O M M E N T

As you did the activity, you will have noticed how hyper-themes make use of nominalisation and noun phrases. You may also have noticed the use of theme–rheme packaging. It is important at this point to emphasise that not all English texts make use of theme as illustrated up to this point. Firstly, such explicit signposting may not be appropriate in all contexts. Secondly, some writers are more skilled than others in using this resource. That is, not all writers are able to harness theme in a way that serves to package and frame their ideas in a communicatively effective manner.

In the next section we will explore further the different types of thematic patterning that may occur in written text. Again, however, it is important to remember that not all English texts will display such patterning.

5.3 Developing meaning across a text: thematic progression

In Book 2 and previous sections in this unit, we saw that information placed in rheme position is often repackaged in a subsequent theme and that this is an important means of developing meaning, particularly within written texts. Such a **zigzag pattern** is common in texts where there are sequences of information organised by reference to time or causes and consequences. These temporal or causal sequences are frequently found in academic and technical writing. Here is an example of such a pattern:

Friction of rotary saws, flywheels, grinders, sanders, belts or pulleys can cause abrasions. An abrasion is simply a loss of skin surface. Broken skin gives easy entry to harmful substances and bacteria.

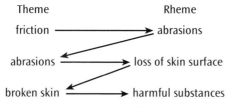

Figure 5 Zigzag pattern (Joyce, 1992, p. 31)

Another thematic pattern which is drawn on to manage information flow is referred to as the **fan pattern**. This pattern involves a clause (typically in hyper-theme position) introducing a number of different pieces of information, each of which is then picked up and made theme in subsequent clauses, for example:

The scheme has two key objectives. The first objective is to deter professional misconduct by migration agents. The second is to provide a mechanism for dealing with complaints against particular migration agents.

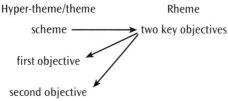

Figure 6 Fan pattern

Such a pattern is often used to organise sets of things such as objectives and reasons. In some (particularly administrative) documents the pattern may be realised in the form of numbered points:

> The scheme has two key objectives:
>
> 1   to deter professional misconduct by migration agents, and
>
> 2   to provide a mechanism for dealing with complaints against particular migration agents.

(Note here the ellipsis of *the first objective is...*, *the second objective is...*)

Below is a further example of the fan pattern (though note that the writer has chosen not to make *cold* a theme):

> The three main reasons babies cry are hunger, cold and illness.
>
> Hunger can be determined by considering when the baby was last fed.
>
> Babies feel cold more acutely than we do and the smaller the baby, the more warmly it should be wrapped up.
>
> Finally, sickness or pain may also be signalled by crying...

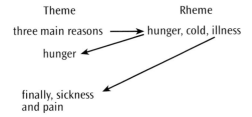

Figure 7 Fan pattern (adapted from Eggins, 1994, p. 305)

A third form of **thematic progression** is one which reiterates or maintains the theme focus rather than developing it (**reiteration pattern**). It is referred to as theme reiteration or the parallel pattern. In this pattern the repetition of a particular element gives a clear focus to the text.

> We collected 2 petri dishes and 40 seeds. We placed a thin layer of soil on one petri dish and some cotton wool on the other. We put in an equal number of seeds in each petri dish and lightly sprayed them with water. We labelled them 'Soil' and 'Water'.
>
> (New South Wales DSE, 1996c, p. 100)

Theme	Rheme (in summary form)
We →	collected dishes and seeds
We →	placed soil and cotton wool in dish
We →	put seeds in dish
<ellipsed theme> →	sprayed with water
We →	labelled

It should be emphasised that theme reiteration as illustrated in the third pattern above may seem relatively unsophisticated. The sample text was, in fact, written by a primary school student. In more sophisticated and well-written text there is usually a discernible patterning of theme based on reiteration alongside other patterns. Here is an extract from an essay on the topic of geography and disease written by a first-year university Geography student. In this text, which would be placed at the highly abstract, written end of the mode continuum, we can see how the reference word *it* is used to refer back to previously mentioned thematised participants (*Trypanosomiasis* and *The tsetse fly*) and thus achieves reiteration whilst avoiding repetition. We can also see that the text makes use of the zigzag pattern (as shown in Figure 5).

> Trypanosomiasis is a disease of the nervous system that affects both human beings and animals. It is caused by parasites called trypanosoma which are transmitted by the tsetse fly. The tsetse fly transmits the disease from one infected person or animal to another. It achieves this by biting the individual so that the disease organisms enter the insect's body, multiply, and move to the salivary glands and mouth. Upon biting another individual, the parasites enter the next victim's bloodstream. The disease leads to fever, headache, chills, swollen lymph glands, a skin rash, weakness and, due to nerve damage, eventual coma and death.
>
> (Hewings, 1999, p. 147)

Theme	Rheme
Trypanosomiasis	…human beings and animals
↓	
It	…tsetse fly
The tsetse fly	…to another
↓	
It	…the individual
so that the disease organisms	…the insect's body
↓	
<they – *ellipted*>	multiply
↓	
and <they – *ellipted*>	…glands and mouth
The parasites	…bloodstream
The disease	…coma and death

Figure 8 The combined reiteration and zigzag pattern in the Hewings text

ACTIVITY 8   (allow about 30 minutes)

In the following text you will notice that the writer does not make a great deal of use of thematic progression. Consequently the information does not flow smoothly: there is no clear sense of ideas and meanings being developed and built up. This places considerable pressure on the reader to work hard to make sense of it. After you have read the text, try to rework some of the sentences so that the overall meaning is retained while making the development of ideas clearer. Consider, in particular, how you might use textual themes as well as the various patterns of thematic progression to improve the text. You may also like to add a macro-theme.

Text 17

In the second half of the nineteenth century, a new art movement was born in France. It was called Impressionism. Paintings captured almost every facet of French life. The exact colours of objects and their shadows were a major focus of Impressionist paintings. They also tried to explore the way light played upon objects. Little dabs of colour producing soft, misty outlines were a new technique. Women and their activities formed a large proportion of the subject matter. The Impressionists were committed to the ideal of realism, producing images of life as they saw it.

(Droga and Humphrey, 2002, p. 127)

COMMENT

After you have completed the activity you might like to compare your version with examples produced by fellow students (see 'Answers to the activities').

5.4 Taking stock

So far in this course you have developed an understanding of how there are three key aspects of mode which influence grammatical choices: (a) the degree of interactivity, (b) the degree of spontaneity, and (c) the communicative distance (i.e. the distance of the language from the action it is describing). We have seen how it is helpful to think about the English language as a continuum – from more spoken-like language at one end through to more written-like language at the other. In particular, we have seen in this unit how spontaneous, conversational English and written texts which have a more interactive style (such as email) show different textual patterning to those which are at the more abstract, reflective end of the continuum.

In the second half of the unit we have concentrated on the grammatical patterns found at the more written end of the mode continuum, focusing in particular on the resources of theme within academic prose. We have seen how writers may make use of hyper-theme and macro-theme as well as clause-level theme to shape and organise ideas in a way that aids the reader to extract key information and follow the main arguments. As we noted earlier, one of our purposes in focusing on writing, and academic writing in particular, is that many students improve their ability to write essays and read texts efficiently once their attention has been drawn to the notion of thematic progression. We certainly hope that you will be able to apply some of the knowledge and skills built up in this unit to your own reading and writing and, if you are a teacher, to your students' reading and writing.

Aside from applying the principle of thematic progression to academic prose, you may be interested in considering how journalists make use of the resources of theme. For example, how do different choices of macro- and hyper-theme, as well as clause-level theme, work in order to make a news report or editorial grab a reader's attention? How do they function to achieve a more or less interactive and spoken style? When you next read a newspaper, consider how effectively journalists organise and package their information. Similarly, if you like reading fiction it may be interesting to think about the literary effects of theme choice (an area you will also explore in the Activities CD-ROM).

In the meantime we will focus on a new emerging channel of communication – computer-mediated communication (cmc) – and explore the effect of this mode of communication on thematic progression. We will also consider the extent to which cmc conducted in an educational environment can be categorised as a form of academic prose.

ACTIVITY 9 (allow about 90 minutes)

Aspects of organisation in online discussion messages

In Chapter 8 of your course reader, *Applying English Grammar*, Hewings and Coffin describe how electronic conferencing is increasingly used for teaching and learning purposes. The authors show how this relatively new channel of communication affects both the use and expression of macro- and hyper-themes.

Before you read the chapter, and particularly if you already have experience of electronic conferencing, try to predict what some of the authors' findings may be. Use the following questions to focus your thinking. Then, as you read the chapter, check your predictions with the results of the authors' research study.

(1) Does electronic conferencing display grammatical features more typically associated with spoken or with written English?

(2) How do you think the resources of theme (including macro- and hyper-theme) might be used to organise information exchanged in electronic conferencing?

ACTIVITIES **CD-ROM** (allow about two hours)

You have now reached the point in the unit where it may be useful to check your understanding of the key concepts that we have covered so far. The CD-ROM Activities for Unit 14 will give you extended practice in identifying macro-theme, hyper-theme and theme in a variety of texts. You will also have the opportunity to think about the communicative effect of making different theme choices.

Conclusion

Think carefully about whether you have achieved a reasonable understanding of both the mode continuum and the way in which theme, hyper-theme and macro-theme contribute to information flow. You should now be beginning to have the confidence to try out your new grammatical tools on different English texts you come across – not just those that belong to the four Longman registers. In particular you should be in a position to judge why some texts are more effectively organised than others, including those that you produce yourself!

Learning outcomes

After completing this unit, you should have developed your knowledge and understanding of:

◆ how texts can be more or less spoken or written, depending on the degree of interactivity and spontaneity and their distance in time and place from the events they are representing

◆ how patterns of theme may vary within a particular Longman register depending on:

   (a) how spoken or how written the language interaction is

   (b) how theme is used to build experiential and interpersonal meaning

◆ how the organising resources of theme are of particular significance in written English and can work at the level of paragraph and whole text as well as at clause level.

In the light of your increased understanding, you should now be able to:

◆ describe how a text draws on theme, hyper-theme and macro-theme to organise and structure information

◆ interpret patterns of theme, hyper-theme and macro-theme in relation to the contextual variable of mode and in terms of their role in building experiential and interpersonal meaning

◆ argue why certain choices of theme, hyper-theme and macro-theme make a text more or less effective

◆ apply your understanding of theme, hyper-theme and macro-theme to make a text more effective.

Key terms introduced and revisited	
channel	macro-theme
communicative distance	
demonstrative	mode
ellipsis	mode continuum
experiential/topical theme	nominalisation
hyper-theme [topic sentence]	noun phrase
interactivity	spontaneity
interpersonal theme	stance
lexical density	stance adverbial
linking adverbial	textual theme
	thematic progression: fan pattern [split pattern theme] reiteration pattern [parallel pattern theme, constant pattern theme] zigzag pattern [linear pattern theme]

Near equivalents are given in [ ].

Answers to the activities

ACTIVITY 1

Table 1

Channel of communication	Text no.	Grammatical features
Face-to-face	2	turn-taking organisation personal pronouns (*you* and *I*) spontaneity phenomena (false starts, hesitations, interruptions, overlap, incomplete clauses) ellipsis (*then <...> did the black lines*) everyday lexis grammatical complexity lexically sparse demonstratives pointing to objects in a shared physical context (*all these things, that little thing*) joint negotiation of ideas reflecting dialogic nature of interaction (*I don't know if I agree; I don't think I would have*)
Telephone	4	turn-taking organisation personal pronouns (*you* and *I*) spontaneity phenomena (false starts, hesitations, interruptions, overlap, incomplete clauses) ellipsis (*or <...> got the painting*) everyday lexis grammatical complexity lexically sparse interrogatives plus responses reflecting dialogic nature of interaction absence of demonstratives pointing to concrete objects and, instead, use of circumstances of location to pinpoint features of interest (*in the middle to the right*) reflecting absence of shared physical context
Email	6	monologic organisation but use of interrogatives (with no immediate responses) personal pronouns (*you* and *I*) ellipsis (*still struggling*) everyday lexis non-standard punctuation use of circumstances of location to pinpoint features of interest (*two thirds of the way*) reflecting absence of shared physical context

TV	3	monologic organisation
		less use of *I* and *you* and more use of third person pronouns, absence of interrogatives
		specialised lexis (*point by point variation in intensity, pictorial surface*)
		demonstratives pointing to things in shared visual space (*this kind of surface, this membrane, these different paints*)
		more grammatically simple and lexically dense reflecting semi-planned nature of speech
Radio	1	monologic organisation
		use of interrogative (*love or hate him?*) but with no expectation of direct response
		less use of *I* and *you* pronouns, absence of demonstratives pointing to things in shared context
Journal	5	monologic organisation with argument being explicitly staged (*First, they create...Second these compositions...*)
		little use of *I* and *you* and more use of third person pronouns
		absence of interrogatives
		specialised lexis (*symphonic composition, signify*)
		absence of demonstratives pointing to things in shared context
		more grammatically simple and lexically dense reflecting polished nature of writing

ACTIVITY 2

The game of rugby is the common feature across all these texts. In some texts the topic of rugby is treated in quite a technical way so it may be helpful for you to skim through this brief glossary of some of the terms. You may also be interested to know that *BTW* (in Text 7) is an increasingly common abbreviation for the phrase *by the way*. And in case you are not familiar with *afterburners,* it is a metaphor borrowed from space travel, referring to *acceleration.*

Third quarter: The 20-minute period immediately following half-time. A match lasts 80 minutes (40 minutes each half).

Dropped a goal: Where the ball is dropped from hand to ground and on contact with the ground is kicked between the posts and over the crossbar (rugby posts form an H shape) for a score of three points.

Penalty: A kick at goal (see above) awarded for an infringement and worth three points if successful.

Referee: Arbiter of match who is helped by two assistants from the touchlines.

Pass: When ball is projected from hands of one player to another, it must travel backwards or sideways, not forwards.

Try: When ball is grounded (by downward pressure from hands, arms or upper body) on or over opposition goal-line and within in-goal area (usually about 10–15 metres long).

Goal-line or try-line: Lines which run at 90 degrees to touchlines at up to 100 m apart. Goal posts are positioned on middle of these lines. Try scored on or over them (see above).

ACTIVITY 3

Here is the theme analysis for the six texts. The completed table follows.

NB: I have inserted subject themes where they are ellipsed in brackets, e.g. <she>.

Text 1

Jackson Pollock[1] – <do you> love him or hate him? In the mid 70's he was in vogue and some people thought he was erm the best thing since sliced bread, others thought he was just throwing paint on canvas in a haphazard, random style. Personally, I've spent some time looking at Jackson Pollock...and looking at his chaotic style gives me some pleasure, <it> gives me some enjoyment. It becomes quite chaotic without without a pattern to begin with and somehow[2] there's detail and pattern revealed the longer[2] you stare at Jackson Pollock. Lavender Mist for instance reveals a kind of aerial photographic style to it, looking like a terrain with pathways and mountains and lakes.

[1]minor clause

[2]*somehow* is a circumstance of manner and *the longer* is a circumstance of time. Both are therefore marked themes.

Text 2

CATHY Well, you know the biggest mystery to me is why on earth this is called Lavender Mist. What... I mean, looking at that. I don't really really understand what all these...all these things are about.

GEOFF   I think...

CATHY I mean that sort of greeny splodge...

GEOFF I think originally looking at the painting the..

CATHY Yeah

GEOFF Oh ... it looks like they ... that bluey colour...

CATHY You mean that erm that little thing just...this thing here...

GEOFF Well there's a kind of turquoise wash, I think..

CATHY Oh right.

GEOFF   I think...

CATHY   <u>Gosh I</u> can't see that at all myself.

GEOFF   <u>I</u> think <u>Jackson Pollock</u> started with the colour, <u>then <he></u> did the black lines then the white on top.

CATHY   Right.

GEOFF   obscuring the Lavender Mist perhaps.

CATHY   <u>Aha, so it</u>'s just sort of coming through.

GEOFF   Yeah.

CATHY   In places.

GEOFF   <u>Yeah, whether</u> you call that turquoise lavender <u>I</u> don't, <u>I</u> don't know <u>if I</u> agree.

CATHY   <u>I</u> don't think <u>I</u> would have, no.

[...]   <u>But it</u>'s not misty, <u>you</u> know, <u>it</u>'s quite a heavy splodgy paint, <u>it</u>'s not got that ephemeral quality of mist or haziness <u>although actually</u> looking at it now, getting a bit of distance from it <u>you</u> can see how it's...

GEOFF   Yeah, <u>I</u> think <u>it</u>'s almost misty in the background with the...

CATHY   Mmm.

GEOFF   ...scrapy, scratchy marks on the top <u>which</u>[1] <u>you</u> know[2] almost sort of, covers up the mist.

[1]*which* is the subject of the dependent clause – *which almost sort of, covers up the mist.*

[2]*you know* is an interrupting clause. Some analysts would treat *you know* as an interpersonal theme commenting on, and framing, the following clause.

Text 3

<u>One of the things that Pollock's getting out of this kind of surface and this way of working,</u> is an extraordinary, almost like, point by point variation in intensity in that surface. <u>He</u> has made a pictorial surface, <u>he</u> has laid down this what you described as this membrane, this skin of paint, er... <u>what feels like every square millimetre, every square Angström unit of it</u> is different from every other. <u>Err, it</u>'s as if this mode of attack has led to erm an extraordinary differentiation of something like the feel of that surface from point to point <u>and the pulverizing of colour that takes place in it,</u> the kind of <u>inmixing of these different paints into one another</u> so that there is almost like,

literally, no level of closeness in the viewing of this picture that finally seems excessive to the way it works. Erm, I see this surface in those terms I have no idea to what extent precisely that responds to a set of intentions Pollock had at that time except that one might say that one basic drive of modernist painting from the beginning, or of a central tradition within it, say starting with Courbet or Manet erm and on into Impressionism erm involves something like wanting to intensify painted surfaces, to give them something like a maximum of a certain kind of presence effect or, as I would prefer to say, presentness effect and Pollock, I think, represents an extraordinary new stage or break through or new paradigm for a certain sort of intensification of the values of of surface.

Text 4

CHRIS I'm really stuggling with this wretched assignment we've got to do, you know the one about erm the Jackson Pollock painting.

BRIDGET Oh yes, oh me too.

CHRIS Are you? Yeah, it's really, I don't know. I'm staring at this painting and I just can't think of anything to say.

BRIDGET No, it's just like a complete blur. Every one bit of it is just like every other bit. It looks like one of those fractal things.

CHRIS Yeah, I mean, I was just wondering if we had a chat about it then maybe it would be useful. But, I don't, I don't know if you've got time now or <you've> got the painting to hand.

BRIDGET Funnily enough, funny you should mention that but I've got it on the desk. I've been poring over it trying to get this assignment written. Erm, yeah, yeah, well I'd be very grateful for any inspiration you can give me[1].

CHRIS Well, just, well, do you like it?

BRIDGET I don't actually. I've got to be honest, I don't like it.

CHRIS Do you think it is, I mean, the thing I noticed erm if you've got it in front of you there's erm a kind of small blue splodge...

BRIDGET Yes.

[2]CHRIS in the middle to the right that seems...

BRIDGET To the right? Wait a minute. I've got... Maybe we've got it different ways up but that says a lot doesn't it, what's top, what's bottom?

CHRIS Yeah.

[1]*you can give me* is an embedded clause – *any inspiration [you can give me]*. Most analysts do not analyse embedded clauses.

[2]This could be treated as a continuation of Chris's previous turn. In this case it would be an embedded phrase post-modifying *a kind of small blue splodge*.

Text 5

The major paintings possess two qualities which relate to both form and content. First, they create order out of chaos. Without obvious patterning they achieve a total symphonic composition and this speaks of the struggle against alienation, fragmentation and disintegration. Second these compositions 'signify' at many levels – they convey by suggestion a multiplicity of 'meanings', meanings that are social, historical and political in character.

Let us take *Lavender Mist* as an example...It is suggestive of an aerial photograph of a city, but it is a city that has somehow been blasted. Here we must remember that this painting was done from above. It is also suggestive of astronomical photographs of nebulae and galaxies (in *Comet, Galaxy* and other works this is explicit, and Pollock is known to have been an avid stargazer) while at the same time close up details of this and other paintings resemble microscopic photos of molecular structures.

Add to these visual associations that these works were painted in the aftermath of Hiroshima and at the onset of the Cold War, and note Pollock's own statement that 'modern art to me is nothing more than the expression of contemporary aims of the age that we're living in ... the modern painter cannot express this age, the airplane, the atom bomb in the old forms of the Renaissance or of any other past culture. Each age finds its own technique.' Also recall again that this technique was to drip, flick and throw the paint onto the canvas from above. Put all this together and I think the connection between the work and the historical advent of the threat of nuclear annihilation is clear.

Text 6

Hi there

<I'm> Still struggling with JP...<I> still can't work out why he called it Lav mist. Maybe it's the reproduction i've got but I definitely can't see any lavender - or mist! the thing I'm wondering about at the moment is a green splodge. <It> seems to stand out from the rest of the painting. It's two thirds of the way up from the bottom of the painting and a little to the right. What do you think? Significant? Or not?

anyway <I'm> just wondering if you want to meet up and talk about it - maybe it might make more sense then?

<u>Are</u> you free this p.m.? Or to-morrow?

<u>Let</u> me know

Cheers

C

Channel of communication	Text no.	Thematic patterning
Face-to-face	2	Largely *I* and *you* pronouns with some thematising of linking words (*well, then, so, although*), only one stance adverbial (*actually*), some wh-interrogatives (*what, whether*)
Telephone	4	Largely *I* and *you* pronouns with some thematising of linking adverbials (e.g. *well, but, if*), two stance adverbials (*funnily enough, maybe*), a number of finites reflecting interrogatives (*are, do, doesn't*).
Email	6	Largely *I* and *you* pronouns with some thematising of linking words (*still, anyway*), several stance adverbials (*actually, maybe*).
TV	3	Greater variety and length of themes with considerable pre- and post-modification of thematised participants (*one of the things that Pollock's getting out of this kind of surface and this way of working is...*), some thematisation of *I* voice, no textual or interpersonal themes.
Radio	1	Variety of themes, including circumstances (*In the mid 70's*) and processes (*looking*), both *Jackson Pollock* and *Lavender Mist* thematised, one stance adverbial (*personally*), only one instance of thematised *I* voice.
Journal	5	Variety of themes including circumstances (*at the same time*), textual themes used to structure argument (*first, second*), a number of processes in imperative mood (*add, note, recall*), only one instance of thematised *I* voice.

ACTIVITY 6

Here are two example paragraphs written by fellow students:

> Logging may bring economic benefits for some people. However, it has some negative impacts on the environment. For example, logging may not only severely affect the vegetation, animals and soils in the rainforest but also have serious effects on the global climate.

> Logging rainforests has detrimental effects upon all aspects of life: the vegetation, animals and birds, and soil. Most disastrous, however, is its effect on global atmospheric and climatic ecosystems.

The original opening paragraph for the essay is as follows:

> There are a number of significant environmental effects of cutting down rainforest trees. Logging has an effect, not only on the vegetation, animals and soils within the ecosystem of the rainforest, but also on global temperatures and future climatic patterns.

ACTIVITY 7

The original text is as follows:

> **What are some of the concerns people have about electronic games? What arguments are put forward in defence of these games?**
>
> The concerns people have about electronic games and the arguments advanced in favour of these games are many and varied. They cover the social, mental, physical and emotional well-being of the people playing the games. In addition, many are ambivalent in their opinions and are voicing both opposing and supporting arguments, making it a complex issue.
>
> The main concern raised about electronic games such as the ultra-violent *Mortal Kombat* is the development of anti-social behaviour in the players. Evidence of anti-social behaviour is observed in the school yard as children try out Kung-Fu-style movements on others. The concern is voiced by psychologists who say that players become desensitised to violent behaviour and hence consider that conflicts are resolved through superior violence.
>
> Others say that rather than creating social problems, the games have some problem-solving within the competition. Dr Julia Robinson, for example, claims that these games can actually help people combat their problems through dealing with conflicts at a distance. She contends that cancer patients and emotionally disturbed patients, for example, can deal with their emotional problems through these games.
>
> Another major issue with respect to the games is the physical and mental development of the user. Those who defend electronic games appear to have the upper hand in this area. The arguments in defence of these games come loosely under the educational banner and are that the players improve their hand–eye coordination skills, and develop their concentration skills and problem-solving abilities.
>
> The opponents of the games point to the apparent negative effects on the user's behaviour. They state that players can become addicted to the games, mood changes are possible, and that the games can even bring on epileptic fits. In addition, the sedentary nature of electronic games can increase the health risks in children.
>
> (Polias, 1993)

ACTIVITY 8

Here are two other examples produced by fellow students:

Example 1

Impressionism was born in France in the second half of the nineteenth century. It was a new art movement committed to the ideal of realism, producing images as they were seen. The production of images as they were seen led to a focus on the exact colour of objects and their shadows. In addition impressionist painters tried to explore the way light played upon objects. For example, they used a new technique of producing soft, misty outlines with little dabs of colour. Finally, the painters' subject matter mainly captured women and their activities.

Example 2

Impressionism, as an art movement, has a number of defining characteristics that distinguish it from other movements in the same sphere: its commitment to the ideal of realism is its most prominent feature.

Impressionism was born as a new art movement in France in the second half of the nineteenth century. Impressionist paintings captured almost every facet of French life, and they focused on two major points: the exact colour and shadows of objects; and the exploration of the way light played on them. These paintings also employed new techniques such as using little dabs of colour to produce soft, misty outlines; and chose women as their main subject matter. The impressionists were committed to the ideal of realism, producing images of life as they saw it.

Unit 15

Making a text hang together: the role of lexical cohesion

Prepared for the course team by Caroline Coffin, with intonation sections by Martin Rhys

CONTENTS

Materials required

While studying this unit, you will need:

> your reference grammar
> the Activities CD-ROM (Section 5 and end of unit).

Knowledge assumed

You should be familiar with the following before starting this unit:

> cohesion
> dysfluency
> field
> given/new information
> intonation terms (from Unit 7)
> lexical density
> marked/unmarked
> mode
> morphology
> nominalisation
> noun phrase
> relational process
> rheme
> taxonomy
> technical term
> tenor
> theme
> theme reiteration
> thing.

This text doesn't hang together very well.

I couldn't follow what he was saying – he seemed to be jumping all over the place.

I'm getting confused over what exactly it is you're referring to…

Introduction

I wonder how often you find yourself saying similar things? I am sure that at some point you have found yourself caught up in a discussion where you have found it hard to keep track of where it was going. Or perhaps you have listened to speeches where it is hard to work out what the main thread is? Maybe too you have come across densely written articles or pieces of fiction where it is not always very clear what is being referred to. In some cases – such as the advertisement below – this may be deliberate. In other cases it may simply be a matter of poor communication. Out of interest, what do you think is being referred to in the advertisement below? Do you think it works to 'hook' you in and make you more aware of, and interested in, the product it is promoting?

(*BBC Homes and Antiques*, August 2002, pp. 16–17)

The advertisement uses two possessive determiners – *our* and *their* – to point to people whose identity is not immediately obvious. However, once we work out that the advertisement is promoting a roasted Mediterranean vegetable sauce produced by the supermarket, Sainsbury's, then we can deduce that:

◆ in the phrase placed above the <u>less</u> appealing sauce (i.e. the one on the left-hand side which has far fewer vegetables), *Their* – in *Their hunt the roast vegetable* – refers to sauces produced by other people (i.e. Sainsbury's' competitors)

◆ in the phrase placed above the <u>more</u> appealing sauce (i.e. the one on the right-hand side which has considerably more vegetables), *Our* – in *Our roast vegetable sauce* – refers to the sauce produced by Sainsbury's.

Because the answer to the puzzling *their* and *our* lies in the small print at the bottom, the advertisement works to hook us into thinking about the text surrounding the visual images and in particular whom the possessive determiners might refer to. Obviously the longer we linger over an advertisement to try to make sense of its message, the more likely we are to remember the product it is promoting.

In the next two units we shall be exploring the way in which both grammar and lexis (lexicogrammar) work to weave together our ideas and thoughts in what is often referred to in commonsensical (as well as technical) terms as cohesive and coherent speech and writing (defined in greater detail later). Because this area of lexicogrammar is concerned with information flow the main contextual domain it relates to is mode. Let us remind ourselves of the relationship between mode, the textual metafunction and lexicogrammar by looking at Figure 1 opposite. Here we can see the territory we have covered so far and where our exploration will take us in the next two units.

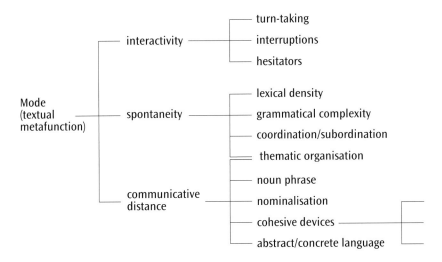

Figure 1 Map of mode

1 WHAT MAKES A TEXT HANG TOGETHER?

ACTIVITY 1 (allow about 15 minutes)

To begin thinking about what people mean when they describe a text as cohesive and/or coherent, read the following two texts. Can you make sense of them easily? Why/Why not?

Text 1

Economics was defined by the late Alfred Marshall, one of the great Victorian economists, as 'the study of mankind in the everyday business of life'. There are other definitions which are discussed later in this book, but Marshall's definition draws attention to that unique feature of human society: that unlike other animals, man provides for his everyday needs by means of a complex pattern of production, distribution and exchange. This everyday business of providing the means of livelihood is called by the general term 'economy'.

Text 2

Outsiders often dismiss this specialised vocabulary as jargon but this is a mistake. Similarly, a decision by a local authority to have only comprehensive schools in its area will divert resources of building accommodation and teaching staff towards this type of education. It was the result of 20 years' study of the industrial developments taking place around him in Britain, which was just passing through the stage known to history as the Industrial Revolution.

COMMENT

It is quite likely that you had little difficulty in understanding Text 1, even if you are not particularly interested in the topic. You were also probably able to guess that it might be an extract from an introductory book on Economics (which it is: Whitehead, 1982, p. 1). Text 1, in other words, is a coherent and cohesive text. But Text 2 is quite different – it is 'non-text'. In fact it was created by copying the first sentence from every fifth page in the introductory book to Economics that Text 1 comes from. You probably found yourself wondering what the passage was about, and might have thought that something was missing or mixed up. Each of the three sentences is a perfectly grammatical English sentence but together they do not form a *text*. This is because the sentences do not relate to each other in any meaningful way.

1.1 Coherence and cohesion

Text, in other words, only becomes text when:

(1) meanings are related or tied together by linguistic devices such as repetition or linking adverbials (referred to as **cohesive devices** or **cohesive ties**)

and/or

(2) meanings in a text make sense in relation to the context of the text as well as the listener's or reader's prior experience and cultural knowledge (this is what is meant by **coherence**).

In relation to (2) it is important to realise that, even where there are no recognisable cohesive signals in a text, a listener or reader may use their cultural knowledge together with their experience of language use to construct coherence. Look at the dialogue below, for example, and see if you can make sense of the interaction:

ANN (SHOUTING) Phone!

BRIAN I'm in the bath

ANN Ok

(Adapted from Widdowson, 1978, p. 29)

Despite the absence of cohesive signals in the text you will probably have succeeded in attributing meaning to this short interchange, i.e. Ann tells Brian that there is someone on the phone who wants to talk to him (a message communicated in a single word – *Phone!*). Brian's response, that he is in the bath, automatically functions to inform Ann that Brian is unable to speak on the phone. To make sense of the interchange you will have (largely unconsciously) drawn on your prior knowledge of similar social situations, as well as your experience of how spoken texts typically 'hang together'. It would sound odd and unnecessarily laboured, in other words, if Brian spelled out the causal link between being in the bath and not being able to speak on the phone (*I'm in the bath and therefore I can't speak on the phone*). Coherence, therefore, should be understood as primarily a mental phenomenon, one that is generated by the experience of a reader or listener rather than by the text itself.

Not all texts, however, rely solely on the reader/listener to create coherence. Often a coherent text is the result of effective use of cohesive devices. Such devices serve to 'glue' together the different meanings that make up a text and help a reader/listener make sense of a situation. For example, they may express logical relationships connecting different parts of a message:

I once acquired a set of recordings of a Bach piano concerto. I was very fond of it, but my mother was forever criticizing and chastising my poor taste [...] *Consequently*, I now hardly listen to Bach.

(Biber et al., 2002, p. 390)

Linking adverbials such as *consequently* create and/or mark the semantic relationship (in the case above, one of cause and effect) which writers or speakers perceive as holding between the utterances they produce. Other cohesive devices such as **reference** signal that the identity of what is being talked or written about can be recovered from the surrounding text. For example, the meaning of *it* in the following sentence can be retrieved by tracking back in the text to the noun phrase it references:

> <u>His great treatise on</u> *The Nature and Causes of the Wealth of Nations* was published in 1776. <u>It</u> was the result of 20 years of study...

In sum, although the absence of cohesive devices does not automatically make a text incoherent (as we saw earlier in the short dialogue), very often such devices play an important role in contributing to the coherence of a text. One of the main reasons for Text 2's incoherence, for example, is the lack of cohesive relations, or cohesive ties, between items. Each sentence is largely self-contained and does not contribute to the interpretation of any other. Thus the text does not hang together as an internally cohesive piece of language. As a result it is unlikely that any reader could make such a random collection of disconnected topics coherent by supplying an overall meaning or communicative purpose (as they could do in the case of the dialogue).

In Units 15 and 16 we will explore some of the most important cohesive resources available in the English language and see how they function to weave together the meanings in a text and so contribute to its coherence. This focus on cohesive devices will, we hope, continue to improve your ability to produce well-organised and coherent texts, whether they be written essays or spoken presentations for your university degree or your professional and/or community life. We also hope that you will continue to develop your skills in working out why some texts flow smoothly and clearly, whereas others make it difficult for you as a reader or listener to see how the meanings connect with each other. Learning to pinpoint where communication has broken down is, after all, a useful first step in repairing and mending such breakdowns.

The weaving or binding together of meanings to create a unified text is sometimes referred to as giving **texture** to a text. Below is a map of the resources, each of which we will cover in turn. Those devices categorised as lexical will be covered in Unit 15 while grammatical devices will be explored in Unit 16. You may be surprised that in a course on English grammar a whole unit is devoted to **lexical cohesion** but, as the course team has always stressed, this course does not make a strong distinction between grammar and lexis. Lexis, as Michael Halliday and Ruquaiya Hasan (1975, p. 281) have stated 'is simply the open-ended and most "delicate" aspect of the grammar of a language'. In other words, both are simply different ways of looking at the same phenomenon, i.e. how English works.

In addition, we will look at some of the intonational devices which contribute to the cohesion of a spoken text.

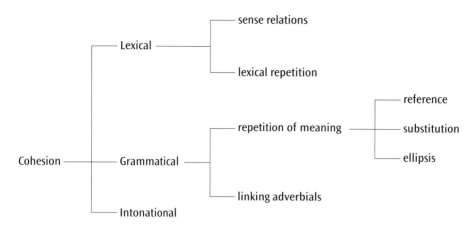

Figure 2 Types of cohesion

❷ USING LEXIS TO MAKE A TEXT HANG TOGETHER

> "You know a word by the company it keeps."
>
> (Firth, 1957, p. 11)

2.1 Lexical chains

Strings of connected words within a text are referred to as **lexical chains**. When several of these chains come together in a text to create an overall impact and meaning, the text is said to be lexically cohesive.

In the following text, which is concerned with explaining volcanic activity, I have underlined all the words which are connected to each other and which form threads of related meaning. (NB: for ease of reference the text has been divided into numbered sections.)

(1) A volcano begins when magma inside the earth forces its way up into the crust. (2) When pressure in the magma builds up, the magma forces its way up, and exits as lava. (3) A volcano also throws up steam and other gases, ashes and dust. (4) It does not

throw up fire. (5) Sometimes <u>material</u> from inside the <u>volcano is thrown</u> 50 or 60 kilometres into the air. (6) In fact the <u>dust and ashes</u> from a <u>volcano</u> may blow around the world for years.

(7) There are three types of <u>volcanoes</u>: an <u>active volcano</u> is one which is <u>erupting</u>; (8) a <u>dormant volcano</u> is one which is '<u>sleeping</u>' — it may not have <u>erupted</u> for many years but could <u>erupt</u> at any time; (9) and an <u>extinct volcano</u> is one which is <u>dead</u> and will not <u>erupt</u> again.

(Shubert, 1998, p. 35)

In Figure 3, we have shown how the two main lexical chains in the text can be displayed. Each sentence or clause complex is numbered in the

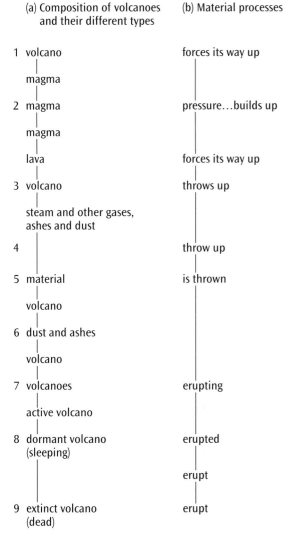

Figure 3 Lexical chains in the 'Volcano' text

left-hand column to show which words/phrases are used at which points in the text.

We can see from the identification of the lexical chains that two major aspects of volcanoes are developed as the text unfolds: (a) the composition of volcanoes (sections 3–6) and the different types of volcano (sections 7–9) and (b) the material processes involved in volcanic eruption. We can see that, together, the two chains build a set of related words concerning volcanic activity. The lexical chains, in other words, provide evidence of the unity of meaning, consistency and tight focus of the text.

Not all texts will show the same degree of consistency and focus. There may be shorter or longer chains and more variety of chains depending on how the meanings of a text are staged and organised. Analysing lexical chains will often provide important insights into a text by telling us such things as:

◆ what is being talked/written about in the text, in that each major lexical chain indicates a topic or part of a topic

◆ how many different things are discussed in the text: are they linked or not? Are they simultaneous or sequential?

◆ whether there is a consistency in what gets talked about, i.e. are there a few major chains or a lot of short, unrelated chains?

Aside from observing that some words or phrases are related to each other in general terms, we can be more precise about the type of relationship that exists between them. For example, whereas some words may simply repeat previous ones, others may relate to each other by providing similar meanings or even opposite meanings. In the following sections, the aim is to familiarise you with different types and patterns of lexical relations that regularly occur in English texts. You will find that analysing texts (including your own!) for lexical cohesion will help you to judge their communicative effectiveness.

ACTIVITY 2 (allow about 45 minutes)

This activity is designed to help you see how lexical cohesive devices contribute to the communicative effectiveness of texts. Within this activity there are five short texts, each of which has been chosen to illustrate a different pattern of lexical cohesion. First, read each text and answer the following questions:

(1) What is the text about (its field)?

(2) What type of relationship exists between the interlocutors (its tenor)?

(3) Is the text more spoken or more written (its mode)?

Text 3

The effects of ageing are particularly obvious in humans, but are not peculiar to us. Ageing occurs in natural populations—as individuals get older they become less fecund and more likely to die. Organisms ranging from yeast to mammals to plants are affected. Cars and washing machines wear out too, which suggests that ageing could be an inevitable consequence of complexity. But at least some things do not age. All organisms living today are descended from lineages that have been going strong for three billion years. Germ lines do not wear out. So if ageing is not inevitable, surely such a universal and ultimately lethal process must have a purpose?

(Gems and Partridge, 2002, p. 921)

Text 4

'I'm not so old', he said, in a musing sort of voice.

'So old as what?'

'Properly considered, I'm in my prime. Besides, what a young and inexperienced girl needs is a man of weight and years to lean on. The sturdy oak, not the sapling.'

It was this point, as said above, I saw all.

'Great Scott, Uncle George!' I said. 'You weren't thinking of getting married?'

(Wodehouse, 1930, p. 27)

Text 5

B: People just don't work Saturday mornings officially in London

[...]

C: Does he come in on Saturdays?

[...]

A: Well most of them seem to come floating in on Saturdays because this...

C: Well I quite enjoy working on Saturdays.

A: M

B: Well I always used to when I was still at Cambridge and one did work Saturdays.

(McCarthy, 1988, p. 189)

Text 6

For years those of us who have played a cat and mouse game with cagey manager Billy Bingham over team selections could always be sure that Donaghy's* name would be the first one down on the sheet. Now, for the first time in over a decade there is uncertainty over the Chelsea veteran's inclusion. Recently the 35-year-old Belfast man has been playing the "sweeper" role in front of the back four.

[* Donaghy is a well-known British footballer who plays for the London-based team, Chelsea.]

(Biber et al., 1999, p. 238)

Text 7

The children want to walk along the parapet a couple of metres above the beach. In this way we proceed past the Delfino verde (the Green Dolphin), then the Orsa maggiore (the Great Bear) until we come to the Medusa. These are the bathing concessions, and the children know all their names on and on along the front towards the centre – Calipso, Sette Pini, La Sirena, Belvedere, Miramare, Aurora – all their names and all their various advantages and disadvantages: the bar at the Delfino verde doesn't have fresh brioches, but the hot showers are truly hot and even have a windscreen of bamboo, an unusual feature in a country where most people will desert the beach if the breeze does anything more than stir the tassels on the sunshades. The Orsa maggiore has hot showers too, and you don't even have to pay here. But there is no windscreen, and the attendant hangs around you to see that you don't push the time switch down more than twice. You get two spurts of no more than forty seconds each. The Medusa has freezing cold showers lined up in a row on a block of cement. They deliver unbelievably icy water in great swishing jets that still the heart as you step under them from burning sand. But the Medusa also has the best terrace bar, with the best *pizzette*, and the best computer games.

(Parks, 1996, pp. 371–2)

COMMENT

Text 3 is an extract from an article on ageing which appeared in the prestigious magazine *Nature*, a publication that is directed at a non-expert readership interested in scientific issues. (In fact you first came across this article in Book 1 Unit 5 when you were examining the use of the passive voice.) The relationship between writer and reader is conversational in places (e.g. note the use of a question) but the mode is clearly written. However, I would locate the text only two thirds of the way towards the written end of the mode continuum as it is not nearly as lexically dense as a research article directed at fellow academics might be.

You will probably have identified Text 4 as a piece of fiction. That is, even though it consists of a conversation between two people, it does not display any of the features of naturally-occurring speech, such as interruptions or hesitations. It also contains a clear authorial intervention (*he said, in a musing sort of voice*).

Text 5 is clearly a transcription of a spoken conversation as evidenced by the speaker turns, the use of the interrogative and the informal linker *well*. (The three dots <...> show that the conversational turns are not immediately sequential.)

Text 6 is an extract from a news text, specifically a sports report on whether or not the footballer Donaghy will be reselected for his London-based Chelsea team. There are several uses of technical terms relating to the specialised field of football (e.g. *"sweeper role"* refers to how a footballer can intercept a loose ball – "sweeping" it up and then distributing it, usually to the defenders or goalkeeper; and *the back four* refers to the defenders in a football team). The use of colloquial expressions (e.g. *cat and mouse game, first one down on the sheet*) and personal pronouns (*those of us*) create an informal, conversational tone. The use of fairly tightly-packed noun phrases, on the other hand, locates the text as belonging to the written mode (e.g. the *Chelsea veteran's inclusion, the 35-year-old Belfast man*). Like Text 3, I would place this text towards the written end of the mode continuum but not at the very end.

You will probably have identified Text 7 as a piece of prose designed to entertain – possibly you thought it was an extract from a novel, based on the amount of description built up through noun phrases (e.g. *great swishing jets that still the heart*, etc.) Or maybe the use of the *I* voice led you to think it was an extract from an autobiography? The text was, in fact, written by a journalist-turned-writer (Tim Parks) who has lived in Italy for a number of years and who writes books recounting his experiences of living there.

Having now established the context for each text, read them a second time in the versions below and think about what type of relationship is operating between the sets of words underlined. What is the communicative effect of this relationship? Then read the short explanation following each text.

Text 3

The effects of <u>ageing</u> are particularly obvious in humans, but are not peculiar to us. <u>Ageing</u> occurs in natural populations—as individuals get older they become less fecund and more likely to die. Organisms ranging from yeast to mammals to plants are affected. Cars and washing machines wear out too, which suggests that ageing could be an inevitable consequence of complexity. But at least some things do not age. All organisms living today are descended from lineages that have been going strong for three billion years. Germ lines do not wear out. So if ageing is not inevitable, surely such a universal and ultimately lethal process must have a purpose?

In Text 3 we have a very clear example of **repetition** where the same lexical item – *ageing* – is repeated five times. This simple restatement of the same item allows the writer to draw out different aspects of the phenomenon. For example:

> Ageing occurs in natural populations…

> …ageing could be an inevitable consequence of complexity.

You may also have noticed how the writer harnesses the resource of theme to create a framework for the text (see Unit 14). That is, by placing *ageing* in theme position (four out of five instances), the writer uses the theme reiteration pattern to maintain *ageing* as a clear focus for the reader. As you would expect in an article which aims to popularise science for a lay audience, the use of repetition helps to leaven what could otherwise be a rather dense and inaccessible piece of academic prose.

As is the case in this text, it is important to note that sometimes a repeated lexical item will be morphologically different (e.g. *age* or *aged* rather than *ageing*).

Text 4

'I'm not so old,' he said, in a musing sort of voice.

'So old as what?'

'Properly considered, I'm in my prime. Besides, what a young and inexperienced girl needs is a man of weight and years to lean on. The sturdy oak, not the sapling.'

It was this point, as said above, I saw all.

'Great Scott, Uncle George!' I said. 'You weren't thinking of getting married?'

In Text 4 we can see that in addition to the repetition of *old*, the lexical items *in my prime* and *of … years* refers back to *old* through a more general process of reiteration. That is, even though *in my prime* and *of … years* are not the exact same lexical items, they carry the same meaning as *old*. The lexical relation highlighted in Text 4 is that of **synonymy**.

Synonymy is the relation between words or phrases with the same or similar meaning. By using the device of synonymy, cohesion is achieved by referring to the same entity in slightly different ways.

We can also note that the use of literary metaphor (whereby one item represents or symbolises another) further reiterates the notion of age, in that *sturdy oak* represents age. Similarly, *sapling* stands for youth and thus reiterates the earlier use of *young*.

Text 5

B: People just don't <u>work</u> Saturday mornings officially in London

<...>

C: Does he <u>come in</u> on Saturdays?

<...>

A: Well most of them seem to come <u>floating in</u> on Saturdays
   because this...

C: Well I quite enjoy working on Saturdays.

A: M

B: Well I always used to when I was still at Cambridge and one
   did work Saturdays.

In this conversational extract we can see an example of the way in which a meaning is repeated in a non-identical form or **relexicalised**. That is, *work* is progressively reformulated as *come in* and *floating in*. According to McCarthy (1987) such relexicalisations, whereby an item is incrementally redefined, are powerful ways of managing conversations. They are often used in conversation for interpersonal effect, as a rhetorical ploy. For example, a speaker can choose to use a similar lexical item as the person they are conversing with but give it a slightly different meaning. This enables them seemingly to agree with their interlocutor whilst simultaneously (and subtly) renegotiating the terms of reference. Thus, in the conversation, whereas *work, come in* and *float in* have the same overall meaning, *float in* redefines the sense of work by giving it a more casual flavour. Such a ploy can, of course, only be exploited in spoken, interactive language. So, already, you are beginning to see how mode affects the way cohesive devices can be used by readers and writers, and you are also beginning to see how cohesive devices, in addition to creating texture, can have interpersonal uses.

Text 6

For years those of us who have played a cat and mouse game with cagey manager Billy Bingham over team selections could always be sure that Donaghy's name would be the first one down on the sheet. Now, for the first time in over a decade there is uncertainty over the Chelsea veteran's inclusion. Recently the 35-year-old Belfast man has been playing the "sweeper" role in front of the back four.

In this report, you have observed how the same referent, the footballer Donaghy, is referred to using different lexical choices – *Chelsea veteran* and *35-year-old Belfast man.*

This type of cohesive device is referred to as **co-reference**. That is, different lexical items are used to indicate the same referent. Such devices are an economical way of communicating information. For example, in this extract the use of co-reference enables the writer to provide the name of Donaghy's football team, age and origins). Evidence from the LSWE corpus shows that this is a relatively common technique in news texts.

Text 7

The children want to walk along the parapet a couple of metres above the beach. In this way we proceed past the Delfino verde (the Green Dolphin), then the Orsa maggiore (the Great Bear) until we come to the Medusa. These are the bathing concessions, and the children know all their names on and on along the front towards the centre – Calipso, Sette Pini, La Sirena, Belvedere, Miramare, Aurora – all their names and all their various advantages and disadvantages: the bar at the Delfino verde doesn't have fresh brioches, but the *hot* showers are truly hot and even have a windscreen of bamboo, an unusual feature in a country where most people will desert the beach if the breeze does anything more than stir the tassels on the sunshades. The Orsa maggiore has hot showers too, and you don't even have to pay here. But there is no windscreen, and the attendant hangs around you to see that you don't push the time switch down more than twice. You get two spurts of no more than forty seconds each. The Medusa has freezing cold showers lined up in a row on a block of cement. They deliver unbelievably icy water in great swishing jets that still the heart as you step under them from burning sand. But the Medusa also has the best terrace bar, with the best *pizzette*, and the best computer games.

In Text 7 it is clear that the writer uses language for semi-literary effect and this is one piece of lexicogrammatical evidence that the text was written to entertain rather than merely inform. For example, lexical choices have been carefully made to evoke contrasting sensations of heat and cold, whilst at the same time the experiences of both heat and cold are intensified through repetition and synonymy.

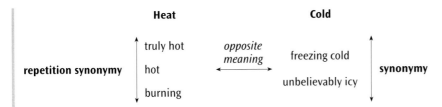

Figure 4 Repetition and synonymy in Text 7

In addition, we have a contrast between the strength of different beach showers – *two spurts of no more than forty seconds each* compared to *great swishing jets*. These sets of contrasts are in turn related to the overall *advantages* and *disadvantages* of the different beach resorts. The relation between words with opposite or contrasting meanings is referred to as **antonymy**. Clearly, such a relation can be exploited to great effect in the self-conscious, reflective mode of creative writing. If we look back to Text 4, for example, we can see the interplay of references to youth and age, such as *inexperienced girl* and *man of weight*.

General comment

Activity 2 has illustrated some of the different ways in which meanings can be lexically reiterated across both written and spoken English. You have seen how such reiteration gives texture to a text and at the same time produces different communicative effects. Although it is not possible always to predict which kinds of lexical cohesion are likely to occur in which Longman registers, Biber et al. (1999, p. 238) observe that synonyms are relatively frequent in the news and fiction registers but rarer in conversation. In the case of synonymy, one possible explanation for this is that creatively-oriented forms of English (such as fiction and news) generally value lexical variation. In conversation, on the other hand, the relative rarity of synonyms can be partly explained by the fact that they are a more ambiguous form of reference than repeated nouns and can therefore cause processing difficulties in the spoken mode.

ACTIVITY 3 (allow about 10 minutes)

The following adapted extract is from a novel by a well-known English writer, Virginia Woolf. She is well known for her unusual, poetic style, and you will find evidence of this in the extract. However, I have changed the original text by removing some of its synonyms and repetitions. As you read the text, think of where you could add synonyms and repetition to give it a more closely-woven texture and thus intensify its poetic effect. You may then like to compare your changes with the original text in 'Answers to the activities'.

In people's eyes, in the trudge; in the uproar; the carriages, motor cars, omnibuses, vans, sandwich men shuffling; brass bands; barrel organs; in the triumph and the jingle and the strange high singing of some aeroplane overhead was what she loved; London; this moment of June.

[...] and she, too, loving it as she did with an absurd and faithful passion, being part of it, since her people were courtiers once in the time of the Georges, she, too, was going that very night to illuminate; to give her party. But how strange, on entering the Park, the silence; the mist; the slow-swimming happy ducks; the pouched birds; and who should be coming along with his back against the Government buildings, most appropriately, carrying a despatch box stamped with the Royal Arms, who but Hugh Whitbread...

(Adapted from Woolf, 1996, pp. 6–7)

2.2 Improving cohesion through taxonomic relations

So far, we have seen how lexical reiteration creates texture through repeating the same, similar or opposite meanings. In addition, lexical reiteration can be used to indicate class–subclass and part–whole relations. In the case of **class–subclass** relations, an item referring to a more general class (the **superordinate**) links to items referring to members of its class. Thus, in the following extract from a History book, *Socialism* is the general class and *Revolutionary* and *Reformist* are both members of the class – they are both types of socialism:

Socialism is the general ideology that capitalism should be replaced by public ownership and control of industry, production and services. There are two broad types, Revolutionary and Reformist.

(Coffin, 1996, p. 104)

Such relationships of class and subclass can be represented visually, as in Figure 5.

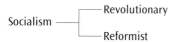

Figure 5

In the continuing section of the history extract, the two types of socialism – revolutionary and reformist – are in turn subdivided into subclasses which can again be visually mapped as exemplified in Figure 6.

Revolutionary Socialism is the idea that capitalism should be overthrown by an uprising of the working people. There are two kinds, Anarchism and Marxist Communism.

Anarchism is the idea that there should be no government at all.

Marxist Communism proposes that the working people should be led by a small party. The party should seize power when the capitalist system starts to collapse. The inevitable collapse of capitalism is part of this Marxist belief.

Reformist Socialism is the belief that revolution is not a good idea and that socialism can be brought about by trade unions and labour parties working within the capitalist system to introduce gradual changes, or reforms.

Figure 6

(Coffin, 1996, p. 104)

ACTIVITY **4** (allow about 15 minutes)

Mapping and visualising relationships built through taxonomies of related meanings can be a useful reading strategy. The text below comes from a Geography textbook aimed at school students. As you read the text, create a diagram as a means of mapping how the different types of rock relate to one another. See 'Answers to the activities' for feedback.

Text 8

There are three main types of **sedimentary rocks**:
◆ **clastic sedimentary rocks**
◆ **chemical sedimentary rocks**
◆ **organic sedimentary rocks**.

Clastic sedimentary rocks are those formed from the *fragments* (clasts) of other rocks.

Chemical sedimentary rocks form when minerals come out of watery solutions as the water evaporates.

Examples:
◆ **limestone**, forming stalagmites and stalactites in caves (the mineral is calcium carbonate)
◆ **gypsum** (calcium sulphate), often found in deserts

◆ **rock salt** (sodium chloride) found in dried inland lakes or in some bays along the seashore.

Organic sedimentary rocks form from parts of animals or plants. When plant matter falls into a swamp, it may eventually become coal. In coral reefs, or on the sea floor, the shells, plates and spines of animals may be cemented together to form limestone.

(Coghill and Wood, 1987)

COMMENT

You will have observed that *sedimentary rocks* is related to *clastic, chemical* and *organic rocks* in the form of a class–subclass relationship and you may also have noticed the effectiveness of thematic patterning in setting out this threeway classification. *Sedimentary,* in other words, is the superordinate term linking to *clastic, chemical* and *organic rocks* as three members of the class. Likewise, *limestone, gypsum* and *rock salt* are members of the class, *chemical rock.*

The relation between subclass and class is referred to as **hyponymy,** with **co-hyponymy** referring to the relation between the members of the same class (e.g. between *clastic, chemical* and *organic sedimentary rocks*). Relations of class to member are given various names in English depending on the field, for example, a *breed* of horses, a *make* of car, a *class* of insects. Common examples include *class, type, kind, variety, genre, sort, category, species, family.* These can be used cohesively between messages, for example:

A: What do you think of my new <u>car</u>?

B: It's great. What <u>make</u> is it?

Not surprisingly, lexical devices that build taxonomies (or **classification systems**) are frequently drawn on in the academic prose register. The more specialised the field, the more specialised the taxonomy. However, it is important to recognise how much of our everyday talk also serves to organise and classify our world. Clare Painter, for example, in her chapter on language and thinking in your course reader, *Applying English Grammar,* has some interesting examples of children developing the linguistic resources for categorising phenomena. The following extract is taken from that chapter:

(S fails to find a picture of a seal in his fish book.)

H: Seals aren't fish, that's why. They're mammals.

S: Are seals mammals?

H: Yes, 'cause they don't lay eggs; they have babies.

(Painter, 1996, p. 17)

Aside from classifying taxonomies, there are also **part–whole taxonomies**. Thus, whereas *bus, train* and *car* are all types or kinds of transport and therefore form a classifying taxonomy, *wheels, brakes, clutch* and *steering wheel* are all parts of a bus (or train or car) and therefore form a part–whole taxonomy. This is illustrated in Figures 7 and 8.

Figure 7 Classifying taxonomy

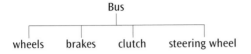

Figure 8 Part–whole taxonomy

A CTIVITY 5 (allow about 15 minutes)

Text 9 below belongs to a specialised register similar to the 'rocks' text in Activity 4 above. That is, although the specific field is *seeds* rather than *rocks*, both texts share the same mode (written), overall purpose (describing a scientific phenomenon) and tenor (expert to non-expert). We can therefore describe such a register as school science (written). Here, knowledge is built up using both part–whole and classifying relations. As you read through the text, complete the diagram in Figure 9 to represent these relations. See 'Answers to the activities' for feedback.

Text 9

Seeds

A seed is the small body produced by plants from which a new plant grows. It is formed as a result of fertilisation and develops from an *ovule*. During the development of the seed, the cells in it are grouped and specialised to form **the shoot, root** and **the first leaves** of the young plant (embryo). Food is passed from the parent plant to the seed, which increases in size as a result. When the process is complete, the seed is ripe and ready for dispersal.

The embryo is the part of the seed that grows into a new plant. It has 3 main parts: **the seed leaves, or** *cotyledons* (either one or two), which are the beginnings of leaves; **the** *plumule*, which becomes the main stem; and **the** *radicle*, which becomes the root. Plants whose seeds have one cotyledon are called monocots, and plants whose seeds have two cotyledons are called dicots.

(Wilkinson, 1985, p. 150)

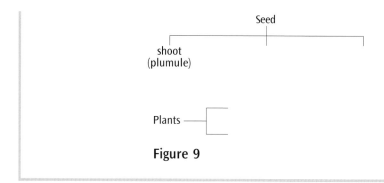

Figure 9

In whole–part taxonomic relationships the relation between a whole (e.g. *plant*) and one of its parts (e.g. *seed* and *shoot*) is referred to as **meronymy. Co-meronymy** is the relation between two parts of the same whole (e.g. *plumule* and *radicle*). As in the case of relations of class to members, relationships of wholes to parts are also given various names in English depending on the field, for example: *part, content, ingredient, constituent, element, component, piece, segment, portion.* Again, part–whole relations can be used cohesively between messages:

A: This book's good.

B: Any part in particular?

As in the case of classification, lexical relations of whole–part feature across all registers. It is interesting to observe, however, the variation in the degree of technicality and specialisation that occurs, in particular, in the academic register. In this register, for example, different fields and different tenor relations (e.g. *expert-to-expert* as opposed to *expert-to-novice*) will result in the use of more or less technicality. Lexical cohesion can thus be seen as a resource which facilitates the construction of both field knowledge and tenor relations.

A CTIVITY 6 (allow about 25 minutes)

In this activity we will look at three examples of 'academic' prose and explore how lexical relations serve to build taxonomies in rather different ways, depending on the degree of abstraction and specialisation found in the text. As you read Texts 10 to 12 create a visual taxonomy making explicit the relationships between the different phenomena. Think too as to whether the relations are class–subclass or whole–part or a combination. When you have finished the activity you may want to compare your taxonomy diagrams with those in 'Answers to the activities'. What role do technical terms (and the relations between them) play in building meaning?

Text 10

Insects are sometimes pests and they are sometimes useful. There are hundreds of insects, e.g. flies, mosquitoes, moths and cicadas. Flies are annoying but also an insect looking very much the same is a bee. They produce honey and wax. They are not pests.

(Adapted from Gerot, 1995, pp. 43–4)

Text 11

The body of an insect is divided into three, the head, thorax and abdomen. The thorax has three pairs of walking legs and can also have two pairs of wings. The most simple insects such as silverfish have no wings. The young are the same as the parents. The winged insects can be put into two groups. In one group, the newly hatched insects look rather like the adults except that their wings are not fully developed. The other group have young called larvae which are quite different from the adult.

(Wilkinson, 1985)

Text 12

The class Insecta is the largest class of animals in the phylum Uniramia. It includes over 750,000 identified species and scientists believe that this figure could double as new insects are discovered and classified. There are over 100,000 known insect species on the Australian continent and surrounding islands.

The class Insecta is divided into two sub-classes. Apterygota comprises the wing-less insects. Pterygota includes all insects which have wings at some stage in their life cycle.

Insects in the sub-class Pterygota are divided into two broad groups. Exopterygota insects undergo incomplete metamorphosis: the wings are developed in the larval stage. Endopterygota insects go through complete metamorphosis: the wings are developed in the pupal stage.

(Wilkinson, 1985)

COMMENT

You probably concluded that two of the texts, 10 and 11, were written by young students. These students (at the age of 11) have limited control over technical, specialised knowledge and so are unable to build complex lexical relations such as those displayed in the professionally written text, Text 12. The writer of Text 10 uses everyday, commonsensical criteria to make a simple classification of insects as either *pests* or *useful*. However, it is not clear which category *mosquitoes, moths* and *cicadas* belong to. The lexical relations are therefore relatively undeveloped. The writer of Text 11, on the other hand, uses technical terms to classify insects by their different structures. The lexical relations are therefore more complex (as can be seen in the taxonomy diagram in 'Answers to the activities'). Text 11 also creates a taxonomy of the different parts that make up the body of the insect. From an educational perspective, the writer of Text 11 is clearly more advanced than the writer of Text 10. Text 12 develops the use of technical terms even further, thus creating a highly specialised taxonomic representation of insect types.

❸ LEXICAL COHESION AND COMMUNICATIVE EFFECTIVENESS

Having explored some of the different ways in which lexical devices build and bind together meanings across texts, let us now (in the next two activities) apply this knowledge to contrast the communicative effectiveness of two texts, both of which are concerned with electronic circuits. (For your information, if you are unfamiliar with the rather specialised field of electronics, an electronic circuit is made up of various components such as wires, resistors, batteries, etc. The circuit has both an input and an output in the form of electrical currents. The output is able to carry out various tasks such as controlling the temperature of a room, specifying the number of messages on an answer machine, or providing a graph on a screen when an electrocardiogram is underway.)

In the case of each of the texts, the purpose for writing and the tenor relations between writer and reader are different. Whereas the professional writer of Text 13 aims to explain to a novice audience the major components of basic circuits, Kevin, the writer of Text 14, is a school student writing in response to the teacher's invitation to write on a subject of personal interest. The contextual variables for each text are therefore different.

A CTIVITY 7 (allow about 20 minutes)

First, read Text 13 and then look at Figure 9. Figure 9 displays Text 13's lexical chains. Think about the implications of these chains regarding:

(1) what is being written about in the text

(2) how many different things are discussed in the text. Are the chains linked or not? Are they simultaneous or sequential?

(3)   whether there is a consistency in what gets talked about, i.e. are there a few major chains or a whole lot of short, unrelated chains?

In particular think about whether the chains point to a successful or an unsuccessful text. Consider too what aspects of the context you need to take into account to make this decision.

Lexical chains are constructed by showing all the lexical items that occur sequentially in a text and which can be related to an immediately prior word. For this reason, each of the sentences in the text are numbered and displayed in the left-hand column. The words are linked by a straight line on which is written the type of relationship between each two words in the chain (e.g. hyponymy, synonymy, repetition). Usually only the main lexical chains are displayed (those with at least three or four words in them). Note that the sentence numbers have been inserted for ease of reference.

Text 13

Components

(1) The major components in any basic circuit include a breadboard, a power source (a battery), resistors, wires, ammeters and voltmeters. (2) As circuits get more and more complex, you begin using components such as capacitors, transistors and switches. (3) All of these components will be explained in this page.

(4) A breadboard is simply a board in which you plug your components into when making a circuit. (5) It is usually a plastic board with holes in it. (6) These holes are connected (inside the board) by metal which allows the current to flow through the components. (7) All holes in the same horizontal line are connected together. (8) Running in a vertical line somewhere on the breadboard are things called 'buses.' (9) These are usually where you would plug your power source and your "ground" into.

(10) Every circuit requires some sort of power source. (11) This is usually in the form of a battery. (12) The symbol for the battery on a schematic diagram is shown in the margin.

(13) If using a regular battery, you will need to solder wires onto the + and − terminals of the battery. (14) Then you may plug these wires into the breadboard. (15) The battery is a type of capacitor with charge stored up on one side (plate). (16) When connected to something else, current will flow.

(Electronics Workshop [online])

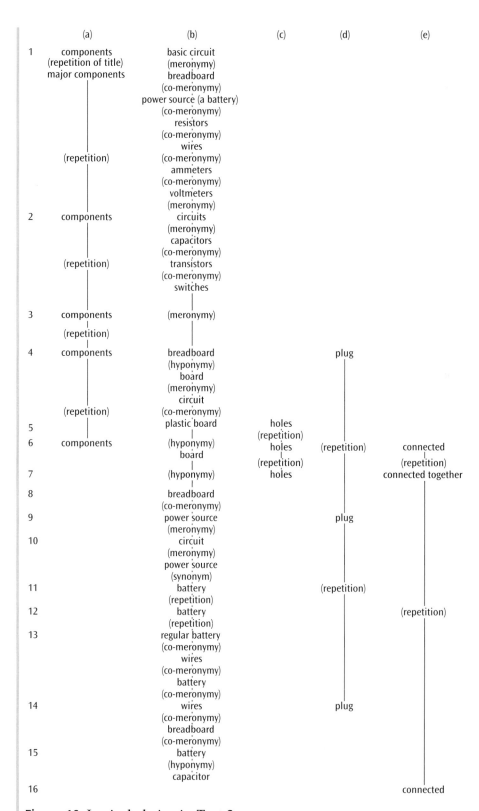

Figure 10 Lexical chains in Text 3

COMMENT

Based on the analysis presented in Figure 14 we can see that a major strength of Text 13 is the way in which the major components of circuits are linked together and are given sustained and focused attention. As the text unfolds, part–whole relations are built up, linking *circuits* with *breadboard, holes, battery* and *wires*. Chain (b) is also clearly related to Chain (a) in that *battery, wires,* etc. are all types of components and therefore co-hyponyms.

The analysis shows that the text is 'thing'-oriented in that there are only two short activity chains. These are concerned with *plugging* and *connecting*. Given that the overall purpose of the text is to set up and explain the taxonomic organisation of a circuit's major components (notice the title – *Components*), this is not surprising. In sum, the analysis shows how the text provides a comprehensive and carefully staged introduction to basic circuits and their component parts.

ACTIVITY 8 (allow about 45 minutes)

Having seen how an analysis of a text's lexical chains illuminates the way in which meanings can be successfully linked together, Activity 8 gives you the opportunity to try out your own analysis on Text 14. To help you we have provided a table showing the three major chains with some examples filled in (Figure 11). On the basis of your analysis, what can you say about the communicative effectiveness of the text? Remember that (as commented on earlier) Kevin, the writer of Text 14, does not have a clear purpose for his text other than to write something on electronics, a topic that is of interest to him.

(When you have completed filling in the lexical chains for Text 14, compare your analysis with the one provided in 'Answers to the activities'.)

Text 14

Electronics

(1) I like electronics because it interests me. (2) I started to like it a few years ago. (3) I took apart old radios and that kind of stuff. (4) My uncle Michael has given me a lot of help and components. (5) You have to have a lot of patience to do the soldering. (6) I have a piece of breadboard. (7) You just push the components' legs in to the board. (8) I still use the soldering iron if the breadboard is not big enough. (9) I've made an electronic clock and have put it into a box. (10) I've got an alarm sign on the display but have not been able to get an alarm fixed up to it yet. (11) At the moment I'm

getting the parts for an electronic organ. (12) It has a keyboard and you have a stylus to touch the metal keyboard. (13) You have an earpiece but can make an amplifier. (14) After that you can make a vibrato circuit.

(Carter, 1996 p. 123)

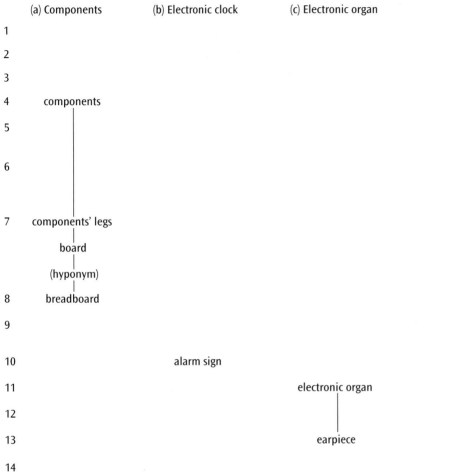

Figure 11 Lexical chains in Text 14

COMMENT

Your analysis of Text 14 will no doubt have revealed a rather different pattern of lexical relations compared to Text 13. Whereas the chains in Text 13 reflect a sustained and technical treatment of circuits, those in Text 14 reflect an uncertainty of focus. Each chain is relatively short and the reader has to work hard to establish the relations between some of the lexical items. In general it seems that the writer has somewhat 'lost the thread' and is drifting from one topic to another without any clear purpose. Whereas in a fast-flowing conversation this might be appropriate, the general expectation is that written texts are more tightly focused and more carefully organised.

The whole notion of purpose is, of course, a central criterion to judging a text's effectiveness. In some ways, because Kevin was not given a clear purpose for his text, it is difficult to make a judgement about his use of lexical cohesion. Perhaps the writing task was meant to serve as an opportunity for him to explore a topic he was interested in as a way of motivating him to write? This raises the interesting and important question of what role writing should play in the educational process. In general, though, I think we can say that Text 14 is not a particularly effective text.

4 LEXICAL COHESION AND REGISTER VARIATION

In Activity 2, we observed that mode has an effect on the type of lexical relations used in texts. For example, we saw that texts at the written end of the mode continuum (and which are no doubt carefully planned and redrafted many times over) often exploit synonyms and antonyms for their literary and creative effect. We also saw that more technical and abstract written texts (such as those found in specialised academic fields) are more likely to build complex and specialised taxonomic relations. In this section we will continue to explore the effect of mode on the use of cohesive devices.

ACTIVITY 9 (allow about 25 minutes)

The purpose of Activity 9 is to illustrate how the cohesive device of repetition can serve a variety of functions within all the Longman registers. From a Longman perspective, the first pair of texts (Texts 15 and 16) would be located in the conversation register and the second pair (Texts 17 and 18) in the academic prose register. However, each of the texts within the pair displays a very different pattern of repetition. As you read the texts:

(1) Think about where you would place them on the mode continuum.

(2) Underline the repetitions.

(3) Think about the communicative effect of the different patterns. Why do you think the speaker or writer uses repetition?

Text 15

[In the following dialogue, Vinnie Jones, Eric Cantona and Mark Hughes are all retired footballers with a reputation for being 'hard men'. Vinnie Jones has exploited this image by going on to star in various films.]

C: Did you see that thing on <unclear>

D: You shouldn't believe that though.

B: Who's Vinnie Jones?

<...>

C: You like Vinnie Jones, don't you?

D: I reckon he er well, <...> probably could –

A: I don't reckon Eric Cantona could.

B: Don't reckon Cantona could what?

A: I don't reckon Cantona could beat him up.

C: Yeah.

B: Nor do I.

A: <unclear> couldn't, but Mark Hughes might.

B: But I don't know why we're talking about this.

(Biber et al., 2002, p. 445)

Text 16

[The following is an extract from the discussion on the artist Jackson Pollock (you first came across texts about him in Unit 14). Here, the art critics Tim Clark and Michael Fried are discussing the special quality of Pollock's style of painting.]

TIM CLARK Yes, all right, OK. An obvious kind of question occurs and it's a question that is sort of generated out of the qualities of an account you really gave...

MICHAEL FRIED A long time ago.

TIM CLARK Yes, a long time ago in the 1960's which enabled a lot of us to look at Pollock in a more productive way, trying to say that, look, in the end, the key quality of this as a picture is a certain evenness and dispersal of energy, an all over-ness, a kind of quality in its deployment of line and colour which you wanted to call optical.

MICHAEL FRIED In the end optical. Pulses of energy move through it but it's a space, as it were, accessible to eyesight alone.

(Open University, 1993)

COMMENT

In Text 15, in which a group of friends are spontaneously discussing the physical prowess of the ex-footballers Hughes, Jones and Cantona, you will have observed what your reference grammar calls *local expressions of repetition*.* As exemplified in Text 15, your grammar book points out that repetitions in conversation are often lexical phrases or **lexical bundles** (see section 13.6 in your reference grammar) whereby speakers repeat partially or exactly what has just been said in the conversation (*I reckon...could, I don't reckon Cantona could, don't reckon Cantona could, I don't reckon Cantona could...*). You could argue that such repetition, rather than serving a cohesive function, works to relieve real-time planning pressure. That is, by repeating certain expressions, the speakers give themselves extra time to gather together their thoughts. You might also argue that repetition functions to clarify or confirm what has previously been said (as seems to be the case in *Don't reckon Cantona could what?*).

> * Your reference grammar distinguishes between repetition that is used cohesively *within* a text (**local repetition**) and words or expressions that are commonly repeated <u>across</u> texts within a particular register (repetition).

Finally, an equally important overall effect of the repetition is to give the conversation unity and cohesion by showing that the speakers are following (or attempting to follow) each other's lines of thought (*I reckon...probably could, I don't reckon Eric Cantona could...*). This in turn contributes to interpersonal solidarity among the speakers.

The next time you participate in a conversation, observe the extent to which you, yourself or your fellow conversationalists use this technique of repetition. Are people buying time? Are they clarifying meaning? Do they sound more or less polished and confident, depending on the amount they repeat themselves? Does this in turn depend on how much pre-planning they have done? For example, they may be telling a story they have rehearsed and told many times over.

Text 16 is an example of a less casual, less spontaneous piece of conversation in which the art critics' more abstract, academic style of speaking reflects the semi-planned nature of the dialogue. Here, repetition functions to give emphasis to certain key points – the fact that historical context is important when considering the interpretation of a painting (*a long time ago*) and the artistic concern with *quality*, including the notion of *optical*. It is particularly interesting to see how repetition in this context allows each speaker to echo the key ideas of the other and to thus create cohesion across conversational 'turns'. The function of the repetition here thus seems to be to draw attention to important ideas (i.e. experiential meanings). At the same time, it reflects how Tim and Michael are following each other's train of thought (a kind of 'inter-thinking') which serves an interpersonal function.

MICHAEL FRIED A long time ago.

TIM CLARK Yes, a long time ago ... you wanted to call optical.

MICHAEL FRIED In the end optical.

It is important to point out that repetition is not always used for cohesive purposes. For example, as commented on earlier, a great deal of repetition in conversation may arise from the fact that it is spontaneously produced, with speakers having to plan and put into action their utterances in real time, 'on the fly'. In the text below, repetitions such as *I, I, I* and *I agree with* (in bold) would not, therefore, be analysed as cohesive devices. Rather, they are more accurately characterised as a type of dysfluency where the need to keep talking threatens to run ahead of mental planning. You may remember that the notion of dysfluency was first introduced in Book 1 Unit 1, and developed in Book 1 Unit 7.

> **I** me – **I** appreci – **I** understand women saying, wait a minute, you know, just cuz I'm a woman I shouldn't have to pay more if I have short hair, and **I agree with that, I do agree with that, I I do agree with that, that's** er th- **that's** obvious, but **very few women, very few women**, have hair that's that short, and **I, an – an – I an – I** mean I think it's a shame that there should have to be a lawsuit over it.
>
> (Biber et al., 1999, p. 54)

Now read the second pair of texts, answering the same set of questions ((1)–(3)) as for pair 1.

Text 17

Food Habits

Kestrels are carnivorous, feeding on small mammals, especially voles, however they are very adaptable to other prey selections. They will eat almost anything they can kill. Their selected prey is either the most abundant or most easily caught of the area. Other prey examples are young rabbits, birds, small bats, lizards, snakes, frogs, insects, earthworms, fish, and crabs. Kestrels can change their hunting style depending on the kind of prey, weather conditions, and their energy requirements. These predators take full advantage of their keen eyesight, sharp claws, and strong beak. They hunt from a perch or from the air. The vertebrate prey is pounced on from a rapid dive, then grabbed by the claws and killed by a bite to the base of the skull. Attacks on less active prey results from slow shallow dives where the kestrel lands and takes the prey directly into its beak.

(McDonnell, 1999 [online])

Text 18

In the Peruvian case study that follows, the degree to which marketwomen are independent petty commodity traders or are undergoing proletarianization is problematic. Also problematic is the degree to which gender may be playing a part in the proletarianization process.

(Biber et al., 2002, p. 405)

COMMENT

Clearly, the texts above would both be located in the Longman academic prose register. However, Text 18 is undoubtedly at the more abstract end of the mode continuum. Evidence for this judgement lies in the writer's combining of nominalisation and tightly packed noun phrases in dense relational clauses (e.g. *Also problematic is the degree to which gender may be playing a part in the proletarianization process*). The repetition of *problematic* across two clauses is a further sign of its relatively sophisticated academic style. Your reference grammar observes that such use of what it calls 'fronting' is, in general, relatively rare in English but where it does occur in academic prose, predicative fronting is the most common form. Your grammar points out (p. 405) that the combination of repetition and fronting is used for focus as well as aiding cohesion by linking clauses (note too the theme–rheme pattern). It also states that *its rarity makes these effects even more conspicuous when they do occur*.

Text 17 is less abstract than Text 18. This is reflected in the greater use of concrete nouns (*kestrels, rabbits, birds*, etc.) and material processes (e.g. *grabbed by, killed by*) although there are also several examples of nominalisations (e.g. *energy requirements, attacks*) and relational processes (*Kestrels are carnivorous, feeding on small mammals*). The form and function of repetition (i.e. *kestrel*) is similar to that exemplified in the text on ageing in Activity 2 where we saw that the simple restatement of an item enables the writer to draw out different aspects of the phenomenon. By placing *kestrel* in theme position and using the theme-reiteration pattern, the writer is able to maintain a clear focus for the reader.

⑤ COHESION AND LEXICAL FOCUS IN SPEECH

Introduction

So far in this unit we have mainly concentrated on cohesion and coherence in written language. I have invited you to examine what is meant by a cohesive or coherent text, and looked at the ways in which cohesion and coherence can be achieved.

Several of the features dealt with so far are of course relevant for both spoken and written English, but our concern in the rest of this unit is to examine the way in which intonation, as a special feature of spoken language, can be used to make a spoken text cohesive. We will discover, for instance, that a shift in **information focus** will signal to the listener that certain information is retrievable from elsewhere in the text or context. Failure to signal this intonationally would result in making the text sound disjointed or as though the speaker does not fully understand what she or he is saying. Failure to perceive such intonation signals renders the text less cohesive for the listener.

We are going to examine two ways in which intonation brings cohesion to a text. The first is when the information focus falls on a lexical item (**lexical focus**); the second is when it falls on a function word (**non-lexical focus**) and will be dealt with in the next unit. Before we pursue either, let us recap very briefly on what we covered in Book 1 Unit 7 in order to remind ourselves of the intonation systems of English. First, read the brief recap section below before you attempt to cover the intonation section in this unit.

Recap

In Unit 7 we learnt that intonation in English is made up of the subsystems of tonality, tonicity and tone. Tonality is how a spoken text gets divided by the speaker into tone-groups, and reflects how the information in the message is distributed into information units. Tone is the selection of pitch contour made at the most prominent point within the tone-group. The most prominent point is known as the tonic syllable, and the location of the tonic syllable comprises the system of tonicity, which is where our main interest lies in this section.

Location of the tonic syllable

There is only one tonic syllable per tone-group. Theoretically, any syllable within the tone-group could be the tonic syllable, as we shall now see. There are five syllables in the following tone-group. It is repeated five times with a different tonic syllable underlined in each case. Try to read each example aloud, changing the location of the tonic syllable as indicated.

15.1   // I taught Welsh in France //

15.2   // I taught Welsh in France //

15.3   // I taught Welsh in France //

15.4   // I taught Welsh in France //

15.5   // I taught Welsh in France //

These audio files are accessed from the Unit 15 page on the Activities CD-ROM.

Now that we can hear where the tonic syllable is located, we need to ask what difference in meaning each location makes. In order to do this, try the following activity.

ACTIVITIES CD-ROM   (allow about 20 minutes)

Now do the activity on context in the Activities CD-ROM.

Information focus

In the same way that tonality (the way an utterance is divided into tone-groups) reflects how a speaker distributes the information in a message into information units, so does tonicity (the location of the tonic syllable) reflect where the information focus is. In 15.1–15.5, where the words are monosyllabic, the tonic syllable and focal item are usually one and the same, though this is by no means always the case. In 15.3, for instance, though the tonic syllable is *Welsh*, a case could be made that the focal item is in fact *taught Welsh*, since this – as opposed to just *Welsh* on its own – is what is linked to *difficult to get work* in the matching context. In other words, in response to someone's assertion that it is *difficult to get work* in France, the speaker of 15.3 counters that he/she has *taught Welsh* there.

Now let us see if we can identify a link between the location of the focal item and the type of context which matches it. 15.3 specifies *France* as given information, whereas 15.2 specifies both *Welsh* and *France* as given. Given information is information which is derivable from elsewhere in the text or context. The focus on *I* in 15.1 suggests that there is a contrast being drawn between the speaker and someone else in the text, which turns out to be *Delyth* from the matching context. The focus on *in* in 15.4 also suggests a contrast, this time between two prepositions: *in* and *outside*.

But what about 15.5? There does not seem to be any implication here for the rest of the text. Nothing is specified as given, and there is no implied contrast. This is because the focal item is the final lexical item in the information unit, which, as we noted in Section 2 of Unit 7, is the unmarked form. It is regarded as unmarked both because of statistical frequency – this is the way it happens around 80 per cent of the time – and because it does not involve a contextual presupposition, i.e. it does not specify any information as retrievable from elsewhere in the text or context.

If focus is unmarked on the final lexical item in the information unit, it will be convenient for our purposes to recognise two marked forms. Focus is marked when it falls on either:

◆   a lexical item which is not the final lexical item in the information unit, which we will, less cumbersomely, call a non-final lexical item

     or

◆   a non-lexical item.

There appear to be different types of implication for the remainder of the text, depending on whether the marked focal item is lexical (as in 15.2 and 15.3) or non-lexical (as in 15.1 and 15.4):

◆   A focal non-final lexical item seems to specify all that follows it within the information unit as given.

◆   Focal non-lexical items imply a contrast with some other item in the text.

This is not to say that marked lexical focus cannot also involve a contrast. Where it does, however, that contrast will usually be supported by choice of tone: either one of the bi-directional ones or a fall or rise of greater width than normal, i.e. a fall beginning from a high point or a rise ending on a high point. Thus, 15.3 would imply the teaching of Welsh as opposed to some other language or subject. Similarly the selection of tones in 15.2 would imply the teaching as opposed to the learning or speaking of Welsh.

For the remainder of this section, we will concentrate on marked lexical focus. Non-lexical focus will be dealt with in the next unit.

Marked lexical focus

The focal item will usually contain new information. Elsewhere in this course you have learnt that given information tends to be delivered at the beginning of a clause, whereas new information goes towards the end. Although we learnt, in Unit 7, that clauses and information units are by no means co-extensive, it is nevertheless to be expected that unmarked focus will fall on the final lexical item in the information unit.

When we talk of the focal item containing new information, this does not necessarily entail that the information will be *factually* new. By new information we mean that which is not considered to be derivable from the text or context. Given information, on the other hand, *is* thus derivable.

Look again at what happens when the focus falls on a lexical item which is not the final lexical item in the information unit:

15.2   // I <u>taught</u> Welsh in France //

15.3   // I taught <u>Welsh</u> in France //

As we saw in Activity 7 on the Activities CD-ROM, focal *Welsh* in 15.3 specifies *France* as given information, i.e. retrievable from elsewhere in the text or context, while in 15.2 focal *taught* specifies both *Welsh* and *France* as given information. It appears, then, that marked lexical focus specifies all that follows it within the information unit as given. Activity 10 will explore this further. Each activity has detailed feedback which will illustrate the ways in which marked lexical focus operates cohesively within a text and context. We will look at the cohesive function of marked non-lexical focus in the next unit.

A CTIVITY 10 (allow about 40 minutes)

These audio files are accessed from the Unit 15 page on the Activities CD-ROM.

Listen to the audio files as you look at the emboldened focal items in the following examples, all of which are non-final lexical items. (The tonic syllable is underlined in each tone-group.)

Make notes for each example on what information is given and where it is retrievable from.

1

15.6   A: // Dylan Thomas <u>Bis</u>tro // Dylan Thomas <u>tea</u>-rooms // Dylan's <u>Di</u>ner // It's turning into a cottage <u>in</u>dustry //

     B: // They've **made** it a cottage industry // al<u>rea</u>dy //

2

15.7   A: // People just don't work <u>Sat</u>urdays // in <u>Lon</u>don //

     B: // Well I quite **enjoy** working Saturdays //

3

15.8   A: // To <u>lis</u>ten to her // you'd never think she came from Lla<u>nel</u>li //

     B: // Maybe <u>not</u>. // But she **looks** Welsh // And I think she **speaks** the language // <u>too</u> //

4

15.9   // They still teach Greek and <u>Lat</u>in there // and I really don't see the **point** of teaching dead languages //

5

15.10   // I **hate** computers // Every time I switch a computer on //
something goes wrong //

6   Situation: two friends walk past a poster advertising the new film
in the *Star Wars* series which it hails as an all-action adventure.
One friend turns to the other and says:

15.11   // I don't **want** to see the new all-action Star Wars film // thank
you //

7

15.12   // I still have a **point** to make // Remember that **party** we had //
Your **sister** came along // She's so good with **children** and things //

8   Situation: at a social gathering or party (... indicates a pause):

15.13   // Anne // let me introduce Robin // ... this is the **doctor** I was
telling you about //

COMMENT

1   Intonation signalled as given: *cottage industry*, retrievable from the
previous speaker's turn, where the same words are used.

2   Intonation signalled as given: *working Saturdays*, retrievable from
the previous speaker's turn. This is another instance where the
same words are used, even though the information signalled as
given contains an inflection (*work, working*).

3   Intonation signalled as given: *Welsh* and *the language*.

Focal *looks* signals *Welsh* as retrievable. Although the word *Welsh*
does not appear explicitly in the preceding text, the information is
retrievable from the sequence *came from Llanelli*. This illustrates that
given information does not need to have been explicitly
mentioned.

Focal *speaks* signals *the language* as given information. Again, these
words do not appear explicitly in the text, but are retrievable from
Welsh in the preceding information unit. The role of the definite
article in *the language* is supporting the specification of a particular
language already mentioned.

4   Intonation signalled as given: *teaching dead languages* is derivable
from *teach* and from *Greek and Latin* in the preceding information
unit. The given *teaching* is inflected from the previous mention and
Greek and Latin are signalled as given by means of the alternative
wording *dead languages*.

Treating information as given can also be used for purposes of
ideological loading. The treatment of information by the speaker as

given entails that such information is retrievable for the listener from the text or context. That is to say, the information must be given for both speaker and listener. This enables the speaker to abuse the notion of given information for ideological purposes by assuming that the listener also perceives it as such – hence the listener agrees to its status as given and hence agrees to the ideology that underlies it. Let us take a relatively harmless example. We might replace the word *dead* with the word *useless* as follows.

> // They still teach Greek and <u>Lat</u>in there // and I really don't see the **point** of teaching useless languages. //

There seems little contention that Latin and Greek are dead in that nobody speaks them any more on a day-to-day basis. However, to say that they are educationally-useless is a contentious statement and one with which several people would disagree. The speaker's presentation of *useless* as given information assumes the listener's acquiescence to this point of view. Intonation is therefore used to ideologically load the statement in favour of the speaker's point of view, and to subtly persuade the listener of its validity.

5   The given information is *computers*. This time the information is retrievable not from what has gone before in the text, but from what is to come. In other words, the information is **cataphorically** (referring forwards) and not **anaphorically** (referring backwards) derivable. This can be seen as a stylistic device by the speaker to arouse the listener's attention. This device would seem to work as follows:

1   The speaker presents information as given by marked lexical focus placement, i.e by assigning the focus to a non-final lexical item.

2   The listener has no means of deriving this information from what has preceded.

3   The listener perceives an irregularity in the treatment of information as given which is not hitherto derivable.

4   The listener seeks to solve this apparent irregularity by awaiting the next part of the speaker's message as clarification.

Another possible context would be in the presence of a malfunctioning computer. In such a case, // I <u>hate</u> computers // would signal information (computers that do not work) as derivable from the situational context. We shall see a further instance of this in the next example.

6   The given information is *see the new all-action Star Wars film*.

This information is not derivable from the text, but from the situational context which the speaker shares with the listener. The speaker is able to treat the information as given because it is retrievable by the listener from the poster which they are both walking past at that moment. Information which refers to something outside the text is said to be **exophorically** derivable.

If the speaker was not a fan of *Star Wars*, we might have the following in the same situation:

15.14   // I don't <u>want</u> to be bored to death // <u>thank</u> you //

where *bored to death* is signalled as given, derivable from the preceding information unit where terminal boredom is derogatively equated to watching the *Star Wars* film. The listener, with shared knowledge of both the situation and the speaker's view of the film, should be able to make the link.

7   There is no given information here. This may seem at first surprising since in all four information units the focus is on a non-final lexical item. Under our normal rules, we expect *make, had, came along* and *things* to be specified as given. The fact that they are not is to do with what has been called the 'relative semantic weight' (Bolinger, 1974) of these words. They are semantically quite empty in that they do not add very much to the meaning of the information unit. They could feasibly be omitted without losing any of the message. Another way of putting it is to say that the empty items are collocationally predictable and, in that sense, empty.

This example seems to be an exception to the general rule about marked lexical focus. However, we still need to be careful since it is the context (and indeed the intonation!) which determines whether a word is semantically empty or not. If we shift the focus backwards in each of the information units:

15.15   // I still have a point to <u>make</u> // Remember that party we
        <u>had</u> // Your sister came a<u>long</u> // She's so good with children
        and <u>things</u> //

we would have a rather different set of meanings. *Things*, for instance, takes on its denotative meaning – not only is she good with children, she is also good with things – rather than the equivalent of 'etcetera' which is what it means in example 15.12.

8   There is no given information for much the same reason as in the previous example. In this context, *telling about* is relatively empty (i.e. collocationally predictable) and the focus is attracted forward to the more significant item *doctor*. If we were to keep the situational context of a party or gathering, and replace *doctor* with

the more generic and less semantically significant *man*, we would expect the focus to revert to the final lexical item which is *telling*:

15.16   // <u>A</u>nne // let me introduce <u>Ro</u>bin // ... this is the man I was <u>tell</u>ing you about //

However, we need to emphasise that it is the context which determines the relative semantic weight of each item. Suppose we were to change the situational context to a hospital, for instance, a context in which doctors are ubiquitous or at least plentiful, then the example would probably change to:

15.17   // <u>A</u>nne // let me introduce <u>Ro</u>bin // ... this is the doctor I was <u>tell</u>ing you about //

The context has now reduced the semantic significance of *doctor* and the focus moves back to the final lexical item which is *telling*.

However, if we were in an environment such as a women's group where the presence of a man would be unexpected, we could expect to find:

15.18   // <u>A</u>nne // let me introduce <u>Ro</u>bin // ... this is the <u>man</u> I was telling you about //

with no presupposition of given information.

Conclusion to lexical focus

You should now be able to recognise a number of English intonation patterns where the information focus is marked, and specify what such patterns entail for the cohesion of the text, i.e. what information is signalled as given and from where in the text or context it may be retrieved. All the examples of marked focus in this section have been to do with lexical items. In the next unit, we will concentrate on examples where the information focus falls on non-lexical or grammatical items.

ACTIVITIES CD-ROM   (allow about two hours)

You have now reached the point in the unit where it will be useful to check your understanding of lexical cohesion. The activities on the Activities CD-ROM will give you extended practice in identifying lexical relations in a variety of texts and in making observations about how they function to make meaning. You will also have the opportunity to make judgements about the effectiveness of a selection of texts.

Conclusion

In this unit we have seen that for readers and listeners to make sense of a text it needs to be both coherent and cohesive. In section 1 we saw that coherence is primarily a measure of the extent to which a reader or listener can make sense of a text in a specific context and that this will often depend on their language experience and familiarity with different social situations. We noted that, unlike cohesion, coherence is not identifiable with any combination of linguistic features.

In Sections 2–4 and in the corresponding CD-ROM activities, you explored a range of lexical cohesive devices which may contribute to the coherence of a text. Your exploration revealed that cohesion is directly attributable to the way a set of sentences is woven together by devices such as repetition, synonymy, etc., and that texts can be more or less cohesive and more or less effective, depending on how they deploy such devices.

In Section 5 and related CD-ROM Activities, you explored the ways in which intonation, and in particular tonicity, operates as a cohesive device within a text by signalling certain information as given or derivable from elsewhere in the text or context.

In Unit 16 we will continue our exploration of cohesion by looking at the 'texturing' function of *grammatical* cohesive devices.

Learning outcomes

After completing this unit, you should have developed your knowledge and understanding of:

◆ the difference between coherent and cohesive text

◆ how patterns of lexical cohesion may vary depending on the mode of a text, i.e. how spoken or how written the language interaction is

◆ how cohesive devices are deployed to build experiential and interpersonal meaning.

In the light of your increased understanding, you should be able to:

◆ describe how a text draws on the resources of lexical cohesion to contribute to the texture and coherence of a text

◆ interpret cohesive patterns in relation to the contextual variable of mode and in terms of their role in building experiential and interpersonal meaning

◆ argue why certain uses of lexical cohesion make a text more or less effective

◆ apply your understanding of lexical cohesion to make a text more effective.

I certainly hope that at the end of this unit you have begun to see how you can apply your grammatical knowledge of cohesion to situations in everyday life. By now you should have gained insight into why some texts hang together better than others. Perhaps it would be interesting to have a look at some of your own pieces of writing and see where they could be made more cohesive?

Key terms introduced and revisited

anaphora [backward reference]	marked
antonymy	meronymy [part–whole]
cataphora [forward reference]	mode
class/subclass	morphology
coherence	new information
cohesion	nominalisation
cohesive device	non-lexical focus
cohesive tie	noun phrase [nominal group]
co-hyponymy [co-class]	part–whole taxonomy
co-meronymy [co-part]	reference
co-reference	relational process
dysfluency	relexicalise
exophoric reference [situational reference]	repetition/local repetition
field	rheme
fronting	superordinate
given information	synonymy
hyponymy [classification]	taxonomy [classification system]
information focus	technical term
information unit	tenor
lexical bundles	texture
lexical chain [lexical string]	theme
lexical cohesion	theme reiteration
lexical density	thing
lexical focus	unmarked

Near equivalents are given in [ ].

Answers to the activities

ACTIVITY 3

In people's eyes, in the <u>swing, tramp and</u> trudge; in <u>the bellow and</u> the uproar; the carriages, motor cars, omnibuses, vans, sandwich men shuffling <u>and swinging</u>; brass bands; barrel organs; in the triumph and the jingle and the strange high singing of some aeroplane overhead was what she loved; London; this moment of June.

[...] and she, too, loving it as she did with an absurd and faithful passion, being part of it, since her people were courtiers once in the time of the Georges, she, too, was going that very night to <u>kindle and</u> illuminate; to give her party. But how strange, on entering the Park, the silence; the mist; <u>the hum</u>; the slow-swimming happy ducks; the pouched birds <u>waddling</u>; and who should be coming along with his back against the Government buildings, most appropriately, carrying a despatch box stamped with the Royal Arms, who but Hugh Whitbread...

(Woolf, 1996, pp. 6–7)

ACTIVITY 4

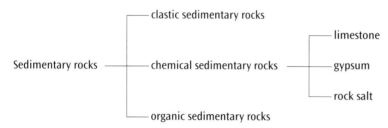

Taxonomy of sedimentary rocks

ACTIVITY 5

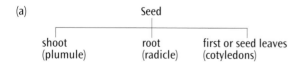

Part–whole taxonomy for plants

Class–subclass taxonomy for plants

ACTIVITY 6

Text 10   (class/subclass, using everyday, commonsensical criteria)

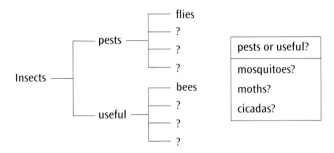

Text 11   (composition or part–whole, using distinct structural features as criteria; NB: use of technical terms)

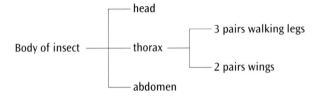

(class/subclass)

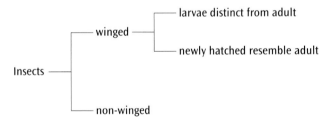

Text 12   (class/subclass; NB: increase in technicality and specialised knowledge)

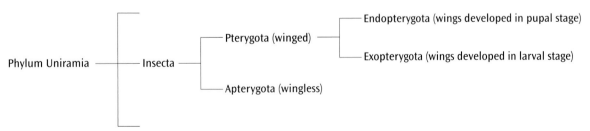

Taxonomy diagrams

ACTIVITY 8
Lexical chain analysis of Text 14

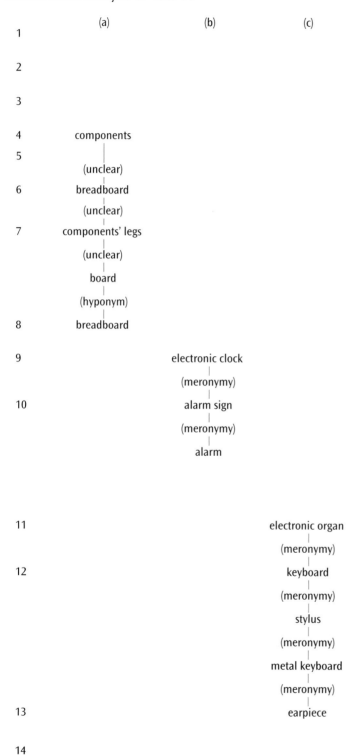

	(a)	(b)	(c)
1			
2			
3			
4	components		
5	(unclear)		
6	breadboard		
	(unclear)		
7	components' legs		
	(unclear)		
	board		
	(hyponym)		
8	breadboard		
9		electronic clock	
		(meronymy)	
10		alarm sign	
		(meronymy)	
		alarm	
11			electronic organ
			(meronymy)
12			keyboard
			(meronymy)
			stylus
			(meronymy)
			metal keyboard
			(meronymy)
13			earpiece
14			

Unit 16

Making a text hang together: the role of grammatical devices

Prepared for the course team by Caroline Coffin with intonation sections by Martin Rhys

CONTENTS

Materials required

While studying this unit, you will need:

> your reference grammar
> the course reader
> the Activities CD-ROM (Section 6 and end of unit).

Knowledge assumed

> conjunctions
> definite articles
> demonstratives
> intonation terms
> pronouns.

Introduction

In the comic strip opposite, Jessica and Katie are discussing the merits of having television programmes specifically designed for children. No doubt many of you have found yourself taking part in a debate similar to the one above. Not necessarily, of course, on the same subject or through the medium of the English language. Nevertheless, it is likely that at some point you have listened to and put forward different points of view on a controversial topic. And in the case of written language or formal debates, you will have had to think particularly carefully about how to weave together a range of different points of view into one cohesive and convincing argument.

You will probably have noticed in Jessica and Katie's discussion various grammatical devices used to link different (and often sharply contrasting) views and ideas, for example, *but, But then again*, etc. These connecting words and phrases are referred to as 'linking adverbials' and will be one of the areas we explore in this unit.

You may remember that in Unit 15 we looked at a number of lexical resources which are commonly used to glue together the meanings in a text. These resources can be grouped together under the headings of sense relations (e.g. meronymy, hyponymy) and lexical repetition. In Unit 15 we also looked at a group of intonational resources that serve to link meanings together.

(Transcribed dialogue between Jessica Coffin and Katie Townsend)

You may also recall from the map of types of cohesion (reproduced below in Figure 1) that there is a third group of linguistic resources which help to make a text hang together. These can be gathered together under the heading of grammatical devices and include those devices such as linking adverbials which we saw illustrated in the discussion above. Grammatical devices will be the focus of this unit although we will also look briefly at the ways in which intonation can establish cohesive relations within spoken texts.

To explore these devices I am going to ask you in the course of the unit to put on different 'hats', that is to see things from different perspectives and evaluate a variety of texts from the point of view of a teacher, an editor and a scriptwriter. I hope you enjoy looking at texts from these different points of view as you explore another area of real-world grammar.

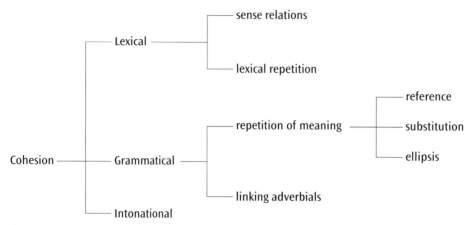

Figure 1 Types of cohesion

 GIVING FEEDBACK

ACTIVITY 1 (allow about 20 minutes)

Reproduced below is a short essay entitled *Should children's TV programmes be taken off air?* It was written by 11-year-old Jessica, who appeared in the cartoon, as part of her preparation for the British national school test known as SATS. It was written under pressure (in 45 minutes) and not surprisingly displays a number of spelling and punctuation errors (which we have retained to keep the full flavour of the text). As you read the essay, consider how you might react to it as a teacher or parent. What advice might you give Jessica in order to improve her text? Think particularly about:

(1) the tenor that Jessica constructs (reflect here on the grammatical devices used, e.g. speech function, pronoun use, lexical choices, etc.)

(2) the organisation of the discussion (here it would be useful to consider her use of theme)

(3) the cohesive quality of the essay (it might be helpful here to underline any examples of the cohesive lexical devices that you came across in Unit 15 and think about how effective they are – see 'Answers to the activities' for feedback on this).

Text 1

Should childrens TV programs be taken of air?

Nearly every household in Britain has the familiar television set. Almost every child has watched a childs programe but the question is should they. Should childrens TV programes be taken of air.

On one hand, the television has been a endless source of education for both young and old. Sesame Street, which is for younger children, has helped many children acquire general knowledge skills such as the alphabet, basic maths problems and has increased the variety of vocabulary. In addition, adults can learn about life in the underwater world or maybe find out about Britain's fascinating past.

Nevertheless, childrens TV can sometimes be a bad influence. Grange Hill features swearing and stealing. Also violent scenes could make children think its cool to fight, which could lead to accidents from them fighting.

However, it has to be recognised that children could start watching unsuitable adult TV if there was no more kids TV. This could show swearing and other things of that sort.

Nonetheless, children could become addicted to the television which would make them stay inside all day which is just lazy and unhealthy; this could make children overweight.

On the other hand, television is a great source of employment. It provides work for adults and children alike. In addition children can improve acting skills by featuring on programes and adults can work but have fun to.

On the one hand to many cartoons can block childrens imagination. Furthermore, when writing storys children sometimes get ideas from programes which can also block imagination.

However, television is also a social thing. People may talk about Eastenders the next day with friends which can bring strong opinions and good discussions. This can improve skills in school.

In conclusion, many people will have there say as there are plenty of arguments on both sides so I'll leave you to decide.

COMMENT

Taking into account Jessica's age and the fact that there was limited time for her to plan and write her essay (students are encouraged to spend 10 minutes on developing a plan, 30 minutes on writing the essay and five minutes on checking it), I think you would probably agree that the essay is reasonably successful. It presents a number of arguments for and against the proposition that children's TV programmes should be taken off air. The arguments are well organised and there is a clear introduction and conclusion even though the opening paragraph (the macro-theme) could have been further developed by previewing the evidence discussed in the body of the essay. At the level of hyper-theme, Jessica makes effective use of its organising capacity to lay out and develop the different sides of her argument. Certainly the teacher made the following comments: 'Well done! You gave very balanced arguments on both sides. Overall very high standard.'

In terms of the tenor, I expect you judged the overall writer–reader relationship as relatively – and appropriately – impersonal and distant. Students are in fact encouraged to adopt a neutral style when they write a factual essay or report. You may, however, also have noticed that, in places, the essay draws on the interrogative structure, a structure more typically associated with spoken interaction (*the question is should they. Should childrens TV programes be taken of air*). You will also probably have noticed some other informal features (e.g. *kids, social thing*) which, combined with the dialogism of the interrogatives and the direct address to the reader in *I'll leave you to decide*, create at times a more engaging, personal style. Perhaps it might be worth pointing out to Jessica that she has successfully engaged with the reader whilst retaining a formal, neutral writer position (there is only one instance of a first person pronoun – *so I'll leave you to decide*). At the same time she might also need to be made aware that too much informality, particularly the use of colloquial lexis, might be perceived negatively by examiners.

No doubt you will have observed that the main form of lexical cohesion in Jessica's essay is repetition (e.g. *children, television*) with some (limited) use of synonymy (*children, kids; employment, work*) and antonymy (*young, old; adult TV, kids TV*). There is no use of hyponymy (e.g. in the form of, say, 'types of children's programmes or types of TV influences such as its effect on health, socialisation', etc.)

Despite the absence of hyponymy which arguably could have led to a more sophisticated discussion (appropriate at a higher level of schooling), the text hangs together very successfully. There is a sustained, focused treatment of the issue under discussion with each argument presented being relevant and 'on topic' (as shown in the lexical chains running throughout the text). Perhaps the main advice you would want to give Jessica (with regard to lexical cohesion) is to try to reduce the amount of repetition. We will see how she could do this in Section 3. Another piece of advice you might want to offer concerns the linking together of arguments. Jessica's teacher did in fact observe that the arguments did not always quite fit together. But how can we pinpoint what is not working for Jessica? How can we be more precise so that she knows what to alter in order to improve her essay?

No doubt you have at some point received vague comments from teachers or lecturers. Do the comments 'poor organisation', 'badly structured' or 'illogical argument' sound at all familiar? And have you ever felt frustrated at not knowing how you can prevent the same comment being made the next time you hand in an assignment?

Just as we were able to articulate some of the grammatical and lexical reasons for the particular tenor adopted in Jessica's essay, we can also use a conscious understanding of grammar to diagnose weaknesses in the logical links between her ideas and her arguments.

ACTIVITY **2**   (allow about 20 minutes)

Now read Jessica's essay again and pull out all the linking phrases (what your reference grammar refers to as 'linking adverbials') that connect ideas and arguments across (but not within) clause complexes and stretches of text. Complete Table 1 below to show how linking adverbials are used to connect ideas in some or all of the following ways:

◆ introducing or contrasting viewpoints (**contrast**)
◆ adding information (**addition**)
◆ pulling ideas together (**summation**)
◆ listing pieces of information (**enumeration**)
◆ restating information (**apposition**)
◆ signalling results or consequences (**result/inference**)
◆ marking contrast or conflict (**contrast/concession**)
◆ signalling a transition to new information (**transition**).

To get you started, I have filled in the first two examples.

Table 1

Linking phrase	Argument/idea	Type of relationship linking ideas
On one hand	television is an endless source of education	contrast
In addition	adults can also learn from children's programmes	addition
Nevertheless		

COMMENT

By completing Table 1 (see 'Answers to the activities') you will have seen how the arguments for and against children's TV are woven together to create a balanced discussion. In particular, you will have seen how the main relationships between the ideas are those of contrast and addition. Column 1 will have highlighted for you how these semantic links were expressed through a variety of linking adverbials.

In general, I would say that Jessica is successful in relating one idea to another. Nevertheless, by looking at the text closely, it is apparent that *nonetheless* is used somewhat confusingly. In addition, we can see that perhaps too many ideas are introduced and too many different viewpoints contrasted. In the future it may be better for Jessica to reduce the number of arguments and develop each of them more fully through exemplification and supporting evidence. As a next step in her writing development she might also be encouraged to use other devices for linking her arguments such as the use of reference (explored later in this unit), for example, *another argument supporting children's TV is...*

In sum we have seen in this section how **metalanguage** – a language for talking about language – can be valuable in pinpointing problems in the way a text has been put together. Such precision on the part of a teacher/editor in showing a student/author where things are going wrong can be extremely constructive in helping them to develop and improve as writers. In other words, although a certain amount of investment may be needed in order to build up a metalanguage, specific instructions such as the following can be very helpful:

> In order to make explicit the logic in your argument, this piece of information needs to be introduced by a result/inference linking adverbial.

Vague comments such as *poorly organised, this essay doesn't hang together, illogical, fragmented,* etc., can leave a student nonplussed as to what they need to do to make their arguments clearer or more logical.

❷ LINKING MEANING LOGICALLY

ACTIVITY 3 (allow about 15 minutes)

You have now begun to see how knowledge of grammatical cohesion can illuminate more precisely whether a text works or not. So, in order to build up a systematic and comprehensive metalanguage for capturing all the different types of linking phrases, let us turn to your reference grammar. Go to Grammar Bite E (pp. 389–96) and read about the six major categories of linking adverbials.

COMMENT

You may at this point be wondering what the difference is between linking adverbials and conjunctions (you first came across the latter in Book 1 Unit 4). Linking adverbials play a similar role to conjunctions in that they connect different parts of a text by explicitly signalling the semantic link (such as *contrast* or *result*). However, unlike conjunctions, which are restricted to joining two clauses together, linking adverbials can bind together meanings across stretches of text:

> Wars are costly exercises <u>because</u> they cause death and destruction. (structural – conjunction)

> Wars cause death and destruction. They can also cause rifts in political alliances. <u>As a result</u> they are costly exercises. (cohesive – linking adverbial)

ACTIVITY 4 (allow about 20 minutes)

This activity is designed to raise your awareness further of the function of linking adverbials. In Texts 2–4 below the linking adverbials are missing. As you read through the texts, complete the following steps:

(1) Think about the field, tenor and mode (the context) of the texts. What are they about? What sort of relationship is being developed between the writer/speaker and the audience? Would you categorise the text as written or spoken or as displaying features of both?

(2) Try to work out what kinds of semantic links exist between the different parts of the text. Are ideas being added, one to the other? Or is there a relationship of cause/consequence?

(3) Select an adverbial linker from the following table for each of the blank spaces. Before you make your choice, consider which linking adverbial is more likely to occur, given typical Longman register distributions (you may want to refer to p. 393 in your reference

grammar). When you have finished, see 'Answers to the activities' for feedback on the adverbial links.

Transition	Contrast/ concession	Result/ inference	Addition
now	yet	as a consequence	and
	on the other hand	then	
		so	

Text 2

Ageing is caused by the accumulation of damage, and no gene has evolved specifically to cause damage and debility. (a) _____ genes do influence the rate of ageing. Birds live longer than comparably sized mammals, which suggests that the rate of ageing evolves. (b) _____ mutations in single genes can increase the lifespans of laboratory animals. Many of these genes have been identified and are known to encode normal constituents of cells and endocrine systems. (c) _____ why has natural selection favoured the wild-type form of the gene rather than a mutant trait that extends lifespan?

(Gems and Partridge, 2002, p. 921)

Text 3

CAROL yes we found carrots first thing obviously you know, I mean, that's what rabbits like, we got some carrots and we got some lettuce and some tomatoes

JIMMY (a) _____ he's had something to eat then

CAROL oh yes definitely

JIMMY he seems to have got away unscathed from the cat

GREG yeah

JIMMY he don't seem to have any injuries

GREG is there any possibility that somebody couldn't actually handle him any more and decided to release him?

JIMMY um, with the condition he's in I wouldn't have thought so, normally they are a bit scratty, if they've been struggling to look after them for a while and (b) _____ decided to let them go, usually when you get them in good condition it's just a simple catch she's broke on her rabbit hutch

JIMMY (c) _____ he's an escapee?

JIMMY I'd say so yeah, he's been very lucky actually because there are foxes round here as well I believe

CAROL yes we do have foxes I see them around sometimes

JIMMY (d) _____ that would have been a problem

CAROL: very lucky (e) _____

JIMMY that would have been a problem for him; he wouldn't have known where to go with him being domesticated. I think if they hadn't have picked him up he wouldn't have lasted very long I don't think.

Text 4

'Darwin, not Wallace, is seen as a scientific hero today because, let's face it, Darwin was the better scientist.' Do you agree?

Darwin, from a contemporary perspective, is seen as a scientist of considerable stature. Wallace, (a) _____ , is largely overlooked. This essay critically examines the factors which account for such a judgement. Rather than focusing on Darwin and Wallace's merits as scientists, a central focus will be the way in which scientific activity and knowledge are valued. In particular I will consider how judgements are historically contingent: across different cultural, social and historical contexts, scientific processes and objectives are valued differently and, (b) _____ , scientists themselves may be perceived as more or less effective. The main argument, (c) _____ , is that science is best understood as a humanly constructed discipline, a historical phenomenon whereby it is not possible to cast its actors (scientists) as 'better' or 'worse' in absolute terms.

COMMENT

You may have noticed that Text 2 is a continuation of the article on ageing which you came across in Book 1 Unit 3 and then again in Unit 15. You may remember that it came from the magazine *Nature*, a publication that is directed at a non-expert audience interested in scientific issues, and that, although the mode is clearly a written one, the writer deliberately adopts a conversational style. The use of adverbial linkers is further evidence of this conversational style in that *and* normally serves as a coordinator to connect words, phrases or clauses within a sentence. Here, however, it serves to connect ideas across sentences (and therefore functions in a similar way to a linking adverbial). If you turn to section 8.4 of your reference grammar (on coordination) you will see that, despite the common prescription prohibiting the use of *and* at the beginning of a sentence, it does in fact occur in sentence- or turn-initial position. You will also see from your reference grammar (p. 393) that *so* is one of the most common linking words in both conversation and academic prose. In speech it is used to move a conversation along and in this text it seems to be functioning in this way as well as marking a step in the writer's reasoning (i.e. result/ inference).

Text 3 is an excerpt from a conversation set in an animal hospital where the speakers are discussing a pet rabbit which has recently escaped from his owners. Not surprisingly, therefore, it exemplifies the most commonly occurring linking adverbials in the Longman conversation register, i.e. *so* and *now*.

Text 4 is the opening paragraph in a discussion essay written at first-year undergraduate level as part of a general arts course. It exemplifies two of the adverbial linkers (*on the other hand*, *then*) that, based on the corpus evidence of LSWE, are extremely common in academic prose. It also exemplifies that, unlike in conversation or in texts adopting a conversational style, adverbial linkers in academic prose frequently occur in medial rather than initial position. Section 11.19 of your reference grammar discusses the positions of linking adverbials more broadly, which you may want to follow up.

In this section, you have increased your awareness of the ways in which adverbial linkers serve to weave together ideas and arguments, and how these are to some extent register-sensitive. That is, they create bridges to previous sections of, and meanings in, a text and act as signposts in the development of a discussion. In the next section we will explore another grammatical device for creating texture – referred to as 'cohesive reference'.

③ DIAGNOSING PROBLEMS OF COHESION IN TEXTS

In my comment on Jessica's use of lexical cohesion in Activity 2, I mentioned that in the future she may need to make sure that there is not too much unnecessary repetition in her writing. This is because repeating the same lexical item again and again may be perceived negatively in some writing contexts. As mentioned in Unit 15, in some registers, such as news and fiction, lexical variation is a stylistic convention.

While excess repetition was not a major problem in Jessica's essay, I felt that in places it was not always necessary for her to repeat the word *children*. In the following two sentences, for example, what could she could have replaced the word *children* with?

> On one hand, the television has been a endless source of education for both young and old. Sesame Street, which is for younger children, has helped many children acquire general knowledge skills such as the alphabet, basic maths problems and has increased the variety of vocabulary.
>
> Nonetheless, children could become addicted to the television which would make them stay inside all day which is just lazy and unhealthy; this could make children overweight.

In answer to my question, you may have come up with synonyms such as *infants* or *girls and boys*. You may also have come up with the idea of simply replacing the noun with a pronoun: *they* or *them* – a simple but effective change.

Pronouns are just one set of grammatical resources referred to as **cohesive reference** that serve to keep track of the participants (i.e. the people and things) in a text as it unfolds. They are used to signal that what they are referring to can be retrieved in a previous or subsequent section of the text. For example, *she* in the sentence below refers back to *my sister Laura*:

> Ten days after the war ended, my sister Laura drove a car off a bridge. The bridge was being repaired: she went right through the Danger sign.

> (Atwood, 2001, p. 8)

Aside from pronouns, other common reference items are definite articles and demonstratives. In the extract above, for example, *the* in *the bridge* signals that *a bridge* in the previous sentence is being referred to.

You may be wondering why it is useful or interesting to study areas of grammar such as pronouns or definite articles and demonstratives. Whilst it may be helpful for teachers or learners of English to be aware of such items, surely most speakers of English have no problems in either understanding or using them? The following activities, however, may make you rethink such an assumption.

A CTIVITY 5 (allow about 10 minutes)

Read the two texts below. They both come from essays written by Open University native-speaker students taking English language courses.

You will notice that in each extract a reference item has been underlined. Try to work out what the reference items are referring to.

Text 5

Although I must agree with Swann that *'a video camera is highly selective'*, in this particular case it undeniably allows us to perceive certain points which can greatly influence our interpretation of what we hear and/or read in a transcript. One of the first things that struck me was that although the class seemed to be fairly homogeneous as far as age was concerned, (all young adults) they appeared to come from a great variety of racial and cultural backgrounds, so here English is by necessity also the lingua franca within the classroom and the possibility of code-switching is eliminated. (see Mercer 2001, P250) Furthermore, this is something which has an enormous influence on how students think and react and what they expect in learning situations.

Text 6

The other debate standard English raises is the issue of whether teachers have the right to dictate how children should speak. When speaking the standard English form children often take on the identity that the language requires.

An extract from a report from the Department of Education and Welsh office highlights this. "formal contexts require particular choices of vocabulary". Standard English not only effects (*sic*) written work but also their verbal speech.

C OMMENT

You will probably have found that in both essays, the student is using the reference item *this* somewhat ambiguously. In Text 5, does *this* refer back to *English is by necessity also the lingua franca* or to *the possibility of code-switching is eliminated* or to something else altogether? And in Text 6, does *this* refer to *children often take on the identity that the language requires*? If so, the extract from the report is not a good illustration.

These extracts from student essays exemplify how even highly competent users of the English language can use reference items in ways that make it difficult for a reader to track what is being referred to. Biber et al. (1999) provide further illustration of reference-retrieval problems in the following corpus extracts from news reports. Can you see what the problems are?

> Ampofo was being outboxed, but then amazingly put his opponent down in the third and fifth rounds. The new champion, who lost the title to Regan a year ago, said: [...]

> A woman and a child had a narrow escape yesterday when their car left the road. The accident happened at about 9.25am at Marks Tey, near Colchester.
>
> (Biber et al., 1999, p. 264)

In the cases above we have examples of what Biber et al. call **indirect reference**, where the connection has to be inferred. Thus in the first text, the reader must do a certain amount of work in order to infer that Ampofo is *The new champion*. In the second text, it must be inferred that the events of the first sentence constitute an accident, i.e. rather than use *the* + lexical repetition (*the narrow escape*), the events are interpreted and referred to as *The accident*.

Biber et al. (1999) also make the point that third person pronouns may at times require a good deal of work on the part of the addressee, particularly in conversation. They use the following conversation extract as an illustration. See if you find any of the references difficult to retrieve.

> Nobody really likes, you know, snow snowmen and things like that. Okay? So we built this snowman round this rock and this car came back cos he came he just came in to hit it and he burst into and broke his bumper, this massive dent in his bumper and he drove round. Cos they did it to me before. I made another one in the park earlier. And they just drove in, knocked it over and ran out. So I put in a rock this time and it was so funny though.
>
> (Biber et al., 1999, p. 331)

I think you would probably agree that the listener/reader has to do a fair amount of work to interpret several of the references. For example, they need to infer that *he* is the driver of the car and *they* the people in the car. In two of the cases, *it* seems to refer to the snowman but in the other cases, the pronoun *it* refers more generally to what happened.

Another potential source of confusion when using or interpreting third person pronouns concerns gender and the issue of gender bias. For example, if the gender of a referent is unknown or irrelevant, which pronoun form do English speakers use? How would you respond to the following comment:

> I went to see *The Piano Teacher* last night with a friend. I thought it was a great film but my friend didn't like it at all.

Would you say?

> Why didn't he?

or

> Why didn't she?

or

> Why didn't he or she?

or

> Why didn't they?

ACTIVITY 6   (allow about 10 minutes)

Your reference grammar has an interesting and useful section on this issue on pages 87–8, which you should now read.

How does the English use of third person pronouns compare with their use in other languages with which you are familiar? In Turkish, for example, there is only one third person pronoun, *o*, which can either mean *he*, *she* or *it* depending on the context in which it is being used. If we use *o* in the following sentence, for instance – *o beni seviyor* (lit. *he/she/it likes me*) – it would be impossible to determine the gender that is being referred to without looking at the overall written or spoken context. This is why, if a person says *o beni seviyor*, it means that they are assuming that the person spoken to knows who is being referred to, and therefore does not have any problems with deducing the gender of the person. If no background information exists, and there is no prior indication of the gender of the person being referred to in the context, a Turkish speaker would not use the third person pronoun generally. In this case he or she would say *bu adam beni seviyor* (*this man likes me*), or use names, e.g. *Ahmed beni seviyor* (*Ahmed likes me*).

By contrast, in many languages, all nouns – whether animate or inanimate – are gendered, and it is not possible to avoid gendering the corresponding pronoun. In French, for example, for a word such as *friend*, *ami* indicates a male friend and *amie* a female friend; any subsequent pronouns pick up on the gender in the form of *il* (masculine: *he*) and *elle* (feminine: *she*).

④ USING REFERENCE EFFECTIVELY

Having explored the pitfalls of reference devices, even when used by experienced English speakers, let us now focus on their effective use.

Activity 5 showed that an analysis of reference can help to pinpoint problems that a reader might have in following a text. If we apply such an analysis to extended texts we can also tell not only whether a reader/ listener will be able to decode easily all the reference items, but we will also be able to see:

♦ *which participants are the major ones*, i.e. who is the text actually concerned with?

♦ *whether the participants stay the same throughout the text*, i.e. if the participants change during the text, at what point are different participants referred to?

In the rest of this section we will consider effective and ineffective uses of cohesive reference.

You may have noticed that I have consistently premodified *reference* with the classifier *cohesive*. This is because reference is a very broad category (as you will see from the entries in your reference grammar) and it is only when reference items enter into **reference chains** that they can be said to function cohesively. Another way of putting this is to say that participants in a text may either be presented as 'new' or presumed as being retrievable from another part of the text. Whenever a writer/ speaker signals to the reader/listener that the identity of the participant is already known (i.e. retrievable from the text), the reference is said to be 'presuming'. It is **presuming** rather than **presenting reference** that creates cohesion in a text. This is illustrated in the following two sentences:

> *I was informed of the accident by a policeman*. (Non-cohesive, presenting, i.e. the reader/listener is not expected to know anything about the participant.)

> *He* (cohesive, presuming) *said the tires may have caught on a streetcar track*. (Here it is presumed that we can work out whom the *he* refers to.)

Marked lexical focus (Unit 15) fulfils a similar presuming function when it presents information to the listener as given, or retrievable from the text. For instance, to quote an example from Unit 15:

> B: // People just don't work Saturday mornings officially // in London //

> C: // Well I quite enjoy working on Saturdays //

(McCarthy, 1998, p. 189)

The focal item *enjoy*, being a non-final lexical item, signals what follows it in the information unit (*working Saturdays*) as given. It is retrievable from the preceding contribution from A.

ACTIVITY 7 (allow about 15 minutes)

Common cohesive reference items are illustrated (underlined) in the corpus examples below. As you read through them:

(1) think about which Longman register the extracts are located in

(2) think carefully about how field, tenor and mode might be influencing the choice of reference items.

Text 7

A teenager who existed on a junk food diet developed scurvy, the bane of seamen two centuries ago, it was revealed yesterday. The 14-year-old, from Northern Ireland, lived on cola, chocolate, hamburgers and crisps.

Her doctor said he had heard of only four or five western teenagers with the disease, caused by a deficiency in vitamin C. The girl did not eat much fruit and was not keen on vegetables, said Dr Kevin McKenna.

Text 8

A: How's the box going?

B: Which box?

A: The new one.

B: Oh that one -

(Biber et al., 1999, pp. 268 and 233)

COMMENT

I am sure you had no difficulty in working out that the first is a text from a news report and the second an extract from a conversation.

In the newspaper report, an unknown teenager is first introduced with a presenting reference – the indefinite article *a*. Once introduced, the teenager can then be treated as 'known' and named by the definite article *the* in later references – *the 14-year-old*, *the girl*. As the corpus evidence in Figure 2 (overleaf) shows, such usage is more common in news than in either academic prose or conversation. One possible explanation is that, compared to pronouns, definite articles as part of a noun phrase are more precise – as well as making it possible to provide extra information about the item referred to (e.g. *the 14-year-old* in the example above).

The use of the combination of definite article and noun phrase (i.e. *the + girl*) to reference items previously mentioned in a text is particularly common in news reports. You may remember this from Activity 2 in Unit 15 where we noted similar use of co-reference in the extract from a sports report on the footballer, Donaghy. In fact, here, as in the news report above, we saw how such use of co-reference provides lexical variation as well as showing different aspects of the person or entity being referred to.

each ■ represents 5%   □ represents less than 2.5%

	CONV	FICT	NEWS	ACAD
backwards reference	■■■■■	■■■■■■	■■■■■■	■■■■■

Figure 2 Percentage use of backward referring or anaphoric reference for definite noun phrases in each register (Biber et al., 1999, p. 266, Table 4.10)

The conversation extract also illustrates the use of the presuming reference *the*. However, in this interchange, it is clear that Speaker A has overestimated the ability of Speaker B to retrieve the item referred to (*the box*) which, presumably, has been mentioned earlier in the same or a previous conversation. This results in B having to seek clarification. A resolves the situation by clarifying which one (*the new one*). Clearly in a spoken, face-to-face conversation, repair work of ambiguous use of reference can take place relatively easily. In the case of written English, in contrast, negotiation of meaning and therefore repair of communication breakdown is rarely possible.

ACTIVITY 8 (allow about 20 minutes)

This activity is designed to show you the variety of grammatical devices available for referring to items in a text cohesively.

In the following three texts you will find a number of grammatical reference devices which link back to items in the text. These include:

♦ personal pronouns (e.g. *he*)

♦ possessive pronouns (e.g. *Is the book hers?*)

♦ demonstrative pronouns (e.g. *Those are difficult*)

♦ definite articles (e.g. *the book*)

♦ demonstrative determiners (e.g. *that book*)

◆ possessive determiners (e.g. _his_ book)

◆ comparatives (e.g. the _other_ book)

◆ place adverbials (e.g. _Here_, we see the main argument)

◆ time adverbials (e.g. Back _then_, times were hard).

Read each text and complete the following steps:

(1) Think about which Longman register the text would be located in.

(2) Identify and underline as many reference items as you can, identify the grammatical form of each and, where possible, use an arrow to show what item they refer to in the text (we have already underlined some examples). To simplify the activity, do not include the definite article as a reference item. See 'Answers to the activities' for feedback on this.

(3) Think about how the field, tenor and mode of the texts might influence the choice of reference items.

Text 9

The universality of the World Wide Web as a platform for communication and interaction relates certainly to its technical aspects and apparently to many characteristics of its available functionalities. Throughout the world, educationally oriented World Wide Web sites have been created, and traffic among these sites includes persons from countries around the globe. Does this mean, however, that the communication and interaction supported by those sites will have the same meaning and level of appropriateness to persons from different cultures and backgrounds?

(Collis and Remmers, 1997, p. 85)

Text 10

[In this text the woman referred to as _she_ is examining a photograph of a man and woman sitting under a tree. The photograph enables the woman to go back in time and evoke a particular period in her life.]

She examines every detail. His fingers bleached by the flash or the sun's glare; the folds of their clothing; the leaves of the tree, and the small round shapes hanging there – were they apples, after all? The coarse grass in the foreground. The grass was yellow then because the weather had been dry.

Over to one side – you wouldn't see it at first – there's a hand, cut by the margin, scissored off at the wrist, resting on the grass as if discarded. Left to its own devices.

The trace of blown cloud in the brilliant sky, like ice cream smudged on chrome. His smoke-stained fingers. The distant glint of water. All drowned <u>now</u>.

(Atwood, 2001, p. 8)

Text 11

CHAIR in the case of many people who are in fact sponsors of these complementary medicines - they want it to be an opponent form of medicine

GP I'd agree with that... I'd agree with that

CHAIR yes

GP I think that we make it a lot worse by being so rigid in our attitude towards... to alternative or complimentary medicine because of opposite... of equal and opposite reactions you naturally get another castle, another entire enclosed castle arising without...which builds an entirely different system and I think this is very dangerous and very unhelpful to the patients.

('Alternative medicine', 1988)

COMMENT

In Text 9, which you probably recognised as a short extract from an academic article, the demonstrative determiner *these* in *these sites* immediately signals that its meaning is retrievable from the preceding text. Corpus findings (Biber et al., 1999, p. 238) show that academic prose has a relatively high frequency of noun phrases with demonstrative determiners, one explanation being that they provide a precise form of reference. The use of demonstrative pronouns such as *this* (e.g. *does <u>this</u> mean*) is also common in academic prose, since academics and students constantly need to reiterate and summarise ideas and entities as arguments are developed.

You will probably have worked out that Text 10 is an extract from a novel and you will have observed the high frequency of possessive determiners and personal pronouns used as reference devices. As you will see from the corpus evidence in your reference grammar (p. 93), the frequency of personal pronouns relative to nouns is far higher in the Longman fiction register compared to news and academic prose. Biber et al. (1999) draw attention to the communicative effectiveness of using pronouns in fiction in the following discussion.

In the novel, the inherent definiteness of personal pronouns means that people and entities are presented as if familiar, even though they have not been introduced, and the reader is forced to be instantly involved in the fictional world.

(Biber et al., 1999, p. 331)

In Text 10, adverbials are used as a means to reference locations in time (referred to as **locational reference**). The reference *then* links to a period in the past, whereas the later use of *now* in *all drowned now* is a cohesive reference which reconnects the reader to the time period constructed in the main narrative of the book.

In the novel from which Text 10 is taken the movement between past and present is a key rhythm and therefore locational reference is constantly drawn on to enable the characters to move in and out of the different time periods. This interweaving of past and present enables the writer to show the significance of past events for the characters' current sense of themselves or to provide the motivation for some contemporary event.

Common location items (which may refer to place as well as time) include *here, there, now, then, these days, at the moment, above, below*.

Another interesting use of reference in Text 10 is the use of *it* in *you wouldn't see it at first* – to refer forward to *a hand*. **Forward referencing** is more technically known as **cataphora** whereas **backward referencing** is referred to as **anaphora**.

You may have recognised Text 11 as an extract from the television discussion on the relative merits of mainstream and alternative medicine which you first came across in Book 1 Unit 7. In the extract we can see how **comparatives** (expressed in this text in the word *different*) can function as a reference device. It is important to note that, with comparatives, the identity of the presumed item is retrieved not because, in itself, it has already been mentioned (or will be mentioned) in the text, but because an item with which it is being compared has been mentioned. Examples of comparatives include *same, similar, different, other, such, more, less, bigger*.

4.1 Creating a map of reference items

ACTIVITY 9 (allow about 20 minutes)

We have now explored a range of reference items so it may be useful at this point to sum up the different types. Look at Figure 3. Work through a piece of your own academic, professional or personal writing and try to find an example for each type. Can you see ways in which you are using grammatical reference more and less effectively?

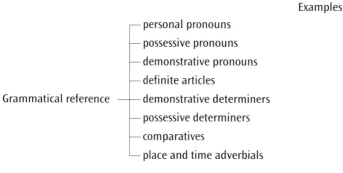

Examples

- personal pronouns
- possessive pronouns
- demonstrative pronouns
- definite articles
- demonstrative determiners
- possessive determiners
- comparatives
- place and time adverbials

Grammatical reference

Figure 3 Different types of reference item

ACTIVITY 10 (allow about 30 minutes)

At this point it will be useful for you to do some further exploration of cohesive reference, using your reference grammar. Use the index there to find out about different types of reference and make notes of any interesting points raised by the authors.

COMMENT

You will have found that your reference grammar has several examples of both backward and forward referencing. In addition, it discusses the use of the definite article, demonstrative determiners and pronouns. From your reading, you will also have seen that reference is often used non-cohesively. Non-cohesive reference occurs when what is referred to can be retrieved from a shared social situation outside the text:

> Finish <u>that</u> cake if you want it. <referring to the cake that the addressee is eating>
>
> (Biber et al., 1999, p. 273)

Situational, non-cohesive reference is particularly common in conversational English where the speakers share the context. In fact, conversational partners are often closely related as family members or friends, and can thus rely on a great deal of shared knowledge, as the following extract illustrates. (There are several further examples of **situational reference** on pages 71 (item E) and 73 (item A) of your reference grammar which you may also want to look at.)

> You know last week my aunty she put her down in **the** kitchen and **the** telephone rang. And **the** telephone's on **the** wall in **the** kitchen.

<unclear> picked it up. All of a sudden she turns round, just sees my little cousin screaming <unclear>. My little cousin's pulled **the** kettle of boiling water down her, all down her back.

(Biber et al., 1999, p. 267)

The corpus evidence in Figure 4 below provides evidence of the extent to which situational reference occurs in conversation compared to the other Longman registers.

each ■ represents 5%   □ represents less than 2.5%

	CONV	FICT	NEWS	ACAD
situational	■■■■■■■■■■ □□		□□	□□

Figure 4 Percentage use of situational reference for definite noun phrases in each register (Biber et al., 1999, p. 266, Table 4.10)

Figure 4 shows that the use of situational reference is much less frequent in the written registers of news, fiction and academic prose. Clearly, language functioning to reconstruct and reflect on events (as opposed to language commenting on action and connecting the ongoing text into the situational context, i.e. conversation) has to work harder to create internally cohesive text.

A key theme of Book 3 is, of course, the variation that occurs within any one Longman register. That is, specific individual texts, even when located in the same Longman register, may vary considerably in how they use language – depending on their specific purpose, their subject matter, the relationship between interlocutors and where they fall on the mode continuum. Later on, and also in the CD-ROM activities, we will explore variation in cohesive devices by analysing several different examples of news, fiction, academic and conversational texts. But before we do this, let us see how the grammatical tools you have acquired so far enable you to make judgements about the effectiveness of texts.

4.2 Diagnosing problems in texts: the role of cohesive reference

ACTIVITY 11 (allow about 30 minutes)

You may remember that in the introduction to Section 4 we said that one of the purposes in acquiring an understanding of cohesive reference was to be able to analyse a text and see:

◆ *whether there is a problem with retrieval*, i.e. can we decode all the presuming reference items?

◆ *which participants are the major ones*, i.e. who is the text actually concerned with?

◆ *whether the participants stay the same throughout the text*, i.e. if the participants change during the text, at what point are different participants referred to?

Now read Text 12, written by the school student Kevin, which you first came across in Unit 15. Wearing your hat of teacher/educator, focus in particular on Kevin's use of reference items and then look at the reference chains shown in Figure 5 opposite.

Reference chains are constructed by linking all presuming reference items with their referents. Reference items and their referents are linked by upward-pointing arrows if the reference is anaphoric and downward-pointing arrows if it is cataphoric. Situational reference items are not included. Think about the implications of the reference chains for Kevin's text in the light of the bullet points listed at the beginning of this activity. Do the chains point to a successful or an unsuccessful text? To answer this you may also want to refresh your memory concerning the lexical cohesion analysis conducted in Unit 15 and consider its role in relation to the analysis of grammatical cohesion.

Text 12

(1) I like electronics because it interests me. (2) I started to like it a few years ago. (3) I took apart old radios and that kind of stuff. (4) My uncle Michael has given me a lot of help and components. (5) You have to have a lot of patience to do the soldering. (6) I have a piece of breadboard. (7) You just push the components legs in to the board. (8) I still use the soldering iron if the breadboard is not big enough. (9) I've made an electronic clock and have put it into a box. (10) I've got an alarm sign on the display but have not been able to get an alarm fixed up to it yet. (11) At the moment I'm getting the parts for an electronic organ. (12) It has a keyboard and you have a stylus to touch the metal keyboard. (13) You have an earpiece but can make an amplifier. (14) After that you can make a vibrato circuit.

(Carter, 1996, p. 123)

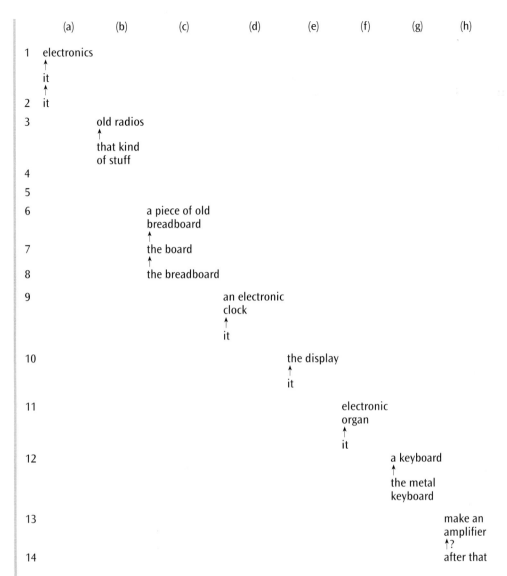

Figure 5 Reference chains in Kevin's text (Text 12)

COMMENT

The identification of reference chains in Text 12 reveals several weaknesses in terms of continuity and cohesion. Most significantly, the shortness and number of the chains reflect a rapid movement from one item to another. The rapid shift from one participant to another means that there are no major people or things that are tracked throughout the whole text. In addition, as we have already seen in Unit 15, the items are not woven together through any clear lexical relations. This indicates that there is a general lack of a sustained development of ideas holding the text together as a unified whole.

In addition, the presuming reference *the* in *the soldering* and *the soldering iron* cannot be retrieved from a previous or subsequent item in the text. Similarly, the use of *the* to introduce *metal keyboard* is slightly ambiguous given that metal has not been previously mentioned. In fact, I think it would have been more effective if the student had written:

It has a metal keyboard and you have a stylus to touch it with.

Likewise the use of *that* in *after that* is rather ambiguous. Does it refer to the possibility of making an amplifier? In sum, the analysis of both lexical and reference chains provides insight into why the text lacks overall texture and cohesion.

ACTIVITY 12   (allow about 30 minutes)

Having seen how an analysis of a text's reference chains can illuminate the way in which meanings are not always successfully woven together, now do the same kind of chain analysis on Text 13 (which also first appeared in Unit 15). Again, as in the previous activity, you should also consider the role of lexical cohesion. After you have completed your analysis think about what insights it provides. See 'Answers to the activities' for feedback.

Text 13

Components

(1) The major components in any basic circuit include a breadboard, a power source (a battery), resistors, wires, ammeters and voltmeters. (2) As circuits get more and more complex, you begin using components such as capacitors, transistors and switches. (3) All of these components will be explained on this page.

(4) A breadboard is simply a board in which you plug your components into when making a circuit. (5) It is usually a plastic board with holes in it. (6) These holes are connected (inside the board) by metal which allows the current to flow through the components. (7) All holes in the same horizontal line are connected together. (8) Running in a vertical line somewhere on the breadboard are things called "buses." (9) These are usually where you would plug your power source and your "ground" into.

(10) Every circuit requires some sort of power source. (11) This is usually in the form of a battery. (12) The symbol for the battery on a schematic diagram is shown in the margin.

(13) If using a regular battery, you will need to solder wires onto the + and - terminals of the battery. (14) Then you may plug these wires into the breadboard. (15) The battery is a type of capacitor with charge stored up on one side (plate). (16) When connected to something else, current will flow.

(*Electronics Workshop* [online])

COMMENT

From your analysis you will have seen how, in Text 13, the number and length of the reference chains are not dissimilar to those in Text 12. However, even though six of the eight chains consist of only one presuming reference item, there is also a chain of three items (*battery*) and one of four items (*breadboard*). In addition, unlike Text 12, there is a main participant – *the breadboard* – which is tracked across the whole text. The chains therefore reflect the organisation of the text which examines, in turn, the main components of circuits and how they work in relation to the breadboard.

From the analysis of lexical cohesion in Unit 15, we have also seen that each of the main participants is taxonomically related and it is this type of cohesion which gives the text overall unity. Reference chains, in other words, serve to complement the overall lexical texture by providing localised cohesion for the discussion of each main component.

Unlike in Text 12, presuming reference items, realised as possessive determiners and definite articles, often accompany repeated noun phrases (e.g. *these components, the breadboard, these holes, the battery*). This makes all referencing precise and unambiguous. Likewise, also in contrast to Text 12, the use of both presenting and presuming references clearly distinguishes which elements of circuits the writer anticipates that the reader is unlikely to be familiar with (*a breadboard, a battery*). In sum, the combination of a lexical chain and reference chain analysis provides strong evidence of, and a clear explanation for, the overall cohesive quality of Text 13.

4.3 Cohesive reference and variation within the Longman registers

So far we have pointed out some of the ways in which cohesive reference is distributed differently in each of the Longman registers. In this section we will begin to explore how, when we look at individual texts, we may find that there is a great deal of variation even where the texts are located in the same Longman register (such as fiction or conversation).

ACTIVITY **13** (allow about 15 minutes)

Now it is time to put on your editor's hat and recap what we have done up to this point. You will need to imagine that you are advising an aspiring novelist about whether or not the opening to their novel will connect with their readers. Will it capture their imagination by drawing them into the fictional world of the novel?

Below are two different versions of the opening to *The Siege*, a novel written by Helen Dunmore which tells the story of the siege of Leningrad during the Second World War. During the blockade, German forces surrounded the city, imprisoning those who lived there and forcing them to confront shelling, starvation and the terrible Russian winter. As the first point of contact with the reader, the opening paragraphs in any novel are, of course, crucial in stimulating their interest and imagination. In *The Siege* the opening aims to make the reader feel familiar with, and intimately connected to, the world set up by the novel. This world – Leningrad at the beginning of spring – is also designed to provide a strong contrast with the ensuing descriptions of a long and hard winter in which the central characters struggle to survive.

As you read Version A, it is important that you, as editor, evaluate how successful the author is in engaging with her reader. Does Helen Dunmore make language choices that will draw the reader into the fictional world of the novel? In particular, does her use of reference devices contribute to the effectiveness of the opening paragraphs? (You may first find it useful to underline each of the reference items.)

Text 14

Version A

June, 1941

It's half past ten in the evening, but the light of day still glows through the lime leaves. They are so green that they look like an hallucination of the summer everyone has almost given up expecting. When you touch them, they are fresh and tender. It's like touching a baby's skin.

Such a late spring, murky and doubtful, clinging to winter's skirts. But this is how it happens here in Leningrad. Under the trees around the Admiralty, lakes of spongy ice turned grey. There was slush everywhere, and a raw, dirty wind off the Neva. There was a frost, a thaw, another frost.

Month after month ice-fishermen crouched by the holes they'd drilled in the ice, sitting out the winter, heads hunched into shoulders. And then, just when it seemed as if summer would forget about Leningrad this year, everything changed. Ice broke loose from the compacted mass around the Strelka.

(Dunmore, 2001, p. 1)

COMMENT

If I were an editor, my thoughts on Helen Dunmore's use of language would be as follows:

First, the use of the present tense – *It's half past ten in the evening* – creates a sense of immediacy. Second, the use of the pronoun *you* in *When you touch them, they are fresh and tender* serves to address the reader directly and thus works to draw them into the fictional world. The literary use of simile in *It's like touching a baby's skin* also evokes a sense of wonder at the preciousness of new life, creating a strong contrast to the ensuing description of the bleak and bitter Russian winter.

Reference devices play an important role in presenting time and place as if the reader's and narrator's perspective on the scene is somehow fused. That is, the use of the definite article in *the evening, the light of day, the lime leaves, the trees around the Admiralty* serves to set up a shared context whereby both writer and reader are construed as inhabiting the same world. The use of *this* in *this year* also assumes shared knowledge (interestingly this reference can also be retrieved from the chapter title – June, 1941). Finally, place adverbials have a similar effect. For example, *here* referring forwards to Leningrad positions the reader as someone already part of the fictional world (*this is how it happens here in Leningrad*). In contrast, if Helen Dunmore had used backwards reference (e.g. *this is how it happens in Leningrad. There...*) the reader would have felt they were being introduced into an unfamiliar world.

In sum, the physical world created in Version A seems to me an effective way of creating an interesting setting for the novel as a whole. The city is brought to life using techniques that remind me of typical film openings – a close focus on an interesting detail with the camera then pulling back to reveal the wider scene. From a grammatical perspective, Dunmore creates this world by initially focusing on the detail of the lime leaves tracked though a chain of four reference items (a 'close shot', if you like). The scene then widens to include a 'panoramic shot' of the Admiralty and the lakes. Here, there are swift changes of scene (or topic) and an absence of reference chains.

A CTIVITY **14** (allow about 15 minutes)

Now read a different version of the opening to the same novel. Imagine Helen Dunmore had submitted this version. As you read it, think about why it is less effective. Focus in particular on its use of reference devices. Then, in your role as editor, think about what feedback an author might find useful.

Text 15

Version B

June, 1941

It's half past ten on an evening in June 1941, but the light of the preceding day still glows through the lime leaves of the trees across the city. The leaves are so green that they look like an hallucination of the summer that the people of Leningrad have almost given up expecting. When the leaves are touched, they are fresh and tender. It's like touching a baby's skin.

Such a late spring, murky and doubtful, clinging to winter's skirts. But this process of spring finally emerging from winter is how it happens in Leningrad. There, under trees which surround the naval academy (the Admiralty), lakes of spongy ice turned grey. There was slush everywhere in the city, and a raw, dirty wind off the Neva, the river that runs through Leningrad. There was a frost, a thaw, another frost.

Month after month ice-fishermen crouched by the holes they'd drilled in the ice, sitting out the winter, heads hunched into shoulders. And then, just when it seemed as if the summer of 1941 would forget about Leningrad, everything changed. Ice broke loose from the compacted mass around the column at the end of one of the islands on the Neva.

C OMMENT

You will probably have observed that in the reversioned opening the reduction in reference items creates greater distance between writer and reader. No longer is the world of Leningrad a shared world and no longer is the reader part of the 'here and now'. Nor are they directly addressed through the pronoun *you*. Rather they are treated as an outsider, someone who needs to have the landmarks spelled out for them. Time and place references are made explicit with the use of *there* rather than *here* as a place adverbial also serving to increase emotional distance. In sum, the absence of assumed, shared knowledge through the use of cohesive and situational reference means that the reader feels less intimately a part of the writer's imaginary world. As a consequence, the opening is less effective in making a reader want to read on.

ACTIVITY 15   (allow about 15 minutes)

Now read an opening to a very different novel called *Thinks...* written by David Lodge. The main focus of this novel is a character called Ralph Messenger – a cognitive scientist concerned with the nature and structure of thought. In the opening scene to the novel, Ralph is tape-recording his own meandering patterns of thought by talking out loud. Thus, whereas the opening paragraphs in the previous novel describe an external world, this one is designed to give the reader insight into the inner workings of the central character. As editor, think about whether it is successful. In what way would it draw a reader into the novel? In particular, do you think that the writer's use of reference contributes to its effectiveness? What feedback might you give the author?

> ### Text 16
>
> One, two, three, testing, testing ... recorder working OK ... Olympus Pearlcorder, bought it at Heathrow in the dutyfree on my way to ... where? Can't remember, doesn't matter ... The object of the exercise being to record as accurately as possible the thoughts that are passing through my head at this moment in time, which is, let's see ... 10.13 a.m. on Sunday the 23rd of Febru – San Diego! I bought it on my way to that conference in ... Isabel Hotchkiss. Of course, Dan Diego, 'Vision and the Brain'. Late eighties. Isabel Hotchkiss. I tested the range of the condenser mike ... yes ... Where was I? But that's the point, I'm not anywhere, I haven't made a decision to think about anything specific, the object of the exercise being simply to record the random thoughts, if anything can be random, the random thoughts passing through a man's head, all right my head, at a randomly chosen time and place ... well not truly random, I came in here this morning on purpose
>
> (Lodge, 2002, p. 1)

COMMENT

Through his grammatical and lexical choices, David Lodge creates a very different orientation to his novel compared to that created by Helen Dunmore. Most strikingly, *Thinks...* is far more spoken in style when compared to *The Siege*.

Clearly, Lodge's opening paragraph is designed to give the reader insight into Ralph's mind, but not necessarily to see the world from his perspective. A distance therefore exists between the main character (it is only later on that the reader finds out it is Ralph Messenger) and the reader. The reader is not positioned to be at the centre of Ralph's world. Rather they find themselves in the role of observer, studying the chaotic internal workings of a cognitive scientist, much in the same way that Ralph himself is attempting to observe and monitor internal thought – from the outside, as it were. Not surprisingly, there is a complete absence of presuming reference. Nor are there any sustained lexical strings. After all, the novelist is attempting to simulate the random thoughts of the main narrator as he flits from one half-formed thought to another. Such use of reference thus helps to achieve the desired effect.

Interestingly, there are two instances of forward reference:

> <u>this moment</u> in time, which is, let's see ... 10.13 a.m. on Sunday the 23rd of Febru

> But <u>that's</u> the point, I'm not anywhere

Personally, if I were giving advice to the author, I would question whether his use of forward referencing captures natural, unplanned thinking. Somehow it almost seems contrived, as though what is being said serves the wider (novelist's) purpose of locating the story in a particular time frame and introducing one of the themes of the book – the nature of random, spontaneous thought. On the other hand, it does serve to create a certain amount of disorientation on the part of the readers – as they struggle to follow the direction of the narrator's thoughts. Perhaps this encourages the reader to 'read on' and find out what the novel is all about.

ACTIVITY 16 (allow about 30 minutes)

Below are two texts. They are both extracts from spoken interactions that you have previously seen. The first is part of the conversation between Jimmy and Greg at the animal hospital (which you first encountered in Activity 4 in this unit) concerning an escaped rabbit. The second text is a continuation of the discussion about alternative medicine which you previously encountered in this unit as well as in Book 1, Unit 7. (Both interactions are available on the Activities CD-ROM, in the video file for Unit 16, and you might find it helpful to watch the interaction first in full.) Underline the cohesive reference items. Are there differences in how reference is used within each of the interactions? Why do you think this is the case? (Before moving to the interpretation stage and answering the question 'Why do you think this is the case?', see 'Answers to the activities' for feedback on the reference analysis.)

Text 17

A: he don't seem to have any injuries

B: is there any possibility that somebody couldn't actually handle him any more and decided to release him?

A um, with the condition he's in I wouldn't have thought so, normally they are a bit scratty, if they've been struggling to look after them for a while and then decided to let them go, usually when you get them a good condition it's just a simple catch she's broke on her rabbit hutch

B: so he's an escapee?

A: I'd say so yeah, he's been very lucky actually because there are foxes round here as well I believe

C: yes we do have foxes I see them around sometimes

A: now that would have been a problem

C: very lucky then

A: that would have been a problem for him; he wouldn't have known where to go with him being domesticated. I think if they hadn't have picked him up he wouldn't have lasted very long I don't think.

('Escaped rabbit', 2002)

Text 18

GP ...and I think as Debra has expressed some of this tonight...she really doesn't see that in fact...or perhaps she does see ...but...I mean... it didn't come over from what she said...that she thinks...or her image... of a...going to a GP with a headache was that she'd get two Paracetamol...Surely it would...might be equally useful for the general practitioner to find out what was about...her headache was about by taking a decent history...erm...I...I find this very worrying...er...er...Debra who seems a delightful person has already fallen...got into the other camp so to speak rather than um

CHAIR Do you...do you...do you feel that about...about...about real...about normal medicine...do you feel that way about it?

DEBRA I was slightly exaggerating... I was slightly exaggerating

CHAIR [attempted intervention]

DEBRA I mean...I...but I do think that...that...that allopathic medicine doesn't have the tools to necessarily find out what the cause of headaches are

GP I think an awful lot of

DEBRA I mean because it doesn't have the questions... because it doesn't have the concepts

GP Well I think a lot of tools are there...perhaps they haven't...you happen to have had the bad luck that no one's used them on you...but I...I think...perhaps...

DEBRA Well

GP a lot of it...the tools are that in fact the patient will very often tell you what is wrong with them...if you give them half a chance – I don't mean give you a diagnosis but they will tell you what the matter is if you give them time.

('Alternative medicine', 1988)

COMMENT

You will probably have noticed that one of the main differences between Texts 17 and 18 is the extent to which reference is used to tie the text into the external context or the ongoing internal text. Text 17 is threaded through with situational (and therefore non-cohesive) reference. This is because the item referred to as *he, him* and *his* (the rabbit), and which generates the main (non-cohesive) reference chain, is clearly and visibly part of the interactants' shared physical context.

Interestingly, where reference is used cohesively in Text 17 it is somewhat ambiguous. For example, in *if they've been struggling to look after them for a while*, it is not completely clear whom *they* refers to. The listener would therefore have to do a certain amount of work to infer that the speaker is probably referring to rabbit owners in general. Likewise, the use of the feminine pronoun *she* in *it's just a simple catch she's broke* is presumably referring to rabbits in general, although again this is not entirely clear and it may be that the speaker is overestimating the obviousness of reference.

Whereas Text 17 is an example of language in action, Text 18 illustrates a less conversational and spontaneous use of spoken language. Rather, it is an example of how language is being used to reflect, rather abstractly, on the strengths and weaknesses of different forms of medicine. Not surprisingly, therefore, there is no use of situational reference. Cohesive reference, on the other hand, plays an important role in contributing to the internal cohesion of the text, tracking participants which have been previously mentioned in the text (e.g. *Debra, tools, patients*). In addition, the fact that the discussion is being conducted specifically for television means that the participants are building an argument which needs to make sense not only to themselves but to a wider audience. Therefore there is greater use of **text reference** to track the development of ideas – *Debra has expressed some of this tonight, I find this very worrying*, etc.

You may of course be thinking that the discussion seems far from coherent as you try to make sense of the decontextualised transcript. This is largely a result of the point made earlier in the course, that spoken language written down will always seem messy and chaotic and will be difficult to follow. However, if you take a look at the video version of the discussion, the participants do not appear to be experiencing any problems in following each other's arguments.

In sum, Activities 12–14 and Activity 15 have illustrated how texts from the same Longman register (fiction in Activities 12–14 and conversation in Activity 15) may display considerable variation in how they deploy cohesive devices. In the case of the conversation texts, we can see that the more abstract the discussion is and the further removed it is from a concrete situation, the less likely participants are to make use of situational reference, and the more likely they are to use cohesive reference. In the case of the fiction texts, the opening paragraphs of the two novels also fall at different points on the mode continuum. Whereas the paragraph from *The Siege* is more written in style, the one from *Thinks...* mimics the spontaneity of unplanned dialogue. However, we can see that, perhaps because Ralph's internal dialogue is not authentic natural speech, there is minimal use of situational reference. In addition, the two novels set up very different fictional worlds and a very different relationship between the narrator/characters and readers. Not surprisingly the use of cohesive reference reflects these different purposes.

Your awareness and understanding of how and why cohesive devices may vary across and within the four Longman registers will be further developed in the Activities CD-ROM for this unit. First, let us consider the role of intonation in contributing to cohesion.

⑤ NON-LEXICAL FOCUS AS A COHESIVE DEVICE

Let us go back to Text 18 from the preceding activity, this time concentrating on the way it is said and not just looking at the ways in which reference functions grammatically. In particular, we will look at the implications for the text and the context when the information focus falls on a non-lexical item.

In Text 19 below, the text is transcribed with intonation in mind. As in all the intonation work on this course, the // represent boundaries of information units or tone-groups; the tonic syllables are underlined; the ... represent pauses.

Now try to read Text 19 aloud to yourself, so that you have some idea of its intonation. This is not an easy task, mainly owing to the dysfluency features within it.

Text 19

GP ...and I think as Debra has expressed some of this tonight //... she really doesn't <u>see</u> that // in <u>fact</u> //... or perhaps she <u>does</u> see // ... but ... I mean ... it didn't come over from what she <u>said</u>//... that she <u>thinks</u> //... or her <u>image</u> ... // of a ... going to a GP with a <u>headache</u> // was that she'd get two Para<u>ce</u>tamol.. // <u>Surely</u> it would ... // might be equally <u>useful</u> // for the general practitioner to find out what was a<u>bout</u>// ... her headache was a<u>bout</u> // by taking a decent <u>history</u> ... // erm ... I ... I find this very <u>worrying</u> //...er ...er ... Debra who seems a de<u>light</u>ful // <u>person</u> // has //al<u>rea</u>dy fallen //... got into the other <u>camp</u> so to speak //... rather than um

CHAIR Do you... do you ... do you feel that about ... about ... about real ... about normal <u>medicine</u> //... do you feel that way a<u>bout</u> it?//

DEBRA I was slightly e<u>xagg</u>erating //... I was slightly e<u>xagg</u>erating //

CHAIR [Attempted intervention]

DEBRA I mean ... I ... but I do <u>think</u> // that ... that ... that   allopathic medicine doesn't have the <u>tools</u> // to necessarily find <u>out</u> // what the cause of headaches <u>are</u> //

GP I think an awful lot of

DEBRA I mean because it doesn't have the <u>questions</u> //... because it doesn't have the <u>concepts</u> //

GP Well I think a lot of tools <u>are</u> there // ... perhaps they haven't ... you happen to have had the bad <u>luck</u> // that no-one's used them on <u>you</u> //... but I ... I think ... perhaps ...

DEBRA Well

GP: a <u>lot</u> of it //... the <u>tools</u> are // that in fact the patient will <u>very</u> often // tell you what is <u>wrong</u> with them //... if you give them half a <u>chance</u> ... //

('Alternative medicine', 1988)

Instead of looking at the cohesive functions of grammatical items in their own right, I now want to examine how grammatical (or non-lexical) items behave intonationally. Or to be more precise, how they behave when they are focal.

You may remember from Unit 15 that focus was neutral or unmarked when it appeared on the final lexical item within the information unit. You also saw that marked lexical focus in the main functioned cohesively to signal information as given. Will non-lexical focus have a similar function? Look at the opening few information units from Text 19:

> // and I think as Debra has expressed some of this to<u>nig</u>ht //... she really doesn't <u>see</u> that // in <u>fact</u> //... or perhaps she <u>does</u> see //

The first three information units are focally unmarked. The final lexical item is focal and no contextual presupposition arises from the intonation. In the fourth, however, focus is marked since the focal item is the auxiliary verb *does*. The cohesive effect of this is twofold. First, it signals *see* as given – it is retrievable from two information units before – but it also implies a contrast between focal *does* and some other item within the text or context. In this case, the contrast is one of straightforward polarity – *does see* as opposed to the *doesn't see* of two units before.

We have a similar polarity contrast further on in Text 19:

> GP // Well I think a lot of tools <u>are</u> there //...

Since the verb *to be* is not a lexical verb, it behaves intonationally as a non-lexical item when focal. One would expect in a neutral situation that the focus would go to *tools*. When it goes instead to *are*, it marks *tools* as given and also implies a contrast. More fully, we mean by this that a focal non-lexical item generally signals the existence within the text or context of another item, that item being derivable by contrast with the focal item. The item which is anaphorically derivable in this instance is Debra's earlier assertion about allopathic medicine not having the tools to find out the cause of headaches. The GP wishes to contradict this assertion directly, and the focal *are* thus provides another polarity contrast – the tools <u>are</u> there as opposed to <u>not</u> being there (allopathic medicine not having them entails they are not there).

During the same conversational turn, the GP continues:

> GP Well I think a lot of tools <u>are</u> there // ... perhaps they haven't ... you happen to have had the bad <u>luck</u> // that no-one's used them on <u>you</u> //...

In the last of these information units, the focal *you* suggests a contrast. It implies that another item of information is given within this text or context, derivable by contrast with the focal *you*. Previous intonation studies (e.g. Halliday (1967) and Crystal (1975)) have claimed that the 'contrastive item' (i.e. that item signalled as derivable by contrast) must belong to the same word class as the focal item, but this is clearly not the case. Consider this example – the contrast is not between *you* and some other personal pronoun, or even any sort of pronoun. The information derivable by contrast is that the tools are there. They exist. The fact that no one's used them on you does not entail that they do not exist.

This illustrates another important point about the focal item: that it is not necessarily confined simply to the word which attracts the focus. Look at the following example:

16.1   // Why bother catching the <u>train</u>? // Why not come in the car with <u>us</u>? //

These audio files can be accessed from the Unit 16 page of the Activities CD-ROM.

The focal *us* in the second information unit is an example of marked non-lexical focus, and it signals information in the text derivable by contrast with it. However, the contrast is not between *us* and another pronoun: it is not a case of coming in the car with *us* as opposed to someone else. The contrast is not between *us* and anything, in fact. The contrast is between *coming in the car with us* and the alternative of *catching a train*. The fact that the focus is on *us* simply signals that a contrast is operative. It does not entail that the focal item alone is one of the terms in that contrast. Here are more examples:

16.2   // The next thing <u>I</u> knew // the entire meal was on the <u>floor</u> //

In 16.2, the contrast is not between what *I* knew and what anybody else knew. Rather it is between what actually happened (*The next thing I knew*) and what might have been expected to happen.

16.3   // well <u>I</u> didn't realise // he was such a good <u>player</u> //

Similarly, in 16.3, although it is perfectly possible for the contrast to be between two pronouns – e.g. *you might have realised this but I certainly didn't* – the likelier contrast is between the fact of the matter and my unawareness of it: *he obviously is a good player, but I wasn't aware of it until now.* The important point is that the contrast that is in operation at any particular point *depends entirely on the context.*

The contrast may either be oppositional (*this as opposed to that*) or additional (*this as well as that*). 16.1, 16.2 and 16.3 are all oppositional:

Coming in the car with us <u>as opposed to</u> going by train.

What happened <u>as opposed to</u> what was expected to happen.

The fact of the matter <u>as opposed to</u> my awareness of it.

Whether the contrast is additional or oppositional is a matter of context. The speaker of 16.3, for instance, might be agreeing with the previous turn:

16.4   A: // I'm starting to change my <u>mind</u> about him // he's starting to look a decent <u>player</u> //

   B: // well <u>I</u> didn't realise he was such a good player // <u>either</u> //

Here the contrast is additional: *I, as well as you, didn't realise how good a player he was.* The adverb *either* functions as an explicit marker of the additional nature of the contrast, in this case two minuses (*I didn't and you didn't*). Two plusses would require *too* or *as well*.

16.5　A:　// I'm starting to change my <u>mind</u> about him // he's starting to look a decent <u>player</u> //

B:　// well <u>I</u> think he's a good player // <u>too</u> //

In both cases, these markers would tend to take their own information units.

ACTIVITIES CD-ROM　(allow about 20 minutes)

Now do the activities on non-lexical focus in the Activities CD-ROM.

Conclusion to non-lexical focus

This section on intonation has examined a selection of ways in which the focal behaviour of grammatical items contributes to the cohesive properties of a spoken text, mainly if not always by indicating the presence of information in the text or context which is derivable by contrast with the focal item. You should now be aware of some of the ways in which English intonation patterns can change by a shift in information focus, and the implications such shifts have for the remainder of the text or context.

⑥ CREATING COHESION THROUGH SUBSTITUTION AND ELLIPSIS

You first came across ellipsis in Book 1 Unit 1, where you saw how it functioned to achieve grammatical reduction, namely in situations where speakers are rapidly processing and responding to the speech of others.

Substitution and ellipsis are both devices used by English speakers to avoid having to repeat redundant or retrievable information. They are really a special kind of reference and often there is considerable overlap between reference, substitution and ellipsis. For example, bridging words like *other, another, more* and *else* fall on the border between reference and substitution. In this section we will review ellipsis and substitution with a focus on their cohesive function. Then you can act as a scriptwriter and consider how conscious awareness of these features can help to create authentic-sounding dialogue.

6.1 Substitution

ACTIVITY **17**   (allow about 10 minutes)

Look at the following texts and work out which items are replaced by another.

Text 20

ASSISTANT Would you like any help?

CUSTOMER Can I try these < > on?

[customer hands assistant a shoe]

ASSISTANT Is that the right size for you?

CUSTOMER I think so. Do you have the other one to these as well?

(Carter and McCarthy, 1994, p. 25)

Text 21

ELLEN Push it out like that.
  Careful of those little roots!
  Well now...
  Now, I'll give you the seed.
  You put...oh!
  Here's yours.
  Now, here, you hold up the leave [sic] and I'll bury it around...
  This got two plants in it!

MOTHER It has < >.
  Do we put them both in?
  I guess we do.
  That's little, isn't it?

ELLEN (nods) Now, my one...too deep

MOTHER No, that's alright.

(Jones, 1996, p. 1)

COMMENT

There are three types of substitution, as exemplified in the texts above:

(1) noun substitution: *Do you have the other <u>one</u> to these as well? Now, my <u>one</u>*

(2) verb substitution: *I guess we <u>do</u>*

(3) clause substitution: *I think <u>so</u>.*

In **noun substitution**, the words used to substitute for nouns are *one*, *ones*, *same*:

> She wore a red shirt and her friend wore <u>one</u> too.
>
> She wore a red shirt and her friend wore <u>the same</u>.

In **verb substitution**, the verb <u>do</u> is used to substitute for other verbs:

> I can't sing as well as she <u>does</u>.
>
> Did anyone lock the door? – Someone must have <u>done</u>. – Yes, I <u>did</u>.
>
> You didn't finish it. – I <u>did</u>.

In **clause substitution**, *so* substitutes for a positive clause and the word *not* for a negative clause:

> Is it going to rain. – The forecast says <u>so</u>.
>
> Is it over? – I hope <u>not</u>?
>
> Is it finished? – If <u>so</u>, we can all go home.
>
> Is it finished? – If <u>not</u>, the boss'll be furious.

For further examples of substitution go to p. 349 of your reference grammar.

6.2 Ellipsis

Ellipsis is the omission of an item from a text when that item can be understood or retrieved when left unsaid. **Cohesive ellipsis** refers specifically to elements which can be recovered from the text rather than the situation. Compare the following, where <...> indicates the ellipted word/phrase:

> <I> Suppose I ought to tell you that shouldn't I?
>
> (Biber et al., 1999, p. 158)
>
> I thought they were on the – seat but they're not <on the seat>.
>
> (Biber et al., 1999, p. 156)

In the first example, the subject *I* is omitted, but it can be supplied from the context and is thus an example of situational ellipsis. In the second example, the circumstance *on the seat* can be retrieved from the previous clause and is therefore referred to as cohesive or textual ellipsis.

ACTIVITY 18   (allow about 30 minutes)

Your reference grammar has many examples of ellipsis occurring in different grammatical environments. Use the index to track down its various functions and uses. Highlight and make notes of what you think are some of the most interesting (or useful) findings. Then compare your findings and observations with those below.

COMMENT

Here are some examples gathered by one of our student testers, Frank Xiao Junhong:

Ellipsis may take place in initial, medial, and final positions. In initial ellipsis, what is omitted may be the subject in a declarative clause, the operator in a question, or subject and operator:

1   // Must be some narky bastards in the rugby club! /There/ [subject]

2   // That too early for you? /Is/ [operator]

3   // Know what I mean? / Do you/ [operator and subject]

4   A: I love French beaches.

   B: Yeah // telling me. /You're/ [subject and operator]

In medial ellipsis, it is particularly common that part of the semi-modal is omitted:

5   Yeah dude, I // gotta start working. /have/

In final ellipsis, any words following the operator can be omitted:

6   A: I suppose Kathy is still living in that same place.

   B: Yeah, she is. /living in that same place/

Sometimes, it is the main verb and complement that are omitted:

7   A1: I'm going out with her at the moment.

   B1: Ah!

   A2: But I should be // by around Tuesday night. /going out with her/

ACTIVITY **19**   (allow about 15 minutes)

Look at the following clauses and decide which grammatical feature is ellipted. If you wanted to make the meaning totally explicit (e.g. for a child or an elementary language learner), what additional words or phrases might you add?

1   The children will carry the small boxes, the adults the large ones.

2   If you could, I'd like you to be back at 4.30.

3   Jim liked the green tiles, I preferred the blue.

4   Will anyone be waiting? Joan will, I think.

5   Should anyone have been told? John should.

See 'Answers to the activities' for feedback.

ACTIVITY **20**   (allow about 20 minutes)

Scripts or dialogues are written for all sorts of reasons – for entertainment (e.g. TV dramas and radio plays), for training purposes, for teaching English, and so on. The script below is taken from a textbook produced for learners of English. It is a written script of a telephone conversation between Linda and a switchboard operator at an English Language College. How far do you think it represents naturally-occurring speech? What might you change to make it more realistic? Think here of the use of ellipsis and substitution as well as cohesive reference. See 'Answers to the activities' for a more realistic version.

Text 22

OPERATOR Good morning. Pembroke College. Can I help you?

LINDA Yes please. I want to speak to a student. Her name is...

OPERATOR I'm sorry. I'm afraid nobody can speak to students today. It's enrolment day. The college is very busy.

LINDA Oh dear! Well, can you take a message?

OPERATOR Well, we *are* very busy...

LINDA Oh *please*! It's very important.

OPERATOR Well, O.K. I'll take the message. I hope it's short!

LINDA Thanks. She's a foreign st...

OPERATOR Just a minute. Now, who is the message *for*?

LINDA Rosa Morello. That's M-O-R-E-double L – O.

OPERATOR Thank you. And who is the message *from*?

LINDA Say 'Linda'. I'm her flatmate.

OPERATOR Yes. And what is the message *about*?

[Linda gives operator the message.]

OPERATOR Is that all now?

LINDA Yes, thanks. Rosa is a foreign student. She's enrolling for English classes.

OPERATOR Thank you. I'll write out the message and send it to the EFL department.

LINDA Thanks very much. 'Bye.

OPERATOR Goodbye. I hope you enjoy the play.

(Davies and Whitney, 1985, p. 30)

COMMENT

You will have seen that just by making a few changes such as avoiding the repetition of *message*, by using cohesive reference devices and using ellipsis, you were able to reduce the stilted and rather artificial tone of the dialogue and make it more lifelike. Nevertheless, you may have decided, as I did in my reversioning (in 'Answers to the activities'), not to overuse ellipsis within the operator's conversational turns in order to maintain a rather formal persona. This decision will, of course, depend on the types of personas and tenor relations that you as a scriptwriter want to establish. For example, if you wanted to create a more informal, relaxed persona for the operator you might start the dialogue as follows:

OPERATOR Morning. Pembroke College. Can I help?

LINDA Yes please. I want to speak to a student. Her name is...

OPERATOR Really sorry but you can't speak to students today – it's enrolment 'n it's really chaotic, everything's all over the place. You know what I mean...

 WRAPPING THINGS UP

Let us pause for a moment and remind ourselves of the different types of grammatical cohesion that we have covered in this unit and what insights they can provide. First let us recall that an analysis of linking adverbials in a text can tell us:

♦ what kind of logical relations structure a text (e.g. result/inference, contrast/concession, etc.)

♦ whether there are points of ambiguity where it is not clear exactly which logical relation is appropriate.

Now, let us remind ourselves that an analysis of cohesive reference can illuminate:

♦ whether there is a problem with retrieval, i.e. *Can we decode all the presuming reference items?*

♦ which participants are the major ones, i.e. *Who/what is the text actually concerned with?*

♦ if there is consistency in participants, i.e. *Do the participants change during the text? At what point do different participants get referred to?*

ACTIVITY 21   (allow about 30 minutes)

Having reviewed the function of linking adverbials and cohesive reference, you will have a chance to apply your understanding of these devices to improve the cohesion of a piece of academic writing.

Look at Text 23 below. It is an essay written by a non-native speaker of English as part of an English language test called the International English Language Testing Systems (IELTS). Candidates' success in this test is deemed to predict their competence in managing the English language demands of academic study. Students have to write a short essay in response to a specific prompt. In the case of the essay, the prompt was as follows:

> Present a written argument or case to an educated reader with no specialist knowledge of the following topic:

> It is now 30 years since man landed on the moon. Since then more and more money has been spent on space research and exploration. Some people think that this is not a good use of our resources and that any hope of establishing human colonies in space is unrealistic.

As you read the essay, you will probably immediately notice that the connections between the different parts of the text are unclear and that it is difficult to make sense of the argument. Bearing in mind the points above, what do you notice about the use – or absence of – linking adverbials and cohesive reference? Try rewriting the text to improve the use of linking adverbials and generally make the text more cohesive. You may also feel that grammatical changes to both the experiential and interpersonal meanings expressed in the essay would improve its overall communicative quality. If you were the student's teacher or friend, what other changes might you suggest they make? Include these changes in your revised version.

Text 23

The previous century was very important for man. Not only we invested every part of the world, also with the help of the science, which had dramatic changes, man for a first time landed on the moon. This was one of the biggest moves for human beings.

This happening, that man landed on the moon, have had many opposite opinion, that is not worth it such a resources, because it can not be possible to leave any human species.

In my opinion I totally agree with these kind of resources. It can not be possible only on earth to have human beings, maybe somewhere very far from earth exists. And this after many years of resource, which until now they will try to find out if this is true that they are human colonies in space. Also some of these resources were concluded that in space leave some king of beings. This thing is like a mystery which I believe that after many years people will solve.

Also the previous years in many countries common people said that they saw a strange thing in the sky which had a strange shape. And science said that it would be possible be some kind of transport which was used by an extra terrestrial. Not only objects, but the same extra terrestrial we saw two years later in our television dead.

I think that all these things the science does not tell without an audience, something they know. But after this entire subject with the human beings in space maybe a mystery for years.

(IELTS Academic Writing Task 2, Version 51)

COMMENT

In 'Answers to the activities' there are two versions of the essay rewritten by fellow students. Look at these to see how they have improved the essay in various ways.

ACTIVITIES CD-ROM (allow about two hours)

You have now reached the point in the unit where it will be useful to check your understanding of grammatical cohesion. Do the activities for Unit 16 on cohesion in the Activities CD-ROM; these will give you extended practice in identifying grammatical cohesive devices in a variety of texts and in making observations about how they function to make meaning. You will also have the opportunity to make judgements about the effectiveness of a selection of texts.

Now let us sum up what we have learned about mode so far:

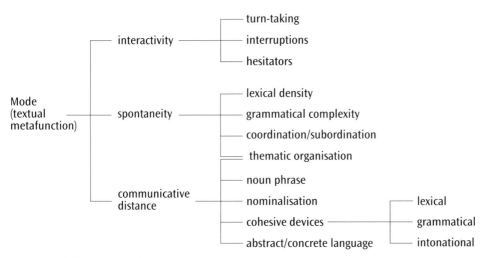

Figure 6 Map of mode

Conclusion

In this unit we have seen how grammatical cohesive devices, when used effectively, help readers and listeners to make sense of a text.

Learning outcomes

After completing this unit, you should have developed knowledge and understanding of:

◆ how patterns of grammatical cohesion may vary depending on how spoken or how written the language interaction is

◆ how cohesive devices are deployed to build experiential and interpersonal meaning

◆ how intonation functions as a cohesive device within spoken texts.

In the light of your increased understanding you should be able to:

◆   describe how a text draws on the resources of grammatical cohesion
    to contribute to the texture and coherence of a text.

◆   describe the ways in which intonation focus on grammatical items
    signals relationships of contrast between items within a text.

◆   interpret cohesive patterns in relation to the context of a text – in
    relation to the contextual variable of mode and in terms of their role
    in building experiential and interpersonal meaning.

◆   argue why certain uses of grammatical cohesion make a text more or
    less effective.

◆   apply your understanding of grammatical cohesion to make a text
    more effective.

Key terms introduced and revisited	
addition	linking adverbial [cohesive connector, connective, linker, conjunctive adjunct, cohesive adjunct]
apposition	locational reference
backward reference [anaphoric]	metalanguage
cohesive ellipsis	presenting reference
cohesive reference	presuming reference
comparative reference	pronoun
conjunction	reference chain
contrast/concession	result/inference
definite article	situational reference [exophoric reference]
demonstratives	substitution (clause, noun, verb)
enumeration	summation
forward reference [cataphoric]	text reference [endophoric reference]
indirect reference	transition [continuative]

Near equivalents are given in [ ].

Answers to the activities

ACTIVITY 1

Text 1

Should childrens TV programs be taken of air?

Nearly every household in Britain has the familiar television set. Almost every child has watched a childs programe but the question is should they. Should childrens TV programes be taken of air.

On one hand, the television has been a endless source of education for both young and old. Sesame Street, which is for younger children, has helped many children acquire general knowledge skills such as the alphabet, basic maths problems and has increased the variety of vocabulary. In addition, adults can learn about life in the underwater world or maybe find out about Britain's fascinating past.

Nevertheless, childrens TV can sometimes be a bad influence. Grange Hill features swearing and stealing. Also violent scenes could make children think its cool to fight, which could lead to accidents from them fighting.

However, it has to be recognised that children could start watching unsuitable adult TV if there was no more kids TV. This could show swearing and other things of that sort.

Nonetheless, children could become addicted to the television which would make them stay inside all day which is just lazy and unhealthy; this could make children overweight.

On the other hand, television is a great source of employment. It provides work for adults and children alike. In addition children can improve acting skills by featuring on programes and adults can work but have fun to.

On the one hand to many cartoons can block childrens imagination. Furthermore, when writing storys children sometimes get ideas from programes which can also block imagination.

However, television is also a social thing. People may talk about Eastenders the next day with friends which can bring strong opinions and good discussions. This can improve skills in school.

In conclusion, many people will have there say as there are plenty of arguments on both sides so I'll leave you to decide.

ACTIVITY 2

Linking phrase	Argument/idea	Type of relationship linking ideas
On one hand	television is an endless source of education	contrast
In addition	adults can also learn from children's programmes	addition
Nevertheless	children's TV can be a bad influence	contrast
Also	violent scenes on TV can lead to fighting and accidents	addition
However	children might watch adult TV if no children's TV is available	contrast
Nonetheless	children could become addicted to the television	contrast (but is in fact an additional 'against' argument)
On the other hand	television is a great source of employment	contrast
In addition	children can improve acting skills and adults can have fun	addition
On the one hand	too many cartoons can block children's imagination	contrast
Furthermore	TV programmes can block children's imagination	addition (but really a more general argument)
However	television is a social activity	contrast
In conclusion	readers need to decide for themselves	summation

ACTIVITY 4

The adverbial linkers are as follows:

Text 2: (a) yet, (b) and, (c) so.

Text 3: (a) so, (b) then, (c) so, (d) now; (e) then.

Text 4: (a) on the other hand, (b) as a consequence, (c) then.

ACTIVITY 8

Text	Reference item	Grammatical form	Referent
9	<u>its</u> technical aspects	possessive determiner	The universality of the World Wide Web
9	<u>its</u> available functionalities	possessive determiner	The universality of the World Wide Web
9	<u>these</u> sites	demonstrative determiner	educationally oriented World Wide Web sites
9	does <u>this</u> mean	demonstrative pronoun	the whole complex of ideas in the previous paragraph
9	<u>those</u> sites	demonstrative determiner	educationally oriented World Wide Web sites
10	<u>she</u> examines	personal pronoun	character in novel mentioned earlier
10	<u>his</u> fingers	possessive determiner	man sitting under tree in photograph
10	<u>their</u> clothing	possessive determiner	man and woman sitting under tree in photograph
10	hanging <u>there</u>	place adverbial	from the tree in the photograph
10	were <u>they</u> apples	personal pronoun	the small round shapes hanging there
10	was yellow <u>then</u>	time adverbial	in the time period when the photograph was taken
10	see <u>it</u>	personal pronoun	forward reference to a hand
10	<u>its</u> own devices	possessive determiner	the hand
10	<u>his</u> smoke stained fingers	possessive determiner	man sitting under tree in photograph
10	all drowned <u>now</u>	time adverbial	the current time period
11	<u>these</u> complementary	demonstrative determiner	the complementary medicines under discussion
11	<u>they</u> want	personal pronoun	Many people who are in fact...
11	they want <u>it</u>		Complementary medicine
11	with <u>that</u>...with <u>that</u>	demonstrative pronoun	The previous point
11	We make <u>it</u>	personal pronoun	The situation
11	entirely <u>different</u> system	comparative	compares an entirely different system through reference back to the system of complementary medicine
11	<u>this</u> is very dangerous	demonstrative pronoun	the existence of two completely separate systems which has just been discussed.

ACTIVITY 12

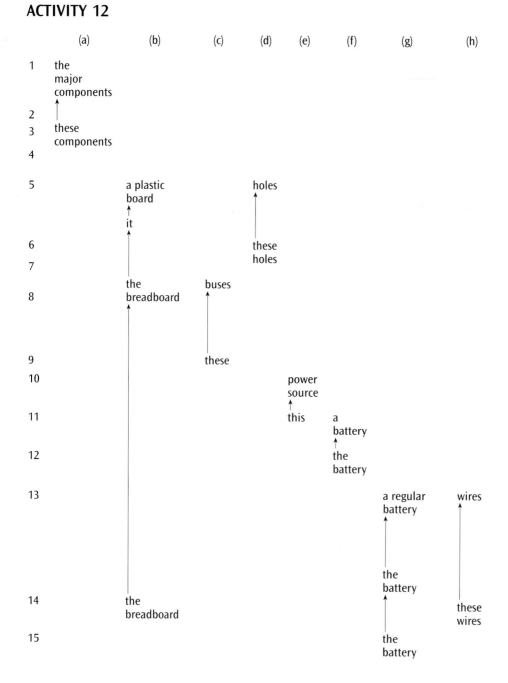

	(a)	(b)	(c)	(d)	(e)	(f)	(g)	(h)
1	the major components							
2	↑							
3	these components							
4								
5		a plastic board ↑ it ↑		holes ↑				
6				these holes				
7								
8		the breadboard ↑	buses ↑					
9			these					
10					power source ↑			
11					this	a battery ↑		
12						the battery		
13							a regular battery ↑	wires ↑
14		the breadboard					the battery ↑	these wires
15							the battery	

ACTIVITY 16

Although you were not asked to underline situational reference, I thought it would be interesting to show the extent to which it is used in the following text and I have therefore highlighted all instances in Text 17.

Text 17

A: he don't seem to have any injuries

B: is there any possibility that somebody couldn't actually handle | him any more and decided to release him?

A: um, with the condition he's in I wouldn't have thought so, normally they are a bit scratty, if they've been struggling to look after them for a while and then decided to let them go, usually when you get them in good condition it's just a simple catch she's broke on her rabbit hutch

B: so he's an escapee?

A: I'd say so yeah, he's been very lucky actually because there are foxes round here as well I believe

C: yes we do have foxes I see them around sometimes

A: now that would have been a problem

C: very lucky then

A: that would have been a problem for him; he wouldn't have known where to go with him being domesticated. I think if they hadn't have picked him up he wouldn't have lasted very long I don't think.

Text 18

GP ...and I think as Debra has expressed some of this tonight...she really doesn't see that in fact...or perhaps she does see ...but...I mean... it didn't come over from what she said...that she thinks...or her image... of a...going to a GP with a headache was that she'd get two Paracetamol...Surely it would...might be equally useful for the general practitioner to find out what was about...her headache was about by taking a decent history...erm...I...I find this very worrying...er...er...Debra who seems a delightful person has already fallen...got into the other camp so to speak rather than um

CHAIR Do you...do you...do you feel that about...about...about real...about normal medicine...do you feel that way about it?

DEBRA I was slightly exaggerating... I was slightly exaggerating

CHAIR [attempted intervention]

DEBRA I mean...I...but I do think that...that...that allopathic medicine
doesn't have the tools to necessarily find out what the cause of
headaches are

GP I think an awful lot of

DEBRA I mean because <u>it</u> doesn't have the questions... because <u>it</u>
doesn't have the concepts

GP Well I think a lot of tools are <u>there</u>...perhaps <u>they</u> haven't...you
happen to have had the bad luck that no one's used <u>them</u> on
you...but I...I think...perhaps...

DEBRA Well

GP a lot of <u>it</u>...the tools are that in fact the patient will very often
tell you what is wrong with <u>them</u>...if you give <u>them</u> half a chance –
I don't mean give you a diagnosis but <u>they</u> will tell you what the
matter is if you give <u>them</u> time.

ACTIVITY 19

Explicit clauses	Ellipsed feature	Comments
1 The children will carry the small boxes, the adults <u>will</u> <u>carry</u> the large ones.	Verb phrase ellipsis. Entire main verb phrase is ellipsed.	This is backward-referencing ellipsis.
2 If you could <u>be back at 4.30</u>, I'd like you to be back at 4.30.	Verb phrase ellipsis. Circumstance of time.	This differs from (a) in that it is forward-referencing ellipsis – it usually only occurs in front-placed dependent clauses. NB: different degrees of ellipsis are possible here: *If you could* *If you could be* *If you could be back*
3 Jim liked the green tiles, I preferred the blue <u>tiles</u>.	Nominal ellipsis. Noun (or head of a noun phrase) object is ellipsed.	
4 Will anyone be waiting? Joan will <u>be waiting</u>, I think	Verb phrase ellipsis. This type is called echoing: it involves repeating an element from the verb group.	
5 Should anyone have been told? John should <u>have been</u> <u>told</u>.	Verb phrase ellipsis.	In complex verb phrases, varying degrees of ellipsis are possible, e.g. *John should have* and *John should have been* are also possible.

ACTIVITY 20

OPERATOR Good morning. Pembroke College. Can I help you?

LINDA Yes please. I want to speak to a student called...

OPERATOR I'm sorry but nobody can speak to students today. It's enrolment day and we're very busy.

LINDA Oh dear! Well, can you take a message?

OPERATOR Well, we *are* very busy...

LINDA Oh *please*! It's very important.

OPERATOR Well, O.K. I hope it's short!

LINDA Thanks. She's a foreign st...

OPERATOR Just a minute. Now, who's it *for*?

LINDA Rosa Morello. That's M-O-R-E-double L – O.

OPERATOR Thank you. And who's it *from*?

LINDA Say 'Linda' – her flatmate.

OPERATOR Yes. And what's it *about*?

(Linda gives operator the message.)

OPERATOR Is that all now?

LINDA Yes, thanks. Rosa's a foreign student enrolling for English classes.

OPERATOR Thank you. I'll write it out and send it to the EFL department.

LINDA Thanks very much. 'Bye.

OPERATOR Goodbye. I hope you enjoy the play.

ACTIVITY 21

Here is the essay rewritten by a student tester from China, Frank Xiao Junhong:

In the past century, we not only explored every corner of the earth but also landed on the moon for the first time in human history, which has triggered everlasting enthusiasm in space research and exploration.

Some people argue that space research and exploration is not a worthwhile enterprise. They do not believe in the possibility of establishing human colonies in space. Therefore they consider this research and exploration a waste of human resources.

However, I hold a different view on space research and exploration. First, research on space may tell us whether there exist other forms of life in places other than the earth. This will be of immense scientific value in various fields. Second, research on space may lead to the establishment of human space colonies. This will greatly improve the earth's living conditions because its resources are being exhausted with the rapid increase in population growth. Third, research on space can also reveal the mystery about the origin of the earth. How the earth came into being remains a mystery to us. So knowledge about space can be valuable in solving this mystery.

In conclusion, I am in favour of space research and exploration though it means heavy investment of human resources. The discussion above demonstrates that its advantages outweigh its disadvantages.

Here is the essay rewritten by a student tester based in the UK, Judy Anderson:

The 20th century was very important for man. Not only did he explore every part of the world, but he also landed on the moon for the first time. This was a dramatic step forward for humankind, and only achieved with the help of science.

However, the whole idea of space travel has become very controversial because of its huge costs. Many feel that it is a waste of limited resources because the possibility of life existing in space is so remote.

Others feel that the expenditure is worthwhile. They believe that there must be life somewhere in the vast expanses of the universe, perhaps a super-being somewhere out there. At the very least, they believe that space is worth exploring in order to establish human colonies there.

The argument for extra-terrestrial life is further fuelled by numerous sightings of strange unidentified flying objects by ordinary people in many different countries. Scientists themselves confirm that these UFOs could possibly be used to transport extra-terrestrials, and a report on television two years ago sensationally showed what appeared to be a dead extra-terrestrial.

Whatever the truth about these matters, the whole subject of life in space holds a fascination for many people. Realistically, however, it is something that will remain a mystery for many years to come.

Review of Book 3

In this book, building on the contextual framework introduced in Book 2, you have extended your understanding of how aspects of the social context can be systematically linked to particular areas of lexis and grammar. Within this (Hallidayan) model, three overarching aspects of any social situation – the field, tenor and mode – are seen as hooking up with three main types of meaning, or metafunctions:

◆ the interpersonal metafunction (which is concerned with social interaction and the exchange of views)

◆ the experiential metafunction (which is concerned with the representation or construal of events and experiences)

◆ the textual metafunction (which is concerned with information flow and the packaging of a message).

In turn these three metafunctions hook up with lexicogrammatical forms, as summarised within the various diagram 'maps' in the units.

You should now have honed your skills in performing a register analysis of a text, for instance determining its tenor by evaluating the use of modality and evaluative language, its field and 'angle on the world' by looking at patterns in agency and affectedness and its mode from its patterns of lexical and grammatical cohesive devices and its use of hyper- and macro- as well as clause-level themes. This type of close analysis has provided you with skills not only to describe and interpret text but to take a critical perspective on the way language is used (and indeed misused). You should by now have a clear sense of how grammatical study has practical value – not only in professional domains (such as translation or teaching), but in everyday life.

In terms of research findings covered, this book has continued to narrow the focus of Book 1's investigation of broad differences between speech and writing, and Book 2's examination of global distinctions between the four Longman registers of conversation, fiction, news and academic prose. You have now seen that there may, in fact, be considerable variation in texts within each of the Longman registers when the specific variables of field, tenor and mode are taken into account. This, I hope, has led you to see that, whilst a corpus made up of texts within a similar semantic domain (such as casual conversation or academic prose) can provide many important insights, it can also elide some of the important differences that are provided by close, detailed analysis of specific texts. It is for this reason that corpus and functional approaches can provide important, complementary perspectives on how grammar works.

Applications (extension study)

If you have time in your study schedule, you may now find it interesting to look at a professional application of some of the grammatical and corpus-based skills and findings introduced so far. Work through Chapter 3 of *Applications: Putting grammar into professional practice* on authorship studies, 'Using grammar to establish the facts' by Barbara Mayor.

This study is **optional** and will not be compulsorily assessed.

CONCORDANCER AND CORPUS CD-ROM
(allow about 2 hours)

If you have carried out the extension study you will have investigated questions of authorship identification and have considered some of the complexities of plagiarism. You will also have had the opportunity to carry out some hands-on concordance searches (in Activity 5). Now explore the topic of plagiarism further by working through the tasks for Book 3 in the *Corpus Tasks* booklet. Completing Task 1 will be a useful means of maintaining and extending your skills in concordancing. To complete the task successfully you do not need to have worked through the extension study.

Key terms from Book 3

As for Books 1 and 2, to help remember and revise terms introduced or revisited in this book, you may find it useful to try to write brief definitions of a few words selected from this list (opposite). Contrast each term with other related terms where relevant, e.g. **anaphora** vs. **cataphora**, and think of an example or two to illustrate the concept, e.g. *Butterflies lay eggs; the eggs hatch into larvae; then the larvae transform into pupae; then the pupae metamorphose into butterflies* as an instance of a zigzag thematic pattern. If you are unsure about any of your definitions or examples, use the indices to Books 1–3 to look up fuller discussions of the concepts. The separate course *Glossary* may also provide useful short definitions and examples of some terms, and your reference grammar will be helpful for certain concepts from *structural* grammar (though most new terms introduced in this book are from *functional* grammar and so will not feature in the reference grammar, or will have slightly different meanings there).

actor	addition	agency and affectedness	anaphora [backward reference]
antonymy	apposition	asserted evaluation	assumed evaluation
authorial presence [persona]	cataphora [forward reference]	channel	class/subclass
coherence	cohesion	cohesive device	cohesive ellipsis
cohesive tie	co-hyponymy [co-class]	co-meronymy [co-part]	communicative distance
comparative reference	conjunction	contrast/concession	co-reference
definite article	demonstrative	dysfluency	ellipsis
enumeration	ergative verb	evaluation	exophoric reference [situational reference]
experienced	experiencer	experiential/topical theme	fan pattern [split pattern theme]
field	fronting	given information	goal
goods and services	hyper-theme [topic sentence]	hyponymy [classification]	indirect reference
information focus	information unit	interpersonal meaning	interpersonal theme
intransitive	lexical bundle	lexical chain [lexical string]	lexical cohesion
lexical density	lexical focus	linking adverbial [cohesive connector, connective, linker, conjunctive adjunct, cohesive adjunct]	locational reference
long passive	macro-theme	marked	material process
mental process	meronymy [part-whole]	metalanguage	modality
mode	mode continuum	morphology	new information
nominalisation	non-lexical focus	non-transactional actor	noun phrase [nominal group]
part-whole taxonomy	personalisation/ impersonalisation	presenting reference	presuming reference
pronoun	question tags	reference	reference chain

reiteration pattern [parallel pattern theme, constant pattern theme]	relational process	relative social status	relexicalise
repetition/local repetition	result/inference	rheme	sayer
short passive	situational reference [exophoric reference]	social contact/distance	stance
stance adverbial	standing	substitution (clause, noun, verb)	summation
superordinate	synonymy	taxonomy [classification system]	technical term
tenor	text reference [endophoric reference]	textual theme	texture
thematic progression	theme	theme reiteration	thing
topic choice [topic selection]	transactional actor	transition [continuative]	transitive
turn management	unmarked	verbal process	zigzag pattern [linear pattern theme]

Near equivalents are given in [ ].

References

'Alternative medicine' (1988). Transcript from an extract from *After Dark Series 2*, Channel 4/ITN Archive.

Atwood, M. (2001) *The Blind Assassin*, London, Virago.

BBC Sport (2003). Transcript from an extract of a live broadcast, Ireland v. England, 30 March 2003.

Beresford, D. (1999) 'South African police open fire on anti-Blair protesters', *The Guardian Unlimited* [online]. Available from http://www.guardian.co.uk.

Biber, D., Conrad, S. and Leech, G. (2002) *Longman Student Grammar of Spoken and Written English Workbook*, London, Pearson.

Biber, D., Johansson, S., Leech, G., Conrad, S. and Finegan, E. (1999) *Longman Grammar of Spoken and Written English*, Harlow, Pearson.

The Birmingham Post (1999) 'A princely foreign lesson', 25 October.

Canadian Hansard, http://www.parl.gc.ca/37/2/parlbus/chambus/house/debates/002_2002-10-01/han002_1215-E.htm.

Carter, R. (ed.) (1996) *Language in the National Curriculum*, Materials for Professional Development [unpublished].

Carter, R. A. and McCarthy, M. (1994) *Language as Discourse: perspectives for language teaching*, London, Longman.

Clark, K. (1992) 'The linguistics of blame: representations of women in *The Sun's* reporting of crimes of sexual violence' in Toolan, M. (ed.) *Language, Text and Context*, London and New York, Routledge.

Cleary, M. (2003) 'England slam the demons', *The Daily Telegraph*, 31 March.

CNN (2001) 'U.S. accuses China over air collision', 2 April 2001. Available from: http://edition.cnn.com [accessed 5 February 2004].

Coffin, C. (1996) 'Exploring literacy in school history', *Write it Right* Series, New South Wales Department of School Education, Metropolitan East Region.

Coghill, G. and Wood, P. (1987) *Science Spectrum 1*, Australia, Heinemann.

Collis, B. and Remmers, E. (1997) 'The world wide web in education: issues related to cross cultural communication and interaction' in Khan, B. (ed.) *Web-based Instruction*, Englewood Cliffs, New Jersey, p. 85).

Davies, E. and Whitney, N. (1985) *Reasons for Reading*, London, Heinemann.

Droga, L. and Humphrey, S. (2002) *Getting Started with Functional Grammar*, Berry (NSW, Aus.), Target Texts.

Dunmore, H. (2001) *The Siege*, Harmondsworth, Viking.

Eggins, S. (1994) *An Introduction to Systemic Functional Linguistics*, London, Pinter.

Electronics Workshop, *Introduction to Electronics – Components*, http://library.thinkquest.org.10784. [Accessed 24 September 2003].

'Escaped rabbit' (2002) in *Animal Hospital* Series, Programme 4, Episode 4, BBC.

Firth, J. R. (1957) 'A synopsis of linguistic theory, 1930–1955'. *Studies in Linguistic Analysis Special Volume*, Philological Society, pp. 1–32.

Gems, D. and Partridge, L. (2002) 'A lethal side-effect', *Nature*, vol. 418, 29 August.

Gerot, L. (1995) *Making Sense of Text*, Cammeray (Aus.), Antipodean Educational Enterprises.

Gittins, M. (1998) 'Computers are bad for you', *PC Basics*, December, pp. 30–31.

Goatly, A. (2000) *Critical Reading and Writing: An introductory coursebook*, London and New York, Routledge.

Halliday, M. A. K. and Hasan, R. (1975) *Cohesion in English*, London, Longman.

Hayward, P. (2003) 'Wilkinson throws doubts aside', *The Daily Telegraph*, 31 March.

Hewings, A. (1999) 'Disciplinary engagement in undergraduate writing: an investigation of clause-initial elements in geography essays', unpublished PhD thesis, Birmingham University.

Hewings, A. and Hewings, M. (2004) 'Impersonalising stance: a study of anticipatory 'it' in student and published academic writing' in Coffin, C. Coffin, C., Hewings, A. and O'Halloran, K. A. (eds) *Applying English Grammar: Functional and Corpus Approaches*, London, Arnold.

Hong Kong Standard (2001) 'US spy plane hits China jet', 11 April 2001. Available from: http://www.hk-imail.singtao.com [accessed 29 September 2003].

Humphrey, S. (1996) 'Migration', *Write it Right* Series, New South Wales Department of School Education, Metropolitan East Region.

IELTS Academic Writing Task 2, Version 51.

International Food Information Council Foundation (1998) 'Caffeine and health: clarifying the controversies', *IFIC Review* [online]. Available from: http://ificinfo.health.org.

Jones, P. (1996) *Talking to Learn*, Sydney, Primary English Teachers Association.

Joyce, H. (1992) *Workplace Texts in the Language Classroom*, New South Wales Adult Migrant English Service.

Katz, I. (2001) 'Controversy over crouching tiger review: an apology', Dimsum [online]. Available from: http://www.dimsum.co.uk [Accessed 25 January 2001].

Kiley, S. and Sherman, J. (1999) 'Bullets wreck Blair visit', *The Times*, 9 January.

Lodge, D. (2002) *Thinks...*, London, Penguin.

Martin, J. R. (2001) 'Language, register and genre' in Burns, A. and Coffin, C. (eds) (2001) *Analysing English in a Global Context*, London, Routledge.

Martin, J. R., Matthiessen, C. M. I. M. and Painter, C. (1997) *Working with Functional Grammar*, London, Arnold.

McCarthy, M. (1988) 'Some vocabulary patterns in conversation' in Carter, R. and McCarthy, M. (eds) *Vocabulary and Language Teaching*, London and New York, Longman.

McDonnell, K. (1999) 'Falco naumanni', The University of Michigan Museum of Zoology Animal Diversity Web, http://animaldiversity.ummz.umich.edu [Accessed 24 September 2003]

Molyneux, J. (1999) 'Expression of an Age', *Socialist Review* [online], Issue 229 (April). Available from: http://pubs.socialistreviewindex.org.uk/sr229/molyneux.htm [Accessed 30 July 2003].

New South Wales Department of School Education, Metropolitan East Region (1996a) 'Exploring Literacy in School History', *Write it Right* Series.

New South Wales Department of School Education, Metropolitan East Region (1996b) 'Exploring Literacy in School Geography', *Write it Right* Series.

New South Wales Department of School Education, Metropolitan East Region (1996c) 'Exploring Literacy in School Science', *Write it Right* Series.

Open University (1993) 'Jackson Pollock: Tim Clark and Michael Fried in conversation', A316 *Modern Art, Practices and Debates*, TV21, Milton Keynes, Open University.

Painter, C. (1996) 'The development of language as a resource for thinking: a linguistic view of learning' in Hasan, R. and Williams, G. (eds) *Literacy in Society*, London, Addison Wesley Longman Limited.

Parks, T (1996) *An Italian Education*, London, Minerva.

Polias, J. (1993) 'Electronic games', Lexis Education [unpublished].

Potter, G. W. (1998) 'Modelling winning performance in invasive team games', unpublished PhD thesis, University of Wales Institute Cardiff and The Open University.

Sainsbury's (2002) [advertisement] *BBC Homes and Antiques*, August 2002, pp. 16–17.

Shubert, D. (ed.) (1998) *Teaching ESL through Science*, Adelaide, Dept of Education, Training and Employment.

Trew, T. (1979) 'What the papers say: linguistic variation and ideological difference' in Fowler, R. (ed.) *Language and Control*, London, Routledge and Keegan Paul.

Whitehead, G. (1982) *Economics Made Simple*, London, Heinemann.

Widdowson, H. G. (1978) *Teaching Language as Communication*, Oxford, Oxford University Press.

Wilkinson, J. (1985) *Senior General Science*, Melbourne, McMillan.

Wodehouse P. G. (1930) *Indian Summer of an Uncle* in Owens, W. R. (ed.) (1991) *The Prose Anthology*, Milton Keynes, Open University.

Woolf, V. (1996) (first published 1925) *Mrs Dalloway*, London, Penguin.

Acknowledgements

Grateful acknowledgement is made to the following sources for permission to reproduce material in this book.

Unit 12

Text

International Food Information Council Foundation 'Caffeine and health: clarifying the controversies', http://ific.org/publications/reviews. Copyright © 2003 International Food Information Council Foundation.

Birmingham Post (1999) 'Leading article a princely foreign lesson', *Birmingham Post*, 26 October 1999. Copyright © Midland Independent Newspapers Plc.

Katz, I. (2001) 'Controversy over crouching tiger review: an apology', http://www.dimsum.co.uk.

Gittings, M. (1998) 'Computers are bad for you', *PC Basics*, December 1998. Copyright © Paragon Magazines.

Unit 13

Text

Kiley, S. and Sherman, J. (1999) 'Bullets wreck Blair visit'. *The Times*. News International Newspapers, Limited. Copyright © 1999 News Group Newspapers Ltd.

Beresford, D. (1999) 'South African police open fire on anti-Blair protesters', *Guardian Unlimited*. http://www.guardian.co.uk. Copyright © 2003 Guardian Newspapers.

Cable News Network (2001) 'US accuses China over air collision', 2 April, 2001. http://www.CNN.com. Copyright © 2001 Cable News Network.

Hong Kong iMail, (2001) 'US spy plane hits China jet', 3 April, 2001. http://www.HK-iMail.Singtao.com.

Unit 14

Text

Johnson, T. *Introduction: Alcatraz.* http://www.csulb.edu/projects/ais/alcatraz/001_001_intro_text.html. Copyright © California State University, Long Beach.

Potter, G.W. (1997) *Modelling Winning Performance in Invasive Team Games.* A doctoral thesis, submitted through the Centre for Performance Analysis, University of Wales Institute. Copyright © Gareth W. Potter.

Molyneux, J. (1999) 'Expression of an age', *Socialist Review*, Issue 229. Copyright © Socialist Review.

Unit 15

Text

Oracle ThinkQuest. (2003) *Introduction to Electronics – Components*. http://library.thinkquest.org/10784/atut2.html. Copyright © 2003, Oracle Help Us Help Foundation.

Illustration

J. Sainsbury Plc. (2002) 'Their hunt the roast vegetable sauce' and 'Our roast vegetable sauce'. Copyright © J. Sainsbury Plc and Sainsbury's Supermarkets Ltd.

Unit 16

Text

'Alternative medicine' (1988). Extract from 'After Dark Series', Channel 4/ITN Archive.

Oracle ThinkQuest. (2003) *Introduction to Electronics – Components*. http://library.thinkquest.org/10784/atut2.html. Copyright © 2003, Oracle Help Us Help Foundation.

Every effort has been made to contact copyright owners, but if any have been inadvertently overlooked, the publishers will be pleased to make the necessary arrangements at the first opportunity.

Course team acknowledgements

The course team wish to thank and acknowledge the assistance of the following in the production of this book.

Michael Hoey (external assessor)

Ron Carter, Susan Feez, Michael Halliday, Geoffrey Leech (general course consultants)

Geoff Thompson (adviser)

Tarek Fakhrel-Deen, Mohammad Awwad, Lewis Mukattash (Arab OU critical readers)

Judy Anderson, Frank Xiao Junhong, Ahmed Sahlane (developmental testers)

E303 Associate Lecturers

Index